Mark—
Best wishes on your new
Adventure— May success
Be the least you achieve!

Mike Coss 8/96

THE SCOUT

THE
SCOUT

RED MURFF
· ·
with MIKE CAPPS

WORD PUBLISHING
Dallas·London·Vancouver·Melbourne

PUBLISHED BY WORD PUBLISHING, DALLAS, TEXAS

The Scout: Searching for the Best in Baseball

Library of Congress Cataloging-in-Publication Data

Murff, Red, 1921–
    The scout : searching for the best in baseball / Red Murff with Mike
    Capps
    p. cm.
    ISBN 0–8499–1299–7
    1. Murff, Red, 1921– . 2. Baseball scouts—United States–Biography.
3. Baseball—United States—History.   I. Capps, Mike, 1950–
II. Title.
GV865.M785A3   1996
796.357'092—dc20   95-43759
[B]   CIP

Printed in the United States of America

6 7 8 9 RRD 9 8 7 6 5 4 3 2 1

(From Red) To every scout who ever drove two hundred miles too fast, dodged an eighteen-wheeler, missed one of his children's special events, or woke up wishing he was at home with his family and instead, because he loves the game, persevered and signed the ballplayer he was after. We're a different breed, gentlemen.

(From Mike) To Dee, who lights up my life every second.

Contents

Foreword

Two men sit inconspicuously behind home plate at a high school baseball game in the cool dampness of an early spring Texas evening. Windbreakers, gloves, and snap-brimmed houndstooth hats cut the settling chill. One man carries a radar gun. Both juggle ballpoint pens, loose-leaf notebooks, and stopwatches. They keep mostly to themselves and have very little to say to anyone else, although their presence causes a stir among the players' parents. No one else notices much about these two quiet spectators.

These men represent baseball's alpha, its bedrock reality. Many who truly know this grand old game believe these hawk-eyed men, these talent scouts, have the sport's toughest job. Their craft is arguably the game's least understood, yet without their remarkable acumen there is no professional baseball. These two are on the prowl for the Atlanta Braves, and the major-league draft is six weeks away. Their objective this night is to pass judgment on a young man's potential to be a first- or second-round draft choice.

Baseball players don't just show up one day at Yankee Stadium, the Astrodome, Fenway Park, or Wrigley Field and begin playing at the major-league level. Someone has to find these kids in high school, college, and amateur ball yards around the world and report any prized finds to the various club executives. With such information in hand a team can then draft a young player, sign him to a contract, and, if he performs like the scout believes he will, the kid has a chance to progress through a club's farm system. If he's good *and* lucky and survives a cut-throat, intensely competitive process of elimination, he may one day end up in the sport that requires more all-around athletic skills than any other: baseball's big leagues. Maybe.

On this night the whispered conversation becomes very serious. The two spot trouble as the young right-handed pitcher goes through his throwing motions.

"Looks like he's favoring that shoulder. He's got a bad hitch. See how his shoulder sort of jerks as he's coming through his delivery?" one questions the other.

"Well, he's still hitting eighty-five on the [radar] gun. But he's been favoring that shoulder since the first time I saw him this year, probably in early March. I'm afraid if we draft him, he'll need the rest of the summer off and then somebody is going to have to help him reinvent that motion of his. That is, if he's not hurt badly."

"Not a first or second rounder then, huh?"

"Not unless he smooths out that delivery and loosens up in the next two weeks."

This kind of insiders' talk between field scout Red Murff and an Atlanta Braves national cross-checker (a scout called in when a team becomes serious about drafting a player to grade him against all other prospects at all positions from across the country) is only a small part of the annual mating dance between major-league baseball and amateur talent—a dance that has been under way in its current form for more than thirty years.

In this particular case the Braves opted not to draft the kid. After watching him pitch, the scouts talked to his parents and coaches and learned that the young man was seriously injured. Red had followed the prospect's progress for three years and disappointedly had to face the realization that his effort wouldn't end happily.

Scouting is a strange secret-society brotherhood. How so? Well, you know who Babe Ruth was, or Lou Gehrig or Joe DiMaggio. Their names and faces have become as American as the flag and apple pie. But you've never heard of the men responsible for finding them. Some fans may have heard about Tom Greenwade, the scout who signed Mickey Mantle, or C. C. Slapnika, the man who discovered Bob Feller. The only reason anyone knows those great scouts is because Feller and Mantle spoke glowingly about them in public and praised them in books. Otherwise no one outside of either scout's club or his immediate circle of friends most likely would ever know about those men.

Much of the scout's job involves operating with intrigue as he moves from town to town, ballpark to ballpark, searching for players. He doesn't want to attract a lot of attention to himself because he doesn't want to give away any information about the ballplayers he's watching.

For the most part scouts are the baseball world's worst self-promoters. Only recently has the Baseball Hall of Fame in Cooperstown acknowledged their existence. The Hall now has an area devoted to the profession, but if life were fair scouts should be given their own separate wing and be inducted the same as any player because their knowledge, input, and acumen mean that much to the game. Major-league scouts are in the business because they truly love baseball and possess a knowledge mixed with an unquestioned, sobering reality that discovering, drafting, and signing baseball talent sometimes boils down to nothing more than a crapshoot.

For most of Red Murff's thirty-three-year career as a professional scout he's known far more success than disillusionment. From thousands of young ballplayers he watched in thousands of ballparks across the United States, South and Central America, and Puerto Rico, Murff had the uncanny ability to find those well-hidden, well-disguised diamonds in the rough destined to one day be the glittering Boys of Summer.

I should know about John "Red" Murff because I was one of those fast-throwing, hard-running, hot-tempered kids when I first met him in 1969 on a sweltering May Saturday at Fireman's Park in Brenham, Texas. Back then Murff was scouting for the

Montreal Expos. As a recent graduate of Fairfield, Texas, High School, I had been invited to an Expos tryout camp by a junior college coach who wanted to give me and a fellow high-school teammate, Steve Wilson, baseball scholarships.

Some big-league teams use these camps to get one final, up-close look at their most promising players just before the June draft. A few college and junior college coaches who have made friends with the scouts running the camps are sometimes allowed in to recruit talent for their programs.

In my case, this particular coach thought I could play defense better than his shortstop, but he wasn't sure I could hit junior college pitching, so he wanted to see how I matched up against some of the fastest high school and junior college talent in Texas and Louisiana. It turned out the coach was wrong. I could hit, but I couldn't play defense.

Everyone attending this particular camp stood in awe of the scout in charge. He was a strapping six-foot-three, 195-pound package of bone, gristle, and short-fused energy and wore a cream-colored Montreal Expos uniform topped off by a Neapolitan ice cream red-white-and-blue cap with a white script M on the crown. Red Murff commanded the attention of everyone—players, parents, coaches, and fellow scouts as he ran this camp of about one hundred hopefuls with all the savoir-faire of a marine boot camp drill sergeant. His pale, redheaded features turned fiery crimson and his blood pressure rose as he ranted, yelled, and cajoled each young player.

"Young man, you better show me the *best* you got, otherwise, you're wasting my time and everyone else's here. This is your one chance. You *gotta* do better!"

Scouts judge potential players' "tools" (their abilities) in five categories—foot speed, arm strength, ability to hit, ability to hit with power, and fielding ability. Murff and his associates conducted drills at this camp that allowed each player to demonstrate his wares. The most important drills to Red for position players (infielders and outfielders) were the running sorties, the races from home to first and the sixty-yard dash.

Eventually I ran the second fastest time in the camp from home to first, but not until Red got in my eighteen-year-old face. The first time I chugged down the first-base line, Murff charged off the mound directly toward me, screaming at the top of his lungs, "You can do better than that, kid . . . you *better* do better than that!"

The next time I did. Much better. I never ran that fast in my life. But out of youthful impatience, I made a hasty decision that sweltering day that changed the course of my life. When I got bored waiting for a turn at bat, I left the camp and the scholarship and walked on at another junior college and (through a series of serendipities) into broadcast journalism.

Red and I didn't cross paths again for nineteen years. That was when a fellow WFAA-TV news producer, John Sparks, and I planned to produce a thirty-minute documentary on the Texas Rangers newest acquisition, future Hall of Famer Nolan Ryan.

We recalled Murff as the man who had discovered Ryan and had given him his shot at professional baseball. So photographer Tom Loveless and I found Red in an Arlington, Texas, hotel room on a Tuesday night after he'd finished his scouting assignment for the day. We rolled tape on Red for more than two hours, asking him dozens of questions about his prized discovery, Nolan Ryan.

During the course of our conversation Red remembered yelling at me at the tryout camp, and we struck up a friendship. Today I proudly call Red Murff one of my best, most trusted, and valued friends, and no one in the world—no king or president or sheik—I've ever interviewed holds my attention more than Red Murff when he tells a good baseball story. When he asked me to help scout for him part time and gave me my scout's card, I was thrilled beyond belief. As part of the team that ran five tryout camps for the Atlanta Braves (similar to the one I had attended in 1969), I learned a great deal about how a talented scout "magically" spots raw talent.

Like life, baseball is a game of what-ifs. What if Red hadn't left his job as a chemical plant supervisor at the "elderly" athletic age of twenty-nine to pursue a professional baseball dream?

What if he had refused to struggle to become a major-league pitcher, only to hurt his back at the age of thirty-four and lose any chance for a lengthy big-league career? Most importantly for baseball fans worldwide, what if Murff hadn't found Nolan Ryan?

Murff's former boss with the New York Mets, Bing Devine, insists that had Red not been so adamant on Nolan's behalf during that first-ever free-agent draft in 1965, the Mets would not have drafted the wild pitching kid from Alvin, Texas. As hard as it is to believe now, Ryan didn't have a single college scholarship offer, and no major-league scout other than Murff believed he would ever pitch in the big leagues.

It was this God-given ability to foresee future athletic performance that made Red a legend in the scouting world. During his career he has signed more than two hundred ballplayers to professional contracts with the Houston Colt .45s, the New York Mets, the Montreal Expos, the Atlanta Braves, and the Chicago Cubs. Four Murff-signed players—Nolan Ryan, Jerry Grote, Jerry Koosman, and Kenny Boswell—played significant roles on the 1969 World Champion New York Mets.

"I didn't know what I had, no one did, only Red Murff," says Nolan.

"If not for Red's persistence, I would never have gone from army private to National League all-star," insists Jerry Koosman.

Baseball executive and former player and manager Bobby Bragan adds, "Red is one of the finest scouts of all time."

"Red may very well have been the best scout ever," says former scouting rival Billy Capps of the Chicago Cubs, who once managed Murff in the minor leagues.

"If they ever open up the Hall of Fame to scouts, Red Murff should be the first one in," said Jerry Grote, former Mets, Dodgers, and Royals all-star catcher.

"I was grateful for Red's support and advice when I was a young player with the Texas League Dallas Eagles, and I admire his perseverance as a major-league scout," adds Bill White, former National League president.

THE SCOUT

Former American League president Bobby Brown called Murff "a super scout."

Roland Hemond, former general manager of the Baltimore Orioles, noted, "The caliber and number of players that Red Murff has signed who have advanced to the big leagues is truly a testimony to a great scout."

And Ann Richards, former governor of Texas, observed, "The sport of baseball just wouldn't be what it is today without Red Murff's enormous influence. I applaud his commitment to helping young players excel."

Without a doubt, scouts are the unheralded heroes of baseball. They travel millions of miles each year, attend thousands of games in high school, college, and amateur parks across the United States, Canada, Mexico, the Dominican Republic . . . or wherever potential talent might be camouflaged. Red Murff was merely making those rounds when he found a young man named Ryan and fifty other big leaguers. In doing so, he has enriched a game loved by fans, parents, and children everywhere.

Mike Capps
September 1995

Red's Random Thought . . .

My scouting style resembled the U.S. judicial system, you know, "innocent till proven guilty." I always figured every young ballplayer I saw was a big-league prospect until he proved to me he was not.

Prologue

Big-league scouts come in all sizes, shapes, and colors. Each of the thirty major-league clubs employs about twenty scouts on a full-time basis, so there are only slightly less than six hundred of us checking out ballplayers in the United States, Mexico, the Caribbean countries, Canada, and now Australia. No matter where we are in the world, we all share the common bond that we do what we do because we love the game of baseball. Period.

Scouts love to be outside in the sunshine, talking and observing the sport and those who play it while communing with others who love it, too, but most of all we love competing with fellow scouts. We win our game by beating the other guy to the best ballplayers. If you look closely, you may see us sitting in the stands at high school and college games. We're the ones in the front rows with notebooks, pencils, stopwatches, and radar guns. We dress casually. We have leathery faces. And we try our best to be inconspicuous. We don't want any attention. That belongs to the ballplayers and the game.

If the focus of our professional attention on a given day is a promising young pitcher, you might see more radar guns in the stands than you have ever seen at the busiest interstate Sunday afternoon speed trap.

We're competitors, so we don't talk to each other a lot. We don't share opinions, or at least I never did, but we watch what's happening on the field *closely*. Most of us have played profes-sionally. A few of us have played in the big leagues. But the majority of us were minor leaguers who became addicted to the game, never wanted to leave it, and yearned to use the knowledge we gained to find real talent.

Most anyone with any kind of baseball experience can spot a kid with big-time ability. The kids who are naturals, the ones who make it look easy, are few and far between, but they're easy to locate. The true art of my craft is talent projection. A top-flight scout must gaze into his crystal ball and forecast how far a young man's talents will take him, how long it will take for those abilities to develop, and to know if he's as good as he will ever be. Because it is an inexact science, scouts have to be modern-day versions of Old West gamblers, no doubt about it.

Don't ever believe anyone who tells you the good players are always discovered and easily evaluated. That's nonsense. We let some great ones slip by occasionally. We almost did with Nolan Ryan.

The story of how Nolan was found explains in great detail how the scouting profession works and sometimes doesn't work. Even though others had written off Nolan because of his scrawny teenage body, I looked at his fastball: he was throwing it harder than any big leaguer I'd ever seen. I didn't disqualify him because of his body. I knew he'd grow. When he filled out I was convinced his fastball could be one of the best of all time.

It was the same story with Jerry Grote. After watching his progress for a couple of years, the Houston Colt .45s had written him off, but I knew in my heart he was a natural-born leader—and lead he did, taking the New York Mets to the world's championship in 1969.

Like an exceptional ballplayer, I was blessed with a special talent. What always set me apart from many of my scouting brethren was an innate ability to project how well a young fellow would progress over his next five years. Nolan Ryan, to me, had obvious talent, but as a high schooler he lacked the size most big-league scouts look for. A kid like Nolan only needed time to grow. He's a good example, but there were many other instances when I believed in young players whom others dismissed and overlooked. I trusted my own gut instincts.

THE SCOUT

I also had an ability to gain a young player's trust and confidence. Maybe because I have always believed one of the biggest responsibilities I had was to develop a trusting, long-term relationship with a prospect, rather than use my position as a big-league scout to exploit a young man for a team. I told every ballplayer I ever signed, "Listen, I may change teams, you may change teams, but I will *always* be the scout who signed you, and I'll always be available to you for playing tips, for advice on getting along with your manager, or just to talk." And I meant it.

I still hear from dozens of these players. Nolan Ryan and I still talk. Jerry Grote and I go hunting every year. Those are lifetime relationships. My personal commitment to their future created a bond of trust between me, a young player, and his folks, and perhaps that part of my reputation played a major role in building my successful career as a professional scout.

Red Murff
Fall 1995

Acknowledgements

From Red: Special loving thanks to my parents for the wonderful competitive genetics they blessed me with that allowed me to achieve far more than my wildest dreams. Thanks to my eight brothers and sisters who let me bat fifth in the family lineup, enabling me to hone sibling rivalry to an art and stoking my competitive fires to the point that simple games and business deals were a piece of cake.

An appreciative note to Abner Doubleday or whomever for inventing a game that allowed my abilities to be tested to the fullest.

Thanks to the special, special friends of baseball, the sportswriters and radio and television play-by-play voices whom I have often criticized, but who wrote glowing reports and painted tremendous word pictures of my exploits for the benefit of those who sat in thousands of living rooms reading, watching, and listening.

I wish to thank my first wife, Irene, who presented me with four beautifully loving daughters—Carol, Patricia, Melinda, and Robin—and my grandsons—Trey, Mark, Patrick, and Jeffrey—and my granddaughters—Erin and Megan—and four special sons-in-law, and *the* special one, my great-granddaughter, Dustin Ryan Monroe.

A very special loving note of undying appreciation to my wife, Sara, who helped me put my shattered life back together, established me as a member of my second family, to my stepson Scott and his wife, Carla, my stepdaughter Betsy, and two incredible grandsons, Ben and Matthew.

To the small community of Burlington, Texas, where I grew up, and its schools, churches, and people who prepared me for life, taught me to live clean, and placed Christianity and the Golden Rule as *the* way to live.

To my special friends from World War II, Aviation Cadets John Blatnik, Bruno Pacini, and Charlie Lopinski. We proved that true, lasting friendship transcends geographical, religious, and ethnic boundaries.

And a final, special tribute to the Reverend Tom Currie, my close personal friend and former pastor of the Brenham Presbyterian Church. Tom taught me that the world is made of two kinds of people: the Jesus-kind and the rest of us. I learned from Tom that, because of my faith, I may have played my life into the cellar at times, but when I leave this world I will become a pennant winner on heaven's all-star team.

From Mike: I owe a deep gratitude to my wife and partner, Dee Covey Capps. I love you so much. You have been my inspiration in so many, many ways.

To our wonderful daughters—Christa, Megan, Kelli, and Karli—for hanging in there with Dad through the tough times.

A special memorial to my late grandfather, Miller Ekas Jr., whose unquenchable thirst for this game rubbed off.

Thanks to Dee's parents, Keith and Barbara Covey, and mine, Doris and Manly Mabry, for all your encouragement, and to my late father, Ben, for his ideals, values, and his greatest lesson: skin color means nothing . . . what's in the heart says it all.

To my cousin, Bill Capps of the Chicago Cubs, next to Red, the world's greatest scout and one of the classiest Christian gentlemen on the face of this earth, a word of thanks for all your help, counsel, and encouragement.

THE SCOUT

A special note of appreciation to the family of my late great junior high coach, Don Emmons, a man who challenged me to give baseball and life all I had. Thanks to my high school coaches, Danny Robertson and Don Reed, college coach Al Hawes, and to Cecil Vega, Owen Finlan, and Paul Aube of the Dallas Amateur Baseball Association, who gave a small-town kid a chance to play long, long ago.

A special note of gratitude to five distinguished gentlemen who ably taught me my craft: Ray Miller, Eddie Barker, Bill Mercer, Marty Haag, and Byron Harris.

And to the memory of Dave Lane, an eternal hero!

A final special note of thanks to my agent, Scott Waxman, and Word Publishing editor Joey Paul for having faith in us and in this project.

Chapter 1

Prowling for Pitchers

I have always prided myself on being able to judge pitchers. I pitched professionally, I coached pitchers, and I know how to work on the mound.

The first thing I look for in a prospective big-league hurler is size, an extremely important attribute. A young man's physical development does not have to be complete, but I do have to make a judgment on how big a kid will ultimately be.

We like a pitcher to be at least six feet tall, sturdily built, but not musclebound, because he needs to have a free and easy delivery. Nothing about a pitcher makes my heart pound faster than a nice, loose motion unleashing an exploding fastball. It's important not to have to strain or "muscle up" to throw the ball, so a young pitcher with a fluid delivery will be less susceptible to arm problems and may have a longer career than a more musclebound pitcher. But height is crucial, because taller pitchers have longer arms and legs. That means he has a better fulcrum from which to launch the ball, and that means he uses less effort than a short-armed pitcher, who really has to work hard on each pitch.

This sounds like we're looking for cookie-cutter dimensions, say six-foot-four and 210 pounds. While that's almost an ideal size, a few inches or pounds either way is okay as long as he has a good sturdy build.

Obviously there are always successful exceptions to any rule, so size is just a guideline, not a hard and fast rule. Remember that Whitey Ford at five-feet-ten struck out a lot of hitters on his guile and an ability to pitch to precise spots. Whitey wasn't by himself sizewise, but not everyone can make up for short stature.

Being left-handed is a great advantage to a pitcher. Throughout baseball, from the peewee leagues to college, most hitters are right-handed and so are most pitchers. For that reason hitters rarely get a chance to compete against left-handed pitchers. Maybe they'll see one in Little League, maybe an occasional lefty in high school. A left-hander's delivery presents an entirely different look to a hitter from that of a right-hander. The breaking ball breaks in a different direction, and lefties usually carry a reputation for being wild, so that tends to make hitters wary.

We'll naturally give a longer look to a left-hander who is not as large as the standard six-foot-plus we like to see in a righty, because hard-throwing left-handers are a scarce commodity.

Besides the left-handed advantage, many other physical attributes come into play for a pitcher. A prospective major-league pitcher should be athletic enough to move off the mound quickly to field his position. He also needs great endurance, especially if he aspires to be a starting pitcher.

Aside from that, what we really want to know is how hard and how fast can he throw? Are his pitches traveling straight or do they have life and movement? In our jargon, does his fastball hop, sink, or move in or out as it speeds toward the strike zone? If the ball is coming in straight, I don't care how fast it's moving, professional hitters eventually will catch up with it and knock the ball all over the park. Any sinking or hopping action on a fastball makes hitting that much more difficult. Ask any hitter.

If a young pitcher has mastered a curve, a slider, or an off-speed pitch, so much the better. We professionals are egotistical enough to believe we can teach a young man a few different pitches. As long as he can throw consistently in the 86–90 mile-per-hour range with some movement, he will always be considered a prospect.

Nolan Ryan was much faster than that from the very first time I saw him. So the question is, How did so many people miss Nolan Ryan and why did they miss him? My fellow scouts had the same chance to see Nolan pitch in high school and in the summer leagues that I did. But they didn't like what they saw.

When Nolan came along we didn't have radar guns, so no one really knew how fast he was throwing. But they didn't know how fast anyone else was throwing either, so in my mind the fact that there were no radar guns doesn't pass for an excuse.

I think the other major-league scouts looked at this skinny six-foot-one, 155-pound high schooler and decided that his body simply did not fit the mold they'd created in their minds for big-league pitchers. Then, through what I call the scouting grapevine, all the scouts began the negative talk about Nolan.

Months after I first saw Nolan I heard the late Paul Richards, the longtime Orioles manager and Houston general manager, tell other scouts that Ryan didn't have a "big enough chest" to be a big-league pitcher. He was "chicken chested," Richards said. A big enough chest? I knew Nolan's chest and the rest of his body would grow into big-league size. Any amateur geneticist could figure this one out. One look at Nolan's dad, Lynn, at six-foot-two and 230 pounds convinced me the younger Ryan would mature into a big, strong man, and time proved me right.

The other amazing fact in this story is that everyone else missed that big blazing fastball. Believe me, he had it, even the first time I saw him during his junior year in high school. Everywhere I go these days, my old scouting competitors like to sit around and say they knew Nolan would be great. The heck they did. My friends have mighty short memories about what really happened. They got into a "group-think" situation and believed what Paul Richards had said about Nolan's chest.

Consequently they left him alone, and that was a lucky break for me.

It wasn't easy to stick to my guns. Nolan pitched some bad ball games during his senior year. It's been well chronicled that he pitched poorly when Mets scouting director Bing Devine came to Alvin, Texas, to see him shortly before that first draft in 1965. That bad outing in front of Devine could have proven to be Nolan's baseball death knell, but it wasn't because I was doggedly determined to prove that Ryan's incredible right arm would one day carry him to the big leagues.

In three decades of scouting I have to say I was never so bent on drafting and signing a ballplayer as I was Nolan Ryan that year. Right after I signed him to his first professional contract, I recall telling him that if he was as good as I thought he was, he would one day make so much money we would both be embarrassed to talk about it. I never made much as a scout or really cared about money, but it was fun to ponder for this kid. At the time I thought we were probably talking about a hundred thousand or so a season. I never dreamed he would make millions of dollars.

In reality, the discovery of Nolan Ryan was simple. A good scout does his homework and makes a judgment. I believed that Nolan could be the best, fastest pitcher anyone would ever see anywhere. He has told me many times over the last thirty years that he never really knew what he had, physically, when he was in high school. But thank God, I did.

Red's Random Thought . . .

Every time I pass by a ballpark I just have to stop.
You never know. The next Nolan Ryan might be there.

Chapter 2

Fate and Chance Are Good Buddies

I've always been a proponent of the notion that God has a master plan for us all, that if we listen closely and pay attention the proper path is all mapped out for us. Call it what you will, chance, fate, whatever, the discovery of Nolan Ryan reinforces the theory that sometimes things are just meant to be.

During the spring of 1964 I was scouting Texas, Oklahoma, New Mexico, and Louisiana for the New York Mets. It was my second scouting job, and I'd only been in the talent procurement business for three years. At the time I lived in Texas City, Texas, a town of about fifty thousand on Galveston Bay, near the Gulf of Mexico, and about thirty-five miles south of Houston. Texas City's main claim to fame occurred in 1947 when a tanker ship exploded and set off a vicious chain of explosions and infernos that killed hundreds and injured thousands. For me, Texas City was a great base for a professional baseball scout. I had easy access to the entire Houston area, southeast Texas, and Louisiana. Within minutes I could be at Houston's Hobby Airport to catch a flight anywhere.

When I woke up early this particular April Saturday morning, I didn't know why but I was full of anticipation as I read the paper over my coffee. I knew that once I had finished the sports section and found out how the Mets and Colt .45s had fared the night before, I was facing an extremely busy day. The first event was a twenty-mile drive to Galveston to see an excellent high school tournament there, then I intended to drive on to Houston that afternoon to catch an early evening game at Texas Southern University.

As a scout I loved tournaments, especially in the early season, because I could go to one ballpark and in the span of four or five hours see at least four teams and seventy or eighty ballplayers. Tournaments saved lots of time, and if I saw one or two good-looking ballplayers, I'd gather as much information on them as I could and then make plans to follow their progress during the year.

High school coaches also love these tournaments for several reasons. First, their players get a lot of game experience early in the season. If a coach is trying to develop younger ballplayers, his freshmen and sophomores, he can fine-tune their play in tournament games. Plus, with the experience his ballplayers are getting, coaches can spot and begin to strengthen weaknesses as they mold and shape their ball clubs before the all-important district games begin.

I rolled up to the Galveston ballpark about an hour before the beginning of the Saturday morning games. Sometime after I sat down, I had a feeling that I was in the wrong place, that I wasn't where I was supposed to be that day. It was the weirdest sensation and one I'd never felt before. It made me feel uneasy, kind of like being in a crowd of tuxedos and you have on a sports jacket and an open collar. Still I went about my usual business and greeted several coaches and fans I knew, visited with some old friends, and managed to sit through two ball games before deciding none of the players on any of the teams interested me. So I went back to my car and headed north on Interstate 45 toward Houston.

As I was driving I suddenly remembered that I had seen something in the newspaper about another tournament being played at Clear Creek High School near the Johnson Space Center. I have no idea what made me remember that tournament, and likewise I have no idea what possessed me to stop there.

I had a cadre of part-time or subscouts who helped give me several sets of eyes at ballparks in my four-state territory. Those guys loved baseball and were experts at giving me a "heads-up" about promising ballplayers, but none of them had told me about any prospects playing at the Clear Creek tournament.

I guess I figured I should drop by Clear Creek to let the coach, Dub Kelly, know that professional baseball people appreciated his efforts in staging the tournament. In my mind Texas baseball coaches have always played second fiddle to football. The folks at Clear Creek had brought Dub in from the Dallas area to build a baseball program, and he spent eight hard years doing just that, despite the problems he had with the football coach. Dub ultimately lost out to the football people and was forced to move on, but I liked his style and his ability to develop young players. Men like Dub Kelly have done a tremendous job instructing and nurturing some great talent, many of whom have gone on to star in the major leagues.

I figured I would make a quick appearance at the ballpark, say my hellos, and then drive on to Houston for the ball game at Texas Southern. I never made it to Houston that day.

Driving into the parking lot at Clear Creek, I noticed that Alvin High School was playing in the game that was under way. As I settled into my seat, the Alvin coach was making a pitching change, and up to the mound walked a gangly, awkward-looking six-foot kid who could not have weighed more than 150 pounds. I had seen a thousand like him during my travels. He was an ordinary, unpolished kid who looked like he was maybe twelve or thirteen years old. I figured he was probably a sophomore or a junior, maybe fifteen or sixteen.

There was nothing remarkable about this youngster at all. Nothing made him stand out from the crowd. Nothing unusual that would have provided the least hint that what I was about to witness was, not a one-in-a-thousand, not even a one-in-a-million, but a once-in-a-lifetime experience.

Before I could say my hellos to the people I knew, I glanced toward the mound as the young pitcher wound up and fired. I could not believe what I had just seen! His one pitch sent my mind spinning, my pulse racing. Was what I had seen real? How in the world could anyone that kid's size throw like that? That bony kid uncorked a better-than-average major-league fastball!

When I say better-than-average major-league fastball, let me explain. In 1964 we had to rely on our own experience and comparison. I had pitched in both the major and minor leagues, had managed in the minors, and had worked closely with lots of professional pitchers. So when it came to judging a fastball's speed, I felt extremely confident in my assessment that this young man had thrown the ball with major-league speed.

As I began fumbling for my game card—a bound, loose-leaf notepad with team rosters, batting orders, and notes on the ballplayers I was watching—I noticed that the only other professional baseball representative in the Clear Creek stands was Mickey Sullivan, then a part-time scout for the Philadelphia Phillies who would later achieve great success as Baylor University's baseball coach. Mickey had seen the same pitch I had seen, but he didn't seem impressed. Or, if he was, he didn't let it show. Perhaps Mickey had been trained as a scout the same way I had been: Don't let your emotions show. Be cooler than cool if you see something that impresses you.

While that little bit of mental oneupmanship was going on between Mickey and me, this kid was winding up again. He uncorked another better-than-major-league-average fastball. This pitch literally jumped off his hand, and it was a strike that split home plate's heart.

Normally when I see exciting talent like this I start taking mental notes. It's a reflex. Relaxed? Yes. Does he have a free and easy motion? Absolutely. Extremely smooth for a kid this young. Legs? Big and strong, but his upper body is skinny.

He wound up again and threw another pitch that looked like it had come from a rocket launcher, this time on the outside corner of the plate for another strike. You could hear it sizzle like a thick slab of ham frying on a red-hot griddle as it roared toward the plate. When the ball slammed into the catcher's mitt, the sound reminded me of a muffled rifle shot. The young hitter couldn't believe what he was seeing—or not seeing—either. He had this sort of empty, glazed-eye stare as he quickly glanced to his coach and then shrugged his shoulders as if to say, What was that? I didn't see a thing!

Now before you go off thinking ole Murff is easily excitable you should understand one thing. I'm a natural skeptic. Most good scouts are, and it serves us well because we think we've seen it all. We want to see a display of big-league talent time and again before we're convinced. We want to make absolutely certain we haven't been deceived before we invite scouting supervisors and cross-checkers into our territory to put a national grade on a prospect.

I didn't even know this kid's name, yet when he turned loose I got excited.

That God had richly blessed this young man was blatantly obvious. That fastball of his was unbelievable. It was the fastest I'd ever seen anywhere. Major leagues, minor leagues, anywhere! And it had life. It jumped off his hand and appeared to hop as it hurtled toward home plate.

Then he wound up again and threw a terrible, awful high school curve that the hitter sliced into right field for a single. But on the next pitch this kid came back with another fastball that exploded into the catcher's mitt. He threw another and another. I sat in stunned silence, my eyes must have been glazed over. I tried to make notes on my worksheet, but I just couldn't. I was speechless and astounded by the display of talent I had seen.

Mickey broke the silence. "Doesn't have much stuff, does he, Red?" I never lied. I told Mickey, "No, he doesn't have a very good curve ball." And he didn't. I have always wondered if the crummy curve ball and the kid's scrawny upper body swayed Mickey's mind. All I know is this skeptical, seasoned ole scout saw enough to believe that I had discovered someone very, very special. A once-in-a-lifetime arm.

After the game I did more homework. I talked with some fans sitting a couple rows back and found out his name was Lynn Nolan Ryan Jr. Everyone on the Alvin team and all the parents called him "Nolie."

Someone told me that Nolie didn't get to pitch much. He said Nolie could throw hard, but he threw the ball all over the place so the coach couldn't rely on him. Another fan told me in deep Southeast Texas parlance that Nolie was "wilder than a March hare."

Unlike so many other days when I'd been bored by a lack of talent at the ballpark, on this day I couldn't wait to get home to fill out my scouting report. I got excited again when I sat down in my office and began to write. I'll never forget my comments. "BEST arm I ever saw ANYWHERE in my life!" I wrote those same words on my game cards several more times during the next year and a half.

The first scouting card I ever sent the Mets on Nolan Ryan was colored red. Red cards indicated that the field scout believed his prospect was a hot, first-rate prospect. And that's what I thought of this young man.

Each time I saw Nolie Ryan, I wrote down the same thing. "BEST arm I ever saw ANYWHERE in my life!" Again I felt more than qualified to make that judgment. Besides my professional experience and having played with the likes of Warren Spahn and Lew Burdette, the night before I had seen the two fastest pitchers in the National League at that time, Jim Maloney of the Cincinnati Reds and Dick "Turk" Farrell of the Houston Astros. Both of those men were big and strong and could throw hard. Nolan Ryan, as a junior in high school, was faster by far than both those fully mature major-league pitchers!

Why had I been picked to find this young man? I couldn't

answer that question initially, but now I'm convinced I was supposed to find him. The discovery of Nolan Ryan would thrill any scout and should have thrilled more scouts than it did. My problem now would be keeping this young phenom under wraps.

Red's Random Thought . . .

I've always considered Hugh Alexander, who worked for the Dodgers and Cubs for decades, to be one of the greatest scouts of all time. Hugh cornered me at the Astrodome a couple of years ago and said, "I'll be dadgummed, Red, if you didn't sign the greatest ballplayer [Nolan Ryan] of all time." I never stopped to think about it in those terms, but if a great scout like Hugh believes it, who am I to say he's wrong?

Chapter 3

Nurturing a Nobody

Since the major-league draft began in 1965, the scouting profession has changed drastically. Before the draft scouts did lots of homework on every ballplayer. We literally babysat our best players. We would follow up a tip from a coach or a former ballplayer about a prospect by quietly traveling to a city or small town close to the player's home and watching him play. If his tools met our standards and we wanted to sign him, we would introduce ourselves and tell him we were interested. Then the fact-finding mission would begin as we tried to learn everything there was to know about the kid. What did he like to do for fun? Besides baseball, what interested him? We wanted to know about his character and his family. We would get to know his parents, his girlfriend, his coaches, his teachers, his best friends. We became a part of his family, and we spent a lot of time visiting him at home. After all that, the player's family knew how sincere we were and realized we were not only interested in signing their son but we also had an interest in the young man himself. That way of doing business gave scouts a sense of security, knowing that they really knew all about the prospect they were signing.

Unfortunately for baseball, it is not that way anymore. The draft has drastically changed the way we do business, but that will be in another chapter.

In the mid-1960s I had the freedom to make my own deals with very little interference from a major-league club. I had my own budget, and in most instances I could set my own price structure for talent. I was more of an executive, an independent businessman representing my team and the game of baseball. Oh, I had bosses to whom I was accountable, but before the draft I was almost a lone wolf, and I liked it that way.

Today a regional scout, such as myself, will find a player and then see him play several times. Then, if I really believe the young man is a prospect, I'll call in a cross-checker. If the young man is a possible number-one draft choice, then the scouting director and possibly the general manager of the club may come to see the youngster, maybe several times.

Grudgingly, I guess I understand the reasoning. With bonuses to these unproven kids running into the million-dollar-plus range, more people have to have a look-see and a say in the drafting of expensive bonus babies. Still I yearn for the good old days before agents, when a man's handshake and his word was his bond. That was the way I did business before the draft.

Fortunately for me, Nolan Ryan came along just as we were beginning the draft process. Actually I saw him for the first time in 1964, the year before that first draft.

Even if I "found" Nolan, give credit to Jim Watson for helping him to grow and develop as a pitching prospect, because this man's participation was crucial. You have never heard of Jim Watson? Well, he was a football man, as were so many other Texas baseball coaches in those days, who had played in the offensive line for the University of Texas in the early 1950s. By the 1960s he found himself coaching the Alvin High School baseball team.

No disrespect to Jim, but he had no idea just what he had in Lynn Nolan Ryan Jr.

Luckily Jim didn't let his ego get in the way of Nolan's development, and because he was such a pro he ended up giving the young pitcher's career a jump-start. Jim could have told me to go away and refused to listen to me, but to his credit he chose to do the opposite and we developed a close working relationship as we advanced Nolan's pitching progress. Jim listened intently, he let me be an unofficial extension of his coaching staff, and above all he learned some solid baseball from me.

I moved slowly and cautiously in building my relationship with the coach, because ego clashes could have irreparably harmed Nolan's growth as a ballplayer. Shortly after Nolan's junior season, I drove to Alvin High School and introduced myself to Jim and his athletic director, Bill Henry. I told them I was a talent scout with the New York Mets, and then I addressed Jim Watson directly.

"Jim, do you know you are coaching one of the ten best arms in the world? Not just one of the ten best in Texas, but in the world?"

I told him there might be some javelin thrower from an Eastern Bloc country who was this young man's equal, or perhaps a South American tribesman who could throw a mean spear. I wanted these Texans to know they had received the blessing of being keepers of a rare find and could be instrumental in cultivating this young man's natural talent.

The funny thing was that Watson didn't know whose natural gift I was talking about. He guessed one name and then another. Then, haltingly, he replied, "You mean *Nolie*, Nolan Ryan?"

"Yes sir," I shot back. "Jim, that Ryan kid is blessed with one of the ten best throwing arms in the world, and I need you to help me develop it."

Remember this is before the draft and I intended to stake my claim early. I wanted to know these men and I wanted them to know me. Selfishly I wanted to secure Nolan Ryan for the New York Mets and hide him from my competitors.

So it was important that his coaches believe that the New York Mets appreciated their hard work and cooperation. I had no way of knowing at that time if other teams were watching Nolan, so whenever the subject of baseball came up around Jim

Watson and Bill Henry, I wanted them to say my name in the same sentence and I wanted them to have complete faith in me.

My main concern was to convince Coach Watson to persuade Nolan to believe in that awesome fastball of his and to use it all the time, especially with runners in scoring position. I told Jim if he could make Nolan understand how great that fastball was, and keep him from throwing a bunch of curves and off-speed pitches, then Watson's team would be playing in the state championship game in Austin in the spring of 1965.

Watson couldn't understand why I did not want Nolan to work on his curve, because he didn't believe high school pitchers could strike out high school hitters without a breaking pitch. I told him that I normally agreed with that, but asked him, "Wouldn't you rather have someone throwing an above-average major-league fastball at high school hitters, than have a high school curve thrown at them?" Watson flashed at the logic and agreed right away. We were in business!

There was a method to my madness since I wanted Nolan developed my way. Despite what you hear from some big-league pitching gurus, weight-lifting coaches, and physical fitness experts, I do not believe lifting weights develops a young man's fastball. I'm convinced that the only way for him to develop that pitch is to throw it properly time and time and time again. A young pitcher has to have confidence in that heater, especially if he's gifted with one that is above average.

While we worked to develop Nolan's fastball, I wanted to practice in relative anonymity. I was so paranoid someone else would find out about him that I begged Jim Watson not to publish the results of Nolan's summer-league performances in the local newspaper. I wanted Nolan under my wraps. I didn't want anyone in professional baseball but Red Murff to know about Nolan Ryan.

I don't think Jim really knew just how awesome Nolan's fastball was, but he came close when he tried to catch for Nolan during warmups. Unfortunately, Jim couldn't get his mitt up quickly enough to catch one of Ryan's screaming missiles and the ball conked him right on the crown of his forehead, knocking the coach flat on the seat of his pants. How it kept from seriously hurting him is a mystery to me, other than to say Jim was a football man. He came away with a firm resolve to *never* try to catch Nolan again, at least not without a football helmet.

We all know now how fast Nolan was in his prime. Once scouts started using radar guns, they clocked him at 100 miles an hour. In 1964 and 1965 I daresay Nolan threw almost that fast as an undeveloped seventeen- and eighteen-year-old.

Nolan's fastball terrorized dozens of high school hitters. I know it did because I heard a lot of his opponents talking about it. The pitch was awesome, it literally slammed into the catcher's mitt before most hitters really realized he'd let go. Scores of Texas high schoolers who faced that incredible heater sat down, thanking their lucky stars they were still alive after wildly whiffing at something they may have heard but probably never saw. The thought of the damage a pitch like that could do was scary for me as an adult, an experienced baseball man, sitting in the stands, so I imagine facing it in the batter's box must have been an absolute nightmare for an inexperienced high school kid.

Once Coach Watson and I developed a rapport, he allowed me to talk to Nolan regularly. Soon I knew we had some problems to overcome. I asked Nolan why he pitched so few innings his junior year. He almost apologetically told me that Watson believed he was too wild and was hurting the team, so he had to come out. That little bit of information told me Nolan had lost confidence in himself and that we would need to do a complete mental makeover. Once a kid, or for that matter even the most seasoned major leaguer, loses confidence and believes he's going to be wild, you can bet he will be. We had to eliminate those negative thoughts.

As I spoke to Nolan about confidence, I remembered my pitching days in the Texas League with the Dallas Eagles and in the National League with the Milwaukee Braves. I recalled how easy it was to fall into that negative thinking trap and how difficult it was to get out. Doubt is infectious, and some pitchers never stop thinking that way.

I asked Watson to never tell Nolan that his pitching was wild and, more importantly, to be extremely positive when Nolan had good control. Bing Crosby sang a song about that once: "Accentuate the positive and eliminate the negative." This was a good lesson for Nolan to learn and a good one for Coach Watson to reinforce.

It seemed the more I talked, the more Nolan listened. As the summer passed, his confidence level rose. As Nolan began to take command of the mound I started to teach him a few tricks of the pitching trade.

First I wanted him to learn to release his fastball with his wrist open and facing the hitter. This allows the wrist to be flexible and enables the pitcher to unleash an extra burst of energy as he drives his arm and wrist downward before releasing the pitch. With that extra power the pitcher's hand and wrist help him create movement on the fastball, that jumping action that makes a live fastball extremely difficult to hit.

I also wanted Nolan to learn the right way to throw a curve. I wanted him to use a karate-chop motion as he drove his arm downward through the arc of his delivery. With the palm of the hand parallel to his head and using the karate-chop motion, the ball naturally curves. The pitcher does not place undue pressure on his fingers, hand, wrist, elbow, or shoulder. In fact, there is no strain on the arm at all.

I wanted this young pitcher to learn to recognize when he had thrown enough in practice. I told Nolan that once he began throwing and felt good and loose, that he had command of his pitches and was ready to go into a ball game, then it was a good idea to stop. I sincerely believe far too many potentially great professional careers never blossomed because some high school or college coach forced a young pitcher to throw too much. I can think of dozens of examples, and I did not want that happening to Nolan.

I especially did not want him throwing hard every day. By nature, eighteen-year-old arms are more fragile than twenty-one- or twenty-five-year-old ones, and a high school senior is not ready to become an everyday reliever. Fortunately I was able to persuade Jim Watson, and because of that I am convinced Nolan developed the way God and Red Murff intended him to.

It wasn't easy to spend so much time on one prospect. Lest you think Nolan was my only responsibility, as a highly competitive New York Mets scout with four states to cover, I had many other young players to watch over, and there were several good ballplayers in the Southwest that year. I had a job to do, but I must confess that I devoted every possible moment in the summer of 1964 to my secret find, Nolan Ryan.

I did my homework. I spent hours in the stands with Nolan's parents, especially his father. I wanted the elder Ryan to know how serious the Mets were about his son and how firmly I believed in Nolan's talent. I also wanted to hear from the senior Ryan what he thought about professional baseball as a career and, fortunately, he signaled his approval. With that knowledge I told him that I would be doing everything in my power to sign his son to a contract with the Mets in the spring of 1965.

During the summer of 1964 I watched Nolan mature, gain confidence in his fastball, and develop a strong faith in himself. While helping Jim Watson, I caught myself in shaking my head in disbelief as I pondered Nolan's awesome gift. As he learned his lessons, Nolan toddled that summer from the high school baseball playpen into a much faster world, that of a top-flight major-league prospect.

As summer of 1964 gave way to fall, I met with one of my subscouts, Red Gaskill, to discuss the players we planned to follow the next spring. In that meeting we began developing strategy for scouting Nolan. I say it was a meeting. When I need to talk strategy, discuss plans, or just think, I head for the nearest duck blind, and that's where Gaskill and I made our plans that year. I don't always shoot anything. Sometimes I never even fire a shot. For me, the duck blind is the greatest place in the world to escape the world's hustle and bustle, to get back to nature, to gain peace of mind, and to make plans in a calm and deliberate way.

This day, like most days, Gaskill and I never fired a shot since ducks weren't our target. We had Nolan Ryan in our sights that day. We had just learned that the scouting profession would undergo a major change in the spring of 1965. For the first time, baseball would conduct a free-agent draft. That meant eligible high school seniors, junior college players, and twenty-one-year-olds who had finished their junior years in a four-year college would be eligible for this historic conscription.

Before the draft, scouts like me could play games and hide our best players, romance their families, keep them under wraps, and then sign them when they graduated. No more. Now all major-league teams would stand on an equal footing. Teams with the worst records would draft earliest. Scouts who once used smooth talk to sell a player's family on their teams now had to convince club executives to draft the players they had discovered.

Gaskill and I knew we would adapt. We swore to each other we would outwork, outthink, and outplan our competition, especially when it came to Nolan Ryan. And I promised Gaskill I would lobby louder and harder and more persistently than I ever had in stating my case for Nolan to the Mets. The draft definitely cost scouts most of our autonomy, but we vowed we wouldn't let that keep us from getting the players we wanted. In this case, Nolan Ryan.

Our plan was simple. We would see every game Nolan pitched during his senior year. Either I would be there or Red Gaskill would. The Mets would see every game Ryan threw. Then we planned to prod scouting director Bing Devine to come to Texas to see our prospect. We were ready.

Red's Random Thought . . .

Just after the first draft in 1965 and before we signed him for the Mets, Nolan won the first game of the state baseball tournament. Then he tried to come back and pitch the second contest. He wasn't having much luck in that second game, and was getting hit pretty good. A part-time scout for another major-league club leaned over to me and said, "Red, I'm glad that big dog is *yours!*" I am too. That "big dog" is headed for the Hall of Fame.

Chapter 4

. . . .

On His Way

In thirty-three years of traveling the roads of Texas, Oklahoma, Louisiana, New Mexico, and assorted foreign countries, I have dodged countless eighteen wheelers, run through hundreds of speed traps (talked myself out of most of them), and put more than a million miles on various vehicles. I average fifty thousand driving miles a year. That's a lot of rubber on the road, a lot of time away from home, and it's not a good way to raise kids or build a happy marriage, but it's a big part of what a scout's life is all about. It's like the old Willie Nelson tune, "On the Road Again," and for better or worse I was hooked on that lifestyle. Instead of making music with my friends, a bunch of us made fast tracks, scouring ballparks for baseball players. While I never shared information on prospects with my fellow scouts on the road, we did have some good times together whenever we could.

Those of us who ran into each other regularly tried our best to have some mealtime together. Sometimes it would be breakfast and a discussion of world and baseball events after a thorough reading of the morning paper before a two-hundred-mile drive to the next ball game, or perhaps we'd catch up over dinner at the next town's best restaurant.

Some of the best times were when we'd decide to have a "hobo supper" in one of our hotel rooms. A hobo supper is relatively simple. One scout would take cold-cut orders from the others, then head for the supermarket. Then we'd have a boisterous picnic in somebody's room. The only hard-and-fast rule was NO talk about the ballplayers we were scouting. So we spun tall tales about the incredible physical skills we exhibited during our own playing days, discussed strengths and weaknesses of former teammates who made it to the big leagues, famous players we'd met (I took great pride in telling everyone about the two times I had met Ty Cobb—I didn't find him to be as nasty or obnoxious as some did), or just plain, simple "how the world could be a better place" bull sessions. Believe me, the older we got, the better ballplayers we were in our younger days. As we aged, you'd have thought most of us would qualify to run the entire country!

Besides these breakfasts and dinners with fellow scouts, I mostly operated alone. It was lonely sometimes, but solitude gave me time to think and make plans and evaluate the players I had seen or was planning to see. I did not want to get into the group-think trap that kept so many scouts from believing in players like Nolan Ryan.

Once I was at a ballpark, I took the time to get to know coaches, the players, and even the fans who often tipped me off on good prospects. I cultivated many wonderful friendships through my travels, some of which have lasted almost forty years. That's what the scouting business is all about: lots of miles, lots of hours alone, lots of camaraderie, and the chance to see some mighty fine ballplayers along the way.

Sometimes the work is tedious. Sometimes days and weeks go by without finding any real ballplayers. Then, lo and behold, you have that once-in-a-lifetime experience of finding a Nolan Ryan, a Jerry Grote, a Kenny Boswell, or a Jerry Koosman. Once you find ballplayers like that, you just have to keep looking, even though sometimes it's like pulling teeth to get your discoveries signed to a major-league contract. Take the case of Nolan Ryan.

THE SCOUT

As good as Red Gaskill and I thought Nolan was, in the spring of 1965 I don't think either of us thought he would be as fabulously successful as he eventually became. We knew the potential was there, but so many things can happen to a youngster along the way to a fruitful big-league career. Family problems, injuries, lack of concentration, so many things can keep a kid from fully developing his marvelous natural ability.

As intimidating as Nolan was to high school hitters that spring, he was by no means a finished product in his senior year. We stood firm in our belief that he possessed one of the ten best arms in the world and that he would improve tremendously once he received regular professional instruction and played against better competition. Even though we had no idea that he would be a cinch candidate for the Hall of Fame, we were convinced that he was definite major-league timber.

You had to admire Nolan. To use an old Texas phrase, he was "chomping at the bit," eager to begin his senior baseball season. He was so ready, he played in a bi-district basketball game on a Friday night and then the next afternoon he pitched ten innings in an intrasquad game and didn't even look winded. Nolan looked ready.

In all candor and honesty, at various times that senior year we were reminded that he was just a kid. He would lose his concentration, he would get wild and get behind in the count, or sometimes he just didn't throw well. But each of the fifteen times a Mets scout saw him pitch that season he always showed us that incredible fastball, and during that entire senior season no major-league club seriously pursued Ryan but the New York Mets.

Nolan's senior year was not without controversy. He threw so cotton-picking hard that he developed a blister on the middle finger of his pitching hand—the power finger, the one that provides the push and drive as the pitcher releases his fastball. I began treating the blister with a reddish yellow gunk called Tuff Skin. It actually worked, but it took six weeks to do the job. In the meantime Nolan didn't throw very well and the other scouts jokingly accused me of picking at Nolan's blister so it wouldn't heal. Now, would I ever do a thing like that? One scout even said, "I figure Murff will miraculously heal Ryan about June 10th" (two days before the draft). Not to worry, he healed long before that.

By the middle of Nolan's senior season other scouts began to take a look at him but never really got interested. Besides listening to Paul Richards proclamation that Nolan's chest wasn't large enough, I think they made another critical mistake. Timing.

I always liked to see Nolan pitch on Tuesdays. His coach scheduled him to pitch the Tuesday game and then the game on Friday. I knew if I saw him on Friday, he'd only be pitching with two days' rest. When I saw him on Tuesdays, he had had an extra day off. So I went to the Tuesday games, and Red Gaskill saw him on Fridays, along with a few other curious scouts. I don't think my competitors saw Nolan at his best, because they likely failed to consider the difference an extra day of rest can make in a young pitcher. It had occurred to me because of my own experience as a professional pitcher.

Unfortunately for the overall good of the game of baseball, most good high school pitchers seldom rest. They are usually the best all-around athletes on the team, so when they are not pitching, the coach almost always uses them as outfielders or shortstops. So they are always on the go, throwing too much, never properly rested, and as a result are rarely able to show the scouts their best stuff.

I took extra precautions to make sure I filled out an extensive report on Nolan each time he pitched, and then I immediately sent it via special delivery to the Mets offices in New York. In each report I made it crystal clear that Nolan's arm was the best I had seen *ever*, so I must have sounded like a broken record to those folks, but I didn't care. I wanted them to know how strongly I felt about this young man.

Early in Nolan's senior year I began lobbying scouting director Bing Devine to see Nolan pitch. I knew there were a couple of other pitchers in other parts of the country who were bigger and stronger than this eighteen-year-old Texan, and I knew those young men were attracting more attention from the Mets. I was afraid if I didn't fight the good fight to get Nolan drafted by constantly haranguing my bosses, the Mets would lose Nolan forever. Finally, after much prodding and cajoling, Devine relented. He was on his way to Texas!

On a Thursday evening in April before Nolan's coach scheduled him to pitch the next night, I ran into Jim Watson at a junior varsity game in Texas City. Bing Devine would be there to watch Nolan the next night. I asked, "Coach, you gonna have Nolan ready to throw his best tomorrow night?"

"No, Red, I'm not. He didn't pitch worth a hoot on Tuesday, he didn't pay any attention to me, he lost his concentration, got wild and I had to take him out of the ball game. So I decided a little 'pay attention to coach' session was in order. First I made him pitch batting practice for at least thirty minutes, maybe an hour, then I ran him until he puked," Watson said very matter of factly.

My heart sank. I was exasperated. "Oh, no. Why did you do that, Jim? Don't you realize the Mets scouting director will be here tomorrow night to see Nolan pitch?"

Bless his heart, Jim had no way of knowing that. He relented and promised to let Nolan pitch in Friday night's game, but for the rest of the junior varsity game and during the entire ride home I sat in stunned silence, my heart in my throat, wondering what effect this "run him until he puked" session would have on Nolan's performance on Friday—but more importantly, what effect would it have on his potential big-league future. I shuddered to think about it.

Early Friday morning I met Bing Devine's plane from New York. Boy, did I feel like a fool. I cannot tell you how upset and embarrassed I was, especially after having spent so much time on the telephone, bragging on Nolan and cajoling Devine into coming to Texas. I wrote so many glowing reports, detailing in no uncertain terms how tremendous Ryan's arm was, and now, it was anybody's guess how good he would be on this night.

Once I picked up Devine and told him the whole story, I began praying, pleading with my Maker to let Nolan perform well. It was little consolation to remember a lesson I'd learned in Sunday school as a kid: Sometimes our most fervent prayers initially go unanswered. Despite my well-intentioned prayers, my worst fears turned into harsh, vivid reality. Nolan's performance was atrocious. He looked weak and lethargic, and he displayed all the characteristics of someone who had been run into the ground the day before. On a critically important evening he displayed absolutely no big-league tools.

Somehow, though, Nolan won the game, but as I talked with Bing Devine on the drive back to the airport, it was quite obvious that my guy had been a major disappointment to the Mets scouting director. Devine told me he liked Nolan's pitching mechanics and he realized the "run until he puked" session hampered his efforts, but my boss was totally unimpressed with my judgment of Nolan's ability.

When we got to the airport, Devine wrote down the name of several of the Mets top pitching prospects. He told me it would be "to my benefit" to hop on an airplane and see what real pitching talent looked like. I did travel to see a couple of those kids, both of whom were drafted well ahead of Nolan, as it turned out. They were excellent pitchers, but they didn't throw as hard as Nolan—nowhere close. Stubbornly I filled out my scouting reports on both young men and noted in boldface letters: CAN'T THROW AS HARD AS RYAN. Looking back, those words might have sounded like sour grapes, but they weren't. They were my true, honest assessment, and I stood firmly by my guns.

In fairness, after we drafted Nolan the next year and he had the chance to pitch in the rookie leagues, Bing Devine became Nolan Ryan's biggest fan. The scouting director later admitted to me that he appreciated my intensity and my solid belief in Nolan's talents because at first he thought I had lost my mind. After that first professional season of Nolan's, my boss had seen enough of that fastball to know what I had seen, and I'm glad he appreciated my stubbornness.

I didn't tell many people about Nolan, not even all my sub-scouts. But then one day I decided to send two subscouts on a secret mission, so secret they didn't know who they were going to see when I assigned them to watch Alvin High School play in the state quarterfinals in Brenham. Tom Bridges and Wade Fatheree were on the case.

Nolan put on a show that night. He threw so hard that any-one who got a foul tip off him was considered a hero. He was that dominant. Wade excitedly left the ball game with one out in the bottom of the seventh inning, headed for the concession stand to get five dollars' worth of change so he could make a person-to-person long distance call to me in Texas City. He was beside himself, believing he had made the scouting find of a life-time, and he just had to tell me what he'd seen.

As he placed his call, the game ended and Nolan walked past him, headed out of the ballpark. Fatheree motioned Ryan over. As my phone was ringing, Fatheree was asking Nolan where Alvin, Texas, was.

Nolan said, "Well, it's about thirty-five miles south of Houston." As I answered the phone, Fatheree told me to wait as he asked Nolan how far Alvin is from Texas City.

Nolan replied, "Less than thirty miles."

Fatheree asked if Nolan knew a Mets scout named Red Murff, and Nolan replied, "Oh, yes sir. Yes sir. Mr. Murff's been working with me for the past two years."

Fatheree realized I already knew about Nolan, so he quickly told me good-bye. He now knew what I had known for two years.

Baseball's first amateur free-agent draft occurred in June 1965. I went to New York along with the other regional scouts to participate. We all gathered at a New York hotel along with representatives from the other seventeen major-league clubs. The commissioner handled the draft, and each team had a chance to draft in inverted order of the way they finished in the standings the previous year.

Each scout came loaded with information on the best players in his region. Each time the Mets turn came to pick, the conversations between scouts, the scouting director, and the general manager got intense, sometimes downright nasty, as each scout fought for his players.

Nolan Ryan's stock with the New York Mets was not high, especially since Bing Devine had seen Nolan perform so poorly earlier that season. Even so, I argued and fussed and fought with my fellow scouts and bosses, trying to get them to draft Nolan. I just knew we were going to lose him!

One round went by, then the second, third . . . then the sixth and seventh. Still I had not been able to convince Devine to draft Nolan.

Finally, when it came the Mets turn in the eighth round, I screamed, "Bing, Nolan Ryan has too much talent for us to leave him! We *have* to take him!" Bing relented. "Okay, if you like him that much, Red, then let's take him."

And we did. Finally . . . finally, I had my man.

The draft took place two days before the start of the Texas high school state tournament. Once the tournament ended for Nolan, I called his family and set up a time to begin contract negotiations. I did not want to rush the Ryans, but I did want them to know the Mets would be making a very fair deal.

The Mets offered Nolan a seven-hundred-dollar-a-month salary, plus a cash bonus of nineteen thousand dollars, which included four semesters of college at one thousand dollars a semester. They also offered an incentive bonus of seventy-five hundred dollars to be paid after Nolan spent ninety days in the big leagues. Nolan's entire signing package amounted to more than twenty-five thousand, a nice sum in 1965 dollars.

Since he had no college baseball scholarship offer, I promised Nolan that if he did not sign with the Mets I would make sure he got a college baseball scholarship. Nolan let me know he was more interested in the money than in college. (During his big-league career he did take a few business courses at Alvin Community College.)

As negotiations wound to a close, I invited sportswriter Steve Vernon to watch Nolan sign his contract. I told Steve he could be there, provided the Ryans gave their okay. I worked closely with Steve on a couple of baseball stories, and I wanted him to see firsthand how the signing process works.

The Ryans approved and afterward I warned Vernon not to speak during the signing. He could watch, but if he uttered a word, he was out of there.

The scene was set. The Ryan family—Nolan, his mother, and his father—along with me, Red Gaskill, and Steve Vernon either sat at the table or in chairs behind us.

All of a sudden, with pen in hand, Nolan balked as he started to sign. I remained calm, watching Nolan's facial expressions, which appeared to be strained. All of a sudden the sportswriter blurted, "Good grief . . . no one ever offered me that much money to do any kind of a job. What's wrong with you, sign the contract!"

I looked at Vernon and was about to motion him out of the room, when I glanced over at Nolan. Whatever fears or trepidations were running through his mind suddenly disappeared with those words, and he immediately put pen to paper and signed.

Whew! A two-year odyssey had ended. I was proud of myself for being so tenacious with my bosses and so persistent with Nolan's coach. The newest Met had clearly learned his lessons.

Even after Nolan found great success as a major leaguer, he came to me for instructional help. In 1986, for example, while Nolan was pitching with the Astros, he'd lost a couple of games in a row. Hitters were catching up with his fastball because it appeared he'd lost just a tiny bit of velocity. For Nolan, a tiny bit of velocity meant his speed had dropped from 97–98 to 95–96 miles an hour. He was still incredibly fast, but not as fast as Nolan had been throwing. I received word through a friend that

Nolan wanted to see me in the Astros dugout several hours before a Houston home game.

When we finally got together, I told him I'd been watching him throw and gave my assessment of his velocity. I suggested he needed another couple of pitches, new surprises to confuse the hitters.

If Nolan's fastball was thrown in the 96–97 mile-per-hour range in those days, his curve ball was a full 15 miles an hour slower, and with its sharp, biting break, really paralyzed hitters. I thought he needed a change-up, a pitch thrown with the same motion as the fastball but released with something taken off so the ball's speed is 10 to 15 miles per hour slower than the fastball. When the change-up is thrown correctly, many a big-league hitter has been sent back to the dugout shaking his head in disbelief.

So Nolan and I went to work on one called the circle change because the pitcher holds the ball by actually making a circle with the thumb and forefinger of his pitching hand. The ball is actually cupped in his hand with the circle at the side of the ball. When this pitch is thrown with a fastball motion it is relatively easy to control yet the pitch drops quickly as it approaches the strike zone and it moves 10 to 15 miles an hour slower than a fastball.

Fortunately the circle change is a pitch that can be picked up quickly, and it took Nolan only about six weeks to master it. I also suggested Nolan learn a pitch college kids called a "cutter." Essentially, a cutter is held like a fastball but as the pitch is released, the pitcher lifts his forefinger and that causes the fastball to cut down and away from a right-handed hitter. So what I did was give Nolan two fastball looks instead of just one.

By adding new pitches to his repertoire, he accomplished exactly what I told him he needed to—give those hitters other troublesome pitches to think about beside his great fastball and curve. The pitches worked almost immediately, and pretty soon he was giving hitters fits and winning ball games. This was part of my "service after the sale" approach to scouting. My role in players' professional development only started with the contract signing. I was always available for advice and guidance.

Besides asking for my advice during his career, Nolan would call me right before he went to spring training so I could watch him pitch. Like a good mechanic who's called in to check out a car before the owner takes it on a long trip, Nolan wanted me to make sure his mechanics were in the proper working order, and he knew from our previous sessions that I could spot anything that was wrong in his delivery. Believe me, I always took those pre-spring training meetings as the highest compliment.

After Nolan made it to the big leagues, I always observed his progress closely through newspaper, television, and radio reports, but I did it from a distance. I never followed him around or bothered him in any way. I always figured if Nolan needed me, he knew where to find me, and that's the way it always worked out.

I did get to see Nolan pitch in some memorable ball games through the years, but in the beginning all was not glory, laud, and honor for our fireballing friend. For instance, I accompanied Nolan's parents, other family members, all his high school coaches, and a cadre of his friends to the Astrodome in 1966 to watch him pitch for the Mets against the Astros. It's funny to look back on that night so long ago now, but I have to tell you, no one had any fun except me. My player had made it to the big leagues, and he was going to be successful. Down deep in my heart I was overjoyed by the thought of Nolan's future. So I was happy as a clam. Meanwhile Nolan was nervous, tense, and anxious, as were his parents, other family members, and his coaches. The Astros whacked him around pretty good. In fact they gave him what we in Texas call a "good country whuppin'."

I joyfully sat down alongside Jim Watson and said, "Isn't this great? Isn't Nolan doing well?"

"He's getting beat," Jim scowled.

"So who cares? Think what's ahead for this boy, Jim."

Somehow I couldn't make everyone understand how incredibly amazing it was just to have Nolan in the big leagues. I guess they learned to believe me later on when Nolan achieved so much success . . . more than even I had ever dreamed of.

While I only saw Nolan pitch in person several dozen times during his career, I always managed to have good fortune when it came to seeing him pitch some memorable games. I didn't see his first four no-hitters because they were pitched for the California Angels. However, something told me to be in the Astrodome for a Saturday afternoon game on September 26, 1981. That afternoon Nolan Ryan became the first pitcher in major-league history to throw *five* career no-hitters. To say I was beaming with pride was the most extreme understatement, but this game provided me with a couple of hilarious moments.

By the seventh inning Nolan was dominating the game. In the bottom of the seventh inning, it was his turn to hit. My wife, Sara, was with me along with her son and his girlfriend. When Nolan stepped into the batter's box, Sara yelled, "Okay, Nolan, hit a homer!"

"Well, Sara." I said, "It's not critical that he hit a home run now. Have you not looked at the scoreboard to see what's happening?"

My remark upset and embarrassed her a little bit, but just as she was about to yell something about his no-hitter, she stopped herself in midsentence. She'd remembered I'd told her that it could be a jinx to talk about a no-hitter during the ball game.

In the eighth inning you could tell Nolan knew what was going on and he appeared to be tensing up just a bit. So was I and so were most of the fans in the stands. Two rows in front of Sara and me sat a man and his wife and their infant son, perhaps fifteen months old. As Nolan wound up to pitch, the baby started screaming and crying. All the fans around the young family were irritated, and the wife leaned over to her husband and suggested they go home.

Her husband paid no attention and the baby screamed louder.

"Let's go home!" she insisted.

Still, the husband refused to look at his wife.

"I said, I wanna go home!" she screamed.

As Nolan continued to pitch, the husband slowly turned to his wife and said very emphatically, "Woman, Nolan Ryan is pitching a no-hitter, and it's the eighth inning, and history may be made here within a few minutes, and if you think I'm leaving this ballpark now, you're out of your mind!"

With that she took a seat, the baby quieted, and the rest is history, except I've often wondered if their marriage survived that night at the ballpark. The family did get to witness a fantastic ball game. On my scorecard, right after Nolan struck out the first two hitters on wicked, biting curve balls, I wrote, "has command of the curve." And did he ever!

I missed Nolan's sixth no-hitter because it happened in Oakland in June 1990, when he was pitching for the Texas Rangers, but I was there for his seventh no-hitter on May 1, 1991, at Arlington Stadium. Who would've ever believed that a forty-four-year-old could still be pitching so well, let along throwing a no-hitter? Nolan made some amazing pitches and literally took my breath away that night. He still had that unbelievable fastball, a nasty curve, the cutter, and the circle change. I have to tell you I grinned every time I heard him grunt when he unleashed that heater.

I missed his five-thousandth strikeout because I knew he'd finish his career with well more than that, but I was there for his three-hundredth career victory, and it took a little luck on my part to pull this one off. Late in July 1990, when it appeared Nolan would get that milestone victory in front of the home-town fans in Texas, I called Rangers general manager Tom Grieve and asked him for some tickets to what I hoped would be a memorable night. Grieve told me he had no tickets, and I don't have to tell you I was extremely disappointed because I knew that if Grieve had really wanted to find me one or two, he could have. As luck would have it, Nolan didn't get his three hundredth that night, so I made reservations at a hotel in Milwaukee, called the Brewers general manager, called my daughter, Robin, and her husband, Bruce, in Chicago, had them meet me at O'Hare

Airport, and we drove up to Milwaukee for the game. Nolan came through! He beat Milwaukee 11–3, and I don't have to tell you I was one happy scout, I mean, how many scouts sign pitchers who win three hundred games?!

After the game Robin, Bruce, and I were escorted into a restaurant at the Rangers hotel where we greeted Nolan and I met George W. Bush and the rest of the Rangers ownership. Bush, the son of the former president, and I renewed an old friendship. His family, father, mother, and brothers sat next to my family in box seats at the Mets games in Houston for five years beginning in 1964. In Milwaukee we talked about old times, his work with the Rangers, and he asked me if I had been in Arlington during Nolan's failed attempt at the three hundredth win, and I politely told him no, because I couldn't get a ticket. I laugh about this now because Tom Grieve overheard the conversation and ran for cover as Bush apologized profusely and told me to call him personally any time I needed any more tickets. I never had another ticket problem as long as Nolan pitched.

In all seriousness I could not imagine in my wildest dreams that Nolan Ryan would've ever been as successful as he became. Nolan made me proud in so many ways during his career, not only as perhaps the greatest pitcher ever, but as a husband, father, and impeccable role model for kids . . . even me. I was blessed in so many ways because of Nolan—still I wonder what would've happened if I hadn't pulled off I-45 and headed for Clear Creek that April Saturday more than thirty years ago.

Red's Random Thought . . .

From the first time I saw him, I knew Jerry Grote could be a major-league catcher. While Johnny Bench always got more publicity because he was a better hitter than Jerry, I will always believe Jerry was the superior catcher, thrower, and handler of pitchers. I am not alone in that judgment.

Chapter 5

Ketch

Some old baseball sage once called the catcher's gear the Tools of Ignorance. Well, it may be dumb and it may be stupid to strap on that livery, chest protector, mask, and shin guards every day and squat down in the hot sun for three hours or more and try to catch fastballs at ninety miles an hour; curves that sometimes skip away in the dirt, and take vicious foul tips off your hands, fingers, or feet, and get body-blocked by base runners trying to score, and generally absorb an incredible physical beating while you're at it. Call it the work of an ignoramus, but no ball club of championship caliber ever won a pennant without an "ignorant" catcher.

The catcher must know where the ball is at all times. A catcher may not be the manager on the field, but he's definitely the manager's eyes. With the help of his skipper and his coaches, the catcher calls each pitch, demands that the man on the mound stay alert and focused on the ball game, and must make sure that all infielders and outfielders are positioned properly.

That's just the beginning. The catcher is responsible for keeping home plate covered at all times and making the proper calls on infield flies, not to mention being unbelievably agile and quick in blocking pitches. If no runners are on second or third base, he must keep any infielder's errant throw from going into the first-base dugout. Ideally he needs to have a great throwing arm, although a catcher can make up for having an average arm by mastering fast footwork and a lightning-quick release of the ball as a runner tries to steal a base.

If you find a catcher who can run, well, that's a rarity. One who can hit or hit with power is also a find. I think catching is the game's toughest position to play for several reasons. The physical toll the job demands is staggering. Broken and twisted fingers are the norm among catchers. Getting the wind knocked out of you is commonplace. Don't forget the wear and tear on the knees, hamstrings, and quadriceps from the constant squatting.

The job is also tough mentally because a catcher must know what each one of his pitchers is capable of in any game situation. Part of the job description includes knowing each opposing hitter's strengths and weaknesses and which base runners are the greatest threats to attempt a stolen base. The catcher has to remember the count on the batter, the number of outs, and, like a chess master, anticipate the play that is about to happen as well as what can occur two or three plays ahead. It's a tough, complicated job.

I've had the opportunity to sign some pretty good catchers who played significant roles on their teams in the major leagues. But I only signed one really great catcher: Jerry Grote. His story goes back to January 1961.

I had just left the Milwaukee Braves organization as a minor league manager and had signed on as a talent scout for the fledgling expansion Houston Colt .45s. The Houston club did not play its first game until April 1962, but in 1961 the team already had executives in place and a stable of scouts combing the country for free-agent talent.

In my new role I began to develop contacts. I called people I knew and trusted all across my assigned territory in Texas and Oklahoma. Some were men I had played professional baseball with through the years. Some were coaches. Some were simply baseball fans who knew talent. They became my lifeline through the years, constantly tipping me off to potential major-league ballplayers.

I was planning my scouting schedule for the spring of 1961 when I got a call from a contact in San Antonio, Andy Anderson. He told me I needed to see a young man from MacArthur High School who had a tremendous throwing arm and could really hit. So when the season rolled around in mid-February, I headed for San Antonio.

When I first saw Jerry Grote during his senior year in high school, he was a shortstop but he had the classic look of a catcher. Stocky body, great arm, fiery temper, and he always knew where the ball was. Jerry acted like a coach on the field, and he had no shortage of self-confidence. This square-jawed, broken-nosed kid walked with a cocky street-fighter's swagger. He was my kind of ballplayer.

When I arrived at the ballpark, Jerry's team was in the field. An opposing hitter slammed a colossal line drive over the left fielder's head. There was no fence to stop the ball from rolling, and it rolled over the chalky, concretelike ground for more than four hundred feet until the left fielder finally ran it down.

When the outfielder reached the ball, Jerry Grote had run from his shortstop's position to a spot in left field about three hundred feet from home plate. He took the relay throw from the left fielder and turned and fired. As he did, the runner rounded third and headed for home. The ball took off like a low trajectory rocket. It tore up grass as it skipped on one hop from just beside the pitcher's mound and slammed right into the catcher's mitt. The runner was out by a good three feet.

Honestly, I thought Roberto Clemente, the late Pittsburgh Pirates outfielder, reputed to have had one of the finest throwing arms of all time, had made that throw. What an arm! No seventeen-year-old I had ever seen could throw like that. This kid did.

I introduced myself to Jerry after the game ended and congratulated him on his throw. He turned out to be a rough, crusty, profane character, even as a teenager. Whoever came up with the term *cocky*, invented it for Jerry Grote. I shook hands with his coach and told him I thought that while Jerry did a good job at shortstop, I believed his ultimate future was behind the plate.

Later on that season I went back to see my prize and there he was, decked out in catcher's livery. He looked like a natural! Once Jerry adjusted to using the gear and became more comfortable at calling pitches, he looked as if he had invented the position.

Believe me, there was no doubt who was in charge on the field to anyone sitting in the stands or anywhere within earshot. From the coach to the outfielders, Jerry had everyone on his toes. If a pitcher became sloppy or lost concentration, the fans in the stands could hear Jerry screaming about it. As a little "wake-up call" a daydreaming pitcher might see the ball coming right back at him from his catcher faster than he'd delivered it to the plate. One way or another Jerry always made his point—Stay alert, pal!

Even as a high school senior Jerry was old-time blood and guts, and he had the best catcher's arm I ever saw, even though some claim that honor belongs to Johnny Bench. Not in my book, and I saw them both. Bench definitely was the superior hitter, the Hall of Famer, the more famous ballplayer, but Jerry's arm was better. Period. He had an extremely quick release. No one ran on him in high school and few did in the big leagues. No self-respecting high school coach would dare send his runners on such a suicide mission and few major-league managers ever did either.

A lot of scouts knew about Jerry Grote but most questioned his hitting ability. I judged him an exceptional high school line-drive hitter and never expected that he'd hit a lot of home runs. In fact I told Jerry's dad that I believed his son would end his career with a lifetime batting average of about .255–.260, with enough power to generate only about seven or eight home runs a year, but I also believed those home runs would come in clutch situations.

To be honest, I had trouble seeing Jerry's hitting feats in high school because I always seemed to be AWOL. Anytime I took a break at one of his games to go to the restroom, to get a Coke, or stop to talk to a fan, that's when Jerry would crush a home run, a triple, or a double. I solved this problem by making a solemn vow to stay in my seat the whole ball game.

I boxed up two professional-stock Louisville Slugger bats and sent them to Jerry, but before I mailed them I took a Magic Marker and drew a pair of eyes on the barrel of each one. I put a note in the box that said, "When you see me in the stands, use the seeing-eye bats and then hit the ball!"

The next time I saw him play was in a tournament in Uvalde, Texas. I noticed Jerry grinning as he came to the plate carrying one of his seeing-eye bats. He looked up in the stands at me, winked, dug into the batter's box, and uncorked a bases-loaded home run. He followed that with a triple and two doubles, all slammed with the seeing-eye bat. That hitting exhibition was all I needed to see. I wanted Jerry Grote for the Houston Colt .45s.

The Houston club promised me they had plenty of money to compete for ballplayers. This was in the days before the draft, so it was open season on everybody. The highest bidder always won. I had some tough competition, since some of the best professional scouts in the history of the game worked the Texas-Oklahoma-New Mexico-Louisiana territory. Scouts like Hugh Alexander with the Dodgers, Bobby Goff with Cleveland, Billy Capps with the Cubs, Fred McAlister with the Cardinals, Dee Phillips with Baltimore, all of us fought for many of the same players.

We were combatants in every sense of the word, and some of my competitors were known to be underhanded in pursuit of a player. In Jerry Grote's case, one of my adversaries told Jerry's dad that his son would be worth a $90,000 bonus, an unbelievable sum in 1961. Remember, this was well before six-figure bonuses were the norm.

All those scouts knew their clubs could not or would not pay that kind of money, but they were playing games with me and the Grote family. They hoped Jerry's dad would garner an inflated sense of his son's worth on the open market so that the first scout (me) to submit a lower bid would end up looking cheap. That trick might have worked on a novice scout, but little did they know I was onto their plan and had my own plan ready.

I did my homework before making an offer to Jerry's dad. On the day I planned to sign him, I knew that my competitors were in Baton Rouge, Louisiana, lining up to make a bid for Dalton Jones, touted as the top prospect in the nation. Jones eventually made it to the big leagues with the Boston Red Sox for a short time, but in 1961 he was the hottest prospect.

The fact my competitors were in Baton Rouge that day worked to my advantage. The Colt .45s had a scout in Louisiana who had been following Jones closely, so I stayed in Texas and pursued Jerry Grote.

That morning I called the elder Grote and told him I was ready to sign his son to a professional baseball contract. He agreed it was time and indicated he preferred the Colt .45s because that meant his son could play in his home state. It always helped working with parents who liked me and my ball club.

Jerry's dad was a man of integrity. For several months he had been dealing with Dodgers scout Hugh Alexander who had begged for the right of first refusal to sign Jerry. He felt he owed a courtesy call to Alexander to let him know the Colt .45s were ready to make a deal.

I told him that Alexander and several other scouts were in Baton Rouge, attempting to sign Dalton Jones. I agreed that he should call Alexander, but I also told him, "Mr. Grote, your son has just as much right to sign a professional contract today as Dalton Jones does, so we should proceed with our business."

I gave him the hotel number in Baton Rouge where Alexander was staying. Once he got the Dodgers scout on the phone, he told him that Red Murff from the Colt .45s was in his home, ready to sign Jerry to a contract.

Alexander treated the elder Grote very rudely and very

abruptly. He said that he was too busy and asked if he could call back in a couple of days. Mr. Grote agreed and then hung up the phone. He thought about it for a moment, almost satisfied with Alexander's answer, until I interrupted.

"Doesn't it appear to you that Alexander is more interested in Dalton Jones than he is your son? Alexander didn't even name a signing bonus price for Jerry. That might seem fair to you, but it's not fair to me and it's not fair to the Houston Colt .45s. We are ready to sign him today, right now, on the spot."

There was no arguing with that. I suggested that he call Alexander back and demand a firm monetary offer from the Dodgers. Alexander played hardball with me at the Grote family's expense, so I decided I'd do the same with him.

This time the Dodgers scout responded angrily. "I told you once," Alexander fumed, "that I am extremely busy now and cannot deal with you."

A determined Mr. Grote persisted. He wanted to hear a firm offer from the Dodgers. After all, he reasoned, the Dodgers have been talking to Jerry for months and it was the Dodgers who asked for right of first refusal, so they should be ready with a bid.

"Okay," Alexander relented. "The Los Angeles Dodgers bid eight thousand dollars for the contract rights to your son. Good-bye." The L.A. scout slammed down the phone, never waiting to hear a response from the stunned father.

Alexander's extremely low offer was devastating. Other scouts had already told the Grotes that Jerry would be in line for a ninety thousand dollar bonus and yet all he heard was a paltry, lowball bid from a scout he thought he trusted.

Meekly he told me about his conversation with Alexander before he dejectedly walked out of the room for a moment. His bubble had burst at the expense of the Los Angeles Dodgers and Hugh Alexander.

"I'm just really too disappointed and too confused to deal with this anymore today," he said. "Jerry and I won't be signing a contract today with you or anybody else."

I left the Grote home, headed north up Interstate 35. About fifty miles outside San Antonio, I stopped and placed a call back to the Grote residence. I said that I did not want the day to end without his receiving a firm monetary bid from the Houston Colt .45s, and I asked if he minded receiving the bid via telegram. I told him I only wanted him to know that fair money was there for his son's services, and that the Houston Colt .45s wanted his son to play for them. This was agreeable, and I sped to the nearest Western Union office.

I offered Jerry a twenty-five thousand dollar signing bonus. Every scout in the Southwest knew that ninety thousand dollars was far too high. I thought my bid was fair for the young catcher.

After looking over our offer, the Grotes decided not to sign. The low bid from the Dodgers helped them lose their taste for dealing with professional baseball people for the time being. Instead, Jerry enrolled at Trinity University for the fall semester of 1961, but he really wasn't college material. He didn't like the classes. He didn't like the atmosphere. Fortunately for us he played college baseball in the spring of 1962 but he didn't play well. Deep in his heart Jerry knew he was not a college man. He was a ballplayer first and foremost, and he knew it. Back then there were no rules governing the signing of college athletes, so we were able to sign him to a professional contract later that year.

Jerry Grote played for a semiprofessional team in Brenham, Texas, during the summer of 1962, then headed out to the Arizona Fall Instructional League, which provides major-league managers and executives the chance to watch top minor-league prospects for an extended period of time. The league also gives major-league players who may be switching positions a chance to get a feel for their new territory under game conditions.

Jerry played extremely well against some pretty fast competition. After the Instructional League season ended, I had a conversation with the manager of the Colt .45s San Antonio club in the Texas League, Lou Fitzgerald. Some of Lou's best players had been promoted to the Colt .45s Triple A team in Oklahoma

City for the 1963 season, and he was looking for replacements. His biggest need was for a catcher, and he had no idea where to find one. Fortunately for Lou, he knew me and I knew just the catcher he was looking for. I told him I'd just seen Jerry Grote play in the Instructional League and I told him Jerry was his man.

"Grote? Good grief, Red, he's only nineteen years old." Fitzgerald shouted. "You're talking about a putting a teenager up against stiff, seasoned, Texas League competition? I don't think so!"

"Grote will do the job," I insisted. Later, Jerry Grote made me a prophet. During the 1963 Texas League season, he made the big jump from rookie league to the Class AA Texas League. With his strong throwing arm, steady bat, and amazing leadership ability, especially at his age and experience level, he led San Antonio to the Texas League pennant and in doing so became a hot major-league prospect.

In my mind I knew beyond doubt that Jerry could be the Colt .45s catcher for the next fifteen years. During the 1964 season he moved up to the big-league club. He caught 130 games for Houston that year and performed extremely well for a major-league rookie at a demanding position—and the kid wasn't even old enough to vote.

For some unknown reason the Colt .45s apparently didn't like him. They signed two other high-priced catchers, and after Grote's first major-league season, they outrighted his contract to their Class AAA Oklahoma City club. Outrighting meant Jerry would never play for Houston again unless every other major-league club refused to offer him a major-league contract. Why Houston did that is beyond me, and I never heard a reasonable, logical explanation from anyone within the organization. Outrighted or not, Jerry Grote was far from done as a major-league catcher.

By the time Grote had been sent down to the minor leagues, I had left the Colt .45s and had gone to work for my old friend Wid Mathews as a scout for the New York Mets. One day while attending a scouts meeting in New York, we were discussing professional players who were available. I knew Jerry's situation and that he was available for the waiver price. So I gave the Mets executives a glowing appraisal of his abilities and urged them to acquire his contract. "Gentlemen," I pontificated, "Jerry Grote can solve New York's catching problems for the next decade and maybe longer."

The Mets listened intently to my assessment and immediately acquired the rights to Jerry's contract, and he did me proud. In fact, he made me look clairvoyant.

With his fiery take-charge attitude, incredible throwing arm, and his consistent, sometimes even powerful bat, he helped lead the Mets to the world's championship in 1969 and back to the World Series in 1973. He also helped the Dodgers go to the World Series later in his career.

Grote impressed everyone except sportswriters. He hated them with a passion. But baseball people—players, managers, coaches, umpires and scouts—always sang his praises.

Character that he is, Jerry Grote stories abound. Like the time he was catching for Houston's entry in the Instructional League. The Colt .45s had signed a hot-shot infielder from UCLA named Ernie Fazio. Fazio played a short time in the big leagues, but he was never the superstar some other Houston scouts thought he'd be.

Anyway, Grote always thought the five-six Fazio had too much mouth for his size, and if there was one trait Jerry detested it was a smart mouth. Grote also believed Fazio was always trying to show him up, and the combative Grote hated that.

During an infield drill Fazio tried to make Jerry look bad on a throw to second base. Professional catchers aim the ball for a low trajectory to the front corner, first-base side of second base. If the ball hits the second baseman's glove at that spot, the runner slides directly into the glove and becomes an easy out.

Fazio made it appear the ball was coming in too low. Instead of waiting for the throw, a disgruntled Fazio moved closer toward home plate. However, the ball was just the intended height and tore into his plastic protective athletic cup, shattering it into tiny pieces, and Fazio passed out. Although he wasn't seriously hurt, Fazio learned one important lesson that day. Don't try to show up Jerry Grote. He meant business, every time he stepped on the field.

Red's Random Thought . . .

In 1963 Mets scouting director Wid Mathews ordered me to sign a high school catcher from a team that was still in the playoffs. I adamantly refused. If the young man signed, he would be ineligible, and it might cause his team to lose a chance at a once-in-a-lifetime state championship. I told Wid that coaches and players were my pipeline to success. I signed the young man after the playoffs.

Chapter 6

What We Do

You'd think it would be easy to give readers a history of scouting. How did this profession evolve? Who were the first scouts? You know the kind of treatise, but there's a little problem. Nobody really knows the whole story.

It has always been an underground brotherhood without the secret handshakes. We are supposed to keep a low profile, so I can only guess how we came into the game. Most of our names and photos are rarely recorded and the only proof that the early ones existed is evidenced by the fact that some extraordinarily talented players were unearthed fairly early in baseball history.

There is no doubt in my mind, for example, that someone with a special eye helped the manager of the first professional club, the Cincinnati Red Stockings, recruit his roster in 1869. But who was he? I'm sure when old Abner Doubleday or some of his cronies needed ballplayers for their fledgling teams, someone was sent out to find gifted athletes, but historians forgot to jot down his name.

Connie Mack, the legendary Philadelphia Athletics manager, always gave credit to his scouts for helping him build his ball clubs, but he seldom identified them or talked much about them as individuals. The old New York Giants boss John J. McGraw did the same thing. One of my mentors, Wid Mathews, worked closely with the legendary Branch Rickey to develop the scouting profession and the farm system with the Brooklyn Dodgers and St. Louis Cardinals and was the fellow Rickey sent as "his man" to make the final evaluation of any ballplayer his team wanted to acquire, but the details on most talent sleuths from back then are sketchy at best.

I can, however, tell you what we do even if I cannot tell you who did it. What most scouts of my generation have in common is the fact that at one time we played and managed in professional baseball but probably didn't make the majors. Big-league executives like Baltimore Orioles general manager Roland Hemond believe being a professional player is essential to becoming a good scout.

"From their on-the-field experience, they know the rudiments: how the game should be played, what physical skills it takes to play the game, and the emotional makeup of young men who are trying to make that first step toward major-league stardom," Hemond says.

Professional managing experience is also a clear advantage for a scout. As they watch their ballplayers perform daily, minor league managers make critical talent judgments. After each ball game they are required to write out a game report on the contribution each player made to the day's contest. He includes a brief synopsis of what happened in the game, who looked good, who didn't, and what is being done to correct problems each player is having with his game. Very simply, the minor-league manager knows who is producing and who isn't, and every day he sends his report card on each of his players to his major-league club's office. His input and his judgment ultimately play a big part in determining what players move up, move down, or are released within a big-league club's minor-league system.

My friend and former competitor Billy Capps (and a cousin of Mike Capps) took what I believe is one of the best, if not the best paths to becoming a scout. He signed his first professional baseball contract after finishing high school in Comanche, Oklahoma, in 1937. He spent the next twenty-three years dedicated to learning how to play the game as a professional third baseman, and he made it as far as Triple A baseball, one level below the big leagues. Billy had spent all that time learning the rudiments, and so he began his career like any craftsman: he became an apprentice first, then a journeyman. Billy's next ten years in the game were spent in the minor-league manager's ranks, applying what he'd learned as a player to handling players in the dugout. He became an expert game strategist, talent evaluator, leader, and above all he learned a sense of autonomy, how to make decisions on his own with little or no input from his superiors.

One step at a time, one year at a time, Billy became a true craftsman. He learned his trade from the ground up and became a baseball expert. In doing so, he built a solid reputation in an occupation he dearly loves. In my opinion he has the perfect background to be a scout. Why has he spent so many years looking for ballplayers? The answer is simple.

"Well, I think I'm like a lot of scouts. I always loved the game and never wanted to leave it, and I really wanted to give something back. Behind God and my family, baseball is my life, " Billy insists. "In 1960 I was tired of the dugout, but I wanted to stay in baseball, so I talked to a friend of mine with the Cubs. I told him, 'Say, if you get an opening for a scout down here in the Southwest, I'd appreciate it if you'd consider me.' Well, this friend knew me pretty well and he really thought with my background I'd make a good scout, and so the Cubs hired me and I've been with 'em ever since."

Billy, like most baseball veterans who want to become scouts, used his experience to optimal advantage and turned a personal contact into a good scouting job. Believe me, Billy is one of the best and a fierce competitor on the scouting circuit. In thirty-five years of scouring the Southwest for talent, he's come up with some great ballplayers. He signed Burt Hooton, a man who won 151 games for the Cubs and Dodgers. He signed Roger Metzger, the outstanding shortstop for the Houston Astros who had his career tragically shortened by an accident that severed some fingers on his throwing hand. Billy Capps also discovered Johnny Bench, the Hall of Fame catcher, but that's a story for a later chapter.

I think Billy would agree with me that in the past few years, we've seen scouts come into baseball with little if any playing experience. That lack of experience results in judgment mistakes made by young scouts who really don't know what it takes to play baseball on the professional level. This scouting business is not as easy as it might appear.

There are a few scouts who have done well with no playing experience, like the late Lee Ballanfant. Lee, however, umpired in the major leagues for more than a decade, so he knew what to look for, but the Lee Ballanfants of the world are few and far between. To be a good scout, it says here in the Murff baseball guide, a scout must have played the game as a professional.

Orioles general manager Roland Hemond agrees. "Scouts have the hardest job in baseball. They must have deep knowledge of what it takes to play the game, and they have to base their judgments on personal experience as professional baseball people," he says.

It's a risky, risky business, and for all intents and purposes a crapshoot. Consider this fact. Only about 5 percent of all ballplayers drafted ever play in the big leagues. Five percent! If you only succeeded 5 percent of the time in your job, you'd be outta there and almost certainly you'd have a bad self-image problem. I've always taken great pride in my percentages. Of the two hundred ballplayers I have signed, more than fifty played in the big leagues, so that gives me a 25 percent success rate.

"Scouts must have the guts of a burglar," says Hemond. "They are baseball's unsung heroes when they go to make a judgment on high school- and college-age ballplayers."

Hemond's absolutely right. It takes nerve to put your reputation on the line after seeing a prospect only a few times under less-than-ideal conditions and then recommend the young high school or college ballplayer to your major-league club, each time knowing that if you're wrong, then maybe you're the one who's out.

It's tough for a scout to project just how good a young player will be when he watches him play against high school or college competition. It's much easier to judge a major-league player's ability when he's measured against major-league players than it is to judge an amateur's talent when you really don't know how good the competition is.

Still a scout who wants to keep his job has to produce excellent finds each year. His success is judged by his major-league club on the progress his players make within the organization. If a scout recommends players who are cut quickly from the lower minor leagues, who don't consistently move up and progress to the higher levels of a minor-league system, who don't make the major leagues occasionally, then that scout won't last long in professional baseball.

They don't make a lot of money for risking their reputations on every ballplayer. A good scout can make forty or fifty thousand dollars a year, plus mileage and expenses, although that's just an average. Most folks would think that's paltry compared to the large salaries awarded to most players. We do it for one reason and one reason only. We love baseball.

Unlike Billy Capps, I took a more circuitous route into the scouting profession. I came back from World War II to my job at Union Carbide in Texas City, Texas. I had signed on there only one month before Pearl Harbor but left when the war began.

By 1950 I had carved out my share of the American Dream. I had a wife, kids, home, car, nice salary, benefits, annuity plan, and, looking at it from the outside, twenty-nine-year-old John "Red" Murff had an excellent future. The problem was my body went to work at the plant every day, but my heart was never at Union Carbide. I never lost the thirst for baseball I had developed as a young boy. Like Moses, I think we all find ourselves lost in a wilderness at one time or another in our lives. That's where I was in 1950.

My parents had always taken me to church when I was a young boy, and I had been taught that prayers ultimately are answered. They might not be answered the way we want them answered, and the answers might not come right away, but they do come. I firmly believe that. Heck, I'm living, breathing proof of it.

In April 1950 a scout named Paul Childs from the Baton Rouge Red Sticks of the Class C Evangeline League helped me answer my baseball prayer. I had been playing ball in some fast, semiprofessional leagues in the Houston-Galveston area. Paul signed me to a contract at the elderly athletic age of twenty-nine. While my friends were settling into their families and careers, I headed out to baseball's back roads, along an uncharted course to what I hoped would be big-league stardom. I took a huge risk, but in my heart and soul I knew it was a chance I had to take.

Five years later, after a few hundred ball games in the minors, another scout played a critical role and helped me answer yet another prayer: getting to the big leagues. Albeit at age thirty-four, an age when many players are either retiring or contemplating giving it up.

In 1955 I pitched for the Dallas Eagles in the Texas League and led the league in victories with twenty-seven. In those days I thought I knew how to pitch, but I had given no thought to baseball scouts or what they did for a living.

Just before a game against Fort Worth, I noticed a group of men who looked like a bunch of gamblers sitting behind home plate. I asked my manager, Dutch Meyer, who they were, and he told me they were major-league scouts, searching the Texas League for prospective big-league talent. As it turned out, one of those men, Earl Halstead of the Milwaukee Braves, had been following my progress since I entered the Texas League in 1953, and he believed I was now ready to pitch in the big leagues.

The Dallas owner, the late Dick Burnett, agreed with Halstead that I was ready and agreed to sell me to the Braves. Problem was, the two couldn't agree on a sale price. Burnett wanted one hundred thousand dollars and three players from the

Braves forty-man roster. Halstead countered by offering forty thousand dollars and three players. After arguing back and forth for several days, the two decided to sit down and play gin rummy with the winner setting the price for the deal. Eight hours later Halstead emerged victorious, and the Braves paid forty grand and three players to acquire my services.

An unfortunate back injury ended my big-league career two years later, but just before the injury I met another scout who played an incredibly influential role in furthering my baseball career. One morning before a game at Wrigley Field, I met a man named Wid Mathews in a Chicago hotel lobby. For the next two hours he conducted a baseball clinic for me, sharing his insight and knowledge.

Wid played briefly in the big leagues, and he survived as a player not because he was blessed with great talent, but because of his tremendous store of knowledge. For example, he knew everything about every player in both the American League and the National League. He knew each hitter's batting average. He knew their strengths and weaknesses on defense. He knew each pitcher's best pitches, how to hit against each one, and he knew how each major-league manager would react in every game situation. What a fountain of baseball wisdom! When I got through talking to Wid that day, I knew in my heart my ultimate role in baseball would be as a scout. Later, Wid hired me as a scout with the Mets.

When I was injured, the Braves returned me to the minor leagues with Wichita in the American Association. Before I arrived, I called manager Ben Geraghty and asked him to allow me to sit by his side during every game I didn't pitch. I wanted him to teach me baseball strategy, game situations, when to pull a pitcher out of a game or leave him in, when to bunt, when to sacrifice, when to hit and run, when to steal. Ben was an unbelievable teacher. With his blessing the Braves hired me in 1960 to manage their Class A Southern Association club in Jacksonville, Florida. There I learned how to judge talent daily, which put the finishing touches to my on-the-field career and made me a well-rounded baseball man. More importantly, all that experience led me into the scouting profession.

In 1960 I had my first shot. Major League Baseball expanded into Texas that year and general manager Gabe Paul interviewed me for a scout's job with the new Houston National League entry, the Colt .45s.

"You're unlike a lot of minor-league managers," Paul told me. "You genuinely like ballplayers. You always give them grades that, in my opinion, are too high for their talent levels, but that means you care about players, and that's an advantage if you want to be a scout. So many minor-league managers aren't able to project how good a player will be in six months or a year down the road. But you are. Your reports include projections, and that's unusual. Most minor-league managers are concerned about winning and winning only, but not you," he said.

Gabe Paul said something to me during that interview that stuck with me throughout my scouting career. "You will be judged on ballplayers that you find, not on ballplayers some other scout finds for you. So make the decisions and judgments yourself! Red, you can't be a good scout if you don't do it all by yourself."

Over the years I listened to other scouts' opinions and listened to the grapevine and gossip mongers, but I never made judgments based on anything anyone else had seen. If I didn't see a particular player with my own eyes, I never filed a report on him.

The scout's job can be complex. We have to stay current on a multitude of constantly changing player acquisition rules, which makes life confusing sometimes but what it all boils down to is whether or not a scout can pick excellent ballplayers year in and year out.

It's a hit-and-miss business, this predicting the future of an eighteen- to twenty-one-year-old. For instance, who would've ever looked at a short, scrawny Pete Rose, all 145 pounds of him as a senior in high school, and predicted he'd eventually set a record for most base hits in a major-league career, eclipsing Ty

Cobb, Babe Ruth, Tris Speaker, Rogers Hornsby, Stan Musial, and Ted Williams?

The scout who ended up signing Rose, Buzzy Boyle of the Cincinnati Reds, once told me, "You gotta give Pete credit. He persistently called me on the phone after his senior year, begging me to sign him. I finally gave in so he'd stop pestering me. I figured, 'What the heck, give him a chance,' and look what happened!"

No scout thought Pete Rose could play. He just didn't have the size, speed, or ability to fit professional baseball's cookie cutter. But he did have heart and hustle! We can never predict just how far those characteristics will take a ballplayer's game, past his God-given talents. I remember when one of my subscouts, Wade Fatheree, was sitting around with a bunch of instructors at one of our tryout camps, and we were talking about speedy baseball players we had seen.

"Well, Rose could do 4.4 to first base," he said.

"Wade, 4.4, that's not even major-league average speed to first," said another instructor.

"Well, shoot." Wade replied, "I'm saying Rose did 4.4 on a walk!"

Mickey Mantle and Whitey Ford may have derisively hung the "Charlie Hustle" moniker on Rose, but in my opinion, baseball could use more Charlie Hustles nowadays.

Some major-league clubs have cut back on the number of scouts they have on the road, so the Major League Scouting Bureau is helping those clubs fill in the blanks. The bureau is paid a flat fee from each major-league team and looks for talent, finds it, evaluates it, and then places their scouting reports in a data bank all major-league clubs can access.

Orioles general manager Roland Hemond believes the bureau is an asset to the overall scouting process.

"Some major-league clubs," he says, "just don't have the monetary resources to put scouts into many remote areas of the country, but the bureau scouts many out-of-the-way places where some teams might not go, and as we all know ballplayers can be found anywhere. Plus, the bureau stages try-out camps all over the country. That's good for baseball, and they find some players at those camps."

Most bureau scouts are fine, but I do not agree that they are the same quality that most major-league clubs employ. It's more accurate to say that the bureau is a proving ground for scouts, kind of like the farm system is for players, because it seems the better bureau scouts always end up working for major-league clubs.

To me the danger comes when the more inexperienced bureau scouts contribute too much overblown information to the scouting grapevine or rumor mill, which can result in players being graded too high. Plus they have no special loyalty to any particular team, so they share their information too readily with college coaches.

"I was concerned," Hemond says, "that when the bureau began, it would turn the scouting process into a combine or central scouting office, and I didn't want clubs to lose the individuality they have in talent procurement."

Hemond and I believe major-league clubs will always need to keep their scouting departments intact and maintain a strong presence in baseball, because it's a down-and-dirty chase to find the best talent, and it's a job that demands the best and most talented scouts.

One of the most-asked questions I got from fans in the stands was, Red, how in the world do you find good ballplayers?

In my younger, more petulant days I told those curious folks it was none of their business, because I just never believed in exposing the general public to my vault of scouting secrets. But I'm retired now, so I really don't mind sharing a few "company secrets."

For me it amounted to wearing out a bunch of shoe leather and establishing personal contacts. I worked myself silly developing a telephone pipeline connecting me with hundreds of youth league, high school, junior college, and senior college coaches. My former scouting territory of Texas, Oklahoma, Louisiana, and New Mexico represented a vast expanse of territory that's home to thousands of young ballplayers, and every year this is a real gold mine of talent. In such an expanse I simply could not get around to every city or town just to have a look, but coaches worked closely and had firsthand knowledge of who could and could not play. That's why I needed them on my side. They gave me extra sets of eyes and ears.

I also developed a lengthy list of former college and professional ballplayers within my region, especially those who stayed in touch with the game. These men gave me an abundance of seasoned, professional eyes at the ballparks in my territory, and I cannot emphasize enough how much I depended on such friends to tip me off to good players.

I spent hundreds of hours at coaching conventions and clinics, and like a good politician I shook hands, made friends, and made absolutely sure those coaches and former players had my business card and my telephone number because I wanted them to be able to reach me twenty-four hours a day, seven days a week if they spotted a ballplayer. I craved information about big-league prospects in my territory, and I felt it was my obligation as a professional baseball representative to meet people on behalf of the entire sport as well as my team.

My instructions to coaches and former players were simple. Let me know who the best ballplayers are in your city or town or county the minute you see one. I wanted the names of anyone between the ages of fifteen and twenty-one. By then you can take a look at his game and begin to evaluate him as a prospect. By the age of fifteen, a young man's foot speed, if he has it, will begin to show. He'll run major-league average speed to first at that age (4.3 seconds). If he possesses a good arm, he'll be able to throw the ball out of the ballpark. A hitter will also be able to hit the ball out of the park at fifteen. If he's a pitcher and a prospect, he'll begin to show you that fastball in the mid- to high eighty-mile-per-hour range. That's how old Todd Van Poppell, who now pitches for Oakland, was when he lit up my radar gun with a ninety-two-mile-per-hour fastball. We can also begin to judge growth at that age. Say a fifteen-year-old is six feet tall and weighs about 150. Just by looking at his parents we can pretty much tell how he will fill out as an adult. While I was interested in fifteen-year-olds, most of my work involved young men between the ages of eighteen and twenty-one simply because they were closer to draft-signing eligibility.

Every scout I know starts in December, before the scouting season begins in January or February, working on a priority list containing the names of each prospect. I may have had fifteen names on that list or ten or five, it didn't matter. Those were the names of young men I planned to follow early in the season.

The names came from my previous year's work watching ball games, when I always made notes on particularly promising young players. The priority list included kids I had seen in try-out camps, during the state playoffs, and the names of young men in major colleges who were about to turn twenty-one years old and therefore become eligible for the draft.

Just before the season began, I mailed my list to my major-league club's draft offices so they had an idea who I would be watching early in the season. Then I called the coaches who had players on my priority list and requested their schedules so I could plan trips to see each youngster early in the year.

A young man could play his way off the list by not performing well. Others could play their way onto the list by showing me potential big-league talent. There was always a surprise or two every year, someone who came out of nowhere to make a name for himself as a professional baseball candidate. It's in this situation that a scout must be flexible in his evaluation and in his thinking process and not cling to a judgment made last week or last year, especially when that call may not hold true today. For instance, if a young outfielder on my priority list at the beginning of the year stopped hitting the ball and could no longer run to first base at or below major-league average speed as he once did, then he is no longer a prospect and I am defeating myself if I continue to push him as one. Remember, every young ballplayer is a prospect to me, until he proves he's not.

I also use my priority list in another way. Whenever national cross-checkers enter the territory, they would sit down with me and we would assign a "national" grade to the prospects on my list, ranking my prospects against all others across the country.

My grading system was a little more rigid than the standard used by most major-league scouts, however most scouts rate position players on a cumulative scale from 20–80, with each player's talents listed in nine categories: arm strength, hitting ability, power, fielding, body size and strength, speed, game knowledge, character, and potential. They receive a grade on a point scale from 2–10.

Let's say I'm grading a junior college outfielder. He's six-one and weighs 180. He has a lean body and is very strong. We'll give him a 7 for his body, which is two points above major-league average. This same young man can really run much faster than major-league average, so he gets an 8 for speed. His arm is major-league average, so he gets a 5 in that category. He hits well for average and gets a 5, he's a legitimate home-run threat, having hit eighteen during his season, so I grade him a 6 for power. His head is always in the game, he never misses a cutoff man, nor throws to the wrong base, so his game knowledge is above average, and he gets a 7 there. He fields his position at major-league average, so that gives him a 5. I believe he'll grow and get a bit stronger, so he gets a 7 for potential. He possesses impeccable character, which is really hard to grade nowadays, and gets an 8 for character.

My outfielder's total point grade is 58. We divide the points by nine categories, and that gives him a 6.0 grade, which on the 20–80 scale makes him a top prospect. Since I've worked with the cross-checker on this grade, my outfielder's 60 will be compared to all other prospects across the country as my team gets ready to develop its list for the draft.

Grading a pitcher is a different task. A subscout of mine, Red Gaskill, now with the California Angels, helped me develop a method for assigning a grade to hurlers. This was back in the spring of 1965, just before we signed Nolan. The previous year, Red and I had found and signed a young pitcher named Jay Carden. Even though we had no radar guns, we estimated Carden threw ninety-three miles an hour. Gaskill insisted Carden threw as hard or harder than Nolan, and while I knew that wasn't the case, I was also convinced we needed to come up with a system for numerically evaluating pitchers. I knew beyond a shadow of a doubt I could prove to Gaskill that Ryan was the faster pitcher and the better long-range prospect.

First we gave a numerical grade for peak velocity. This is the top fastball speed a pitcher exhibited. I felt confident I knew what certain pitches in every speed range looked like because I had seen Bob Feller's fastball clocked on an elaborate speed measuring device, and I had seen others measured as well. Don't forget, I had a professional pitching background myself.

80–82 mph	1 grade point
83–84 mph	2 grade points
84–85 mph	3 grade points
85–86 mph	4 grade points
86–87 mph	5 grade points
88–89 mph	6 grade points
90–92 mph	7 grade points
93–95 mph	8 grade points
96–98 mph	9 grade points
99+ mph	10 grade points

On the same grade point scale, we then graded a pitcher's "comfort zone," or the speed at which he comfortably threw most of his fastballs. For comparison purposes Nolan Ryan at his fastest was clocked at more than 100 and sometimes as high as 102 miles an hour, but his comfort zone was about 97 or 98 miles an hour. Sandy Koufax threw 97–98 miles an hour, with a 94–95 comfort zone. Nowadays, the "Big Unit" Randy Johnson with the Mariners tops out at 95–96, with a comfort zone of 92–94.

We also graded a pitcher's curve or breaking ball, his off-speed pitch or change-up, his body size, and character on the same scale.

From what I had seen of Nolan and of Red Gaskill's favorite prospect, I convinced Red of Nolan's superiority by grading them this way:

Nolan		Jay
17	Age	21
10	Peak Velocity	8
9	Comfort Zone	7
3 (potential 7)	Breaking Pitch	5
2 (potential 6)	Control	4
no grade	Off Speed	4
(potential 6)	Body Size	5
6 (potential 9)	Character	5
39 (at 17)	Total	38
(potential 50)		

Since Jay was already twenty-one years old when we graded him, I felt he'd reached his full potential. Therefore, once Nolan reached his potential, he'd grade out a full twelve points higher. I knew by looking at them who the better prospect was, and the grading system proved it. I used this same system for almost three decades, and while the observations of others were sometimes right and sometimes wrong, my little system never let me down.

Red's Random Thought . . .

Gosh, I miss the days before the draft. We were scouts, businessmen, and we were a bigger part of the player procurement process. The draft changed the face of baseball, and not for the better.

Chapter 7

The Conscription

I hate to sound like all the old-timers who talk about the good ole days because in a lot of ways those days weren't always that great. For major-league scouts, however, the draft meant lots of change for us in dozens of ways and it turned out that the pre-draft days were better for us.

Before the draft began in 1965, before the days of all the buck-passing bureaucracy, the bureau, and the scouting grapevine, I had the autonomy to sign whomever I wanted. My club gave me a budget, and the bonuses for each player I signed came from that pile of money.

When I came across a truly hot prospect, one attracting attention from several teams, I always let my scouting supervisor know about it—as long as I didn't think they were likely to talk to other teams about him. In essence, I was a lone wolf, and I liked it that way.

Former Orioles general manager Roland Hemond says it more precisely: "The market was strictly open. Scouts spent more time with fewer prospects, perhaps seeing one player ten to fifteen times before signing. Evaluations, in those days, were much more thorough."

Nowadays, if I find a prospect I'm really interested in, the bureaucracy involved in acquiring that player's services is staggering.

There's no lock on my chance to draft him, and a lot of people have to agree with my opinion. After I discover the player and recommend him to my club, a national cross-checker comes in to grade my player against all others in the country. This helps a team establish a graded, numerical pecking order for its coveted players. This is a critical list that is established as a ready reference for draft day. If my prospect grades high, the scouting director and perhaps the general manager will take a look to help determine how high the young man should be drafted. Early on in the search, there's no sense spending a lot of time getting to know only a few players. I have to be familiar with dozens. I never know when someone within my club's management ranks will hear talk from the scouting grapevine about a player who I don't really like, and as the field scout I have to be able to talk about the kid in question.

The draft has made it more difficult to scout a young player's character. We just don't have the time now to get to know the young men as well as we once did, which leads to needless mistakes like a drug problem, trouble with the law, or refusal to take direction from coaches.

Baseball management probably believes all these checks and cross-checks are necessary in this day of million-dollar-plus bonuses paid to unproven players, but the simple fact is, no one is courageous enough to take the blame for making a mistake, so everyone has to share in the foul-up. This weird, unsound theory is based on the premise that the general manager can fire any one of us, but he can't fire all of us.

Let's be honest. The main reason the draft was instituted more than thirty years ago was the simple fact that general managers and scouting directors were jealous of the field scouts' independence. They believed we spent too much on ballplayers, and they were convinced they could save money for the owners, who were complaining that bonuses paid to free agents were raging out of control. In those days a ninety to two hundred thousand dollar bonus was the range with which we worked. So the general managers and scouting directors talked the owner-ship rules committee into instituting a draft with the stated promise that it would save bonus money for each club.

But there's a note of irony here. The draft didn't save any major-league club a dime. Not one. If you don't believe me, just look at how bonuses have escalated through the years. Now first-round draft choices garner million-dollar-plus bonuses, paid and often wasted on unproven young men. Thirty years after the first free-agent draft in 1965, bonuses rage out of control. I blame the advent of baseball's additional bureaucracy, the involvement of player agents, and "money for nothing" morals displayed by both agents and players. The draft simply did not accomplish what the lords of baseball intended.

The draft didn't do much to enhance the careers of guys like me either. As Roland Hemond says, "The draft has meant that individual scouts get far less credit than they should for finding players."

For instance, before the 1989 draft the Orioles New England scout, Leo Labosiere, really pushed to get Jeff Bagwell drafted in the second round, but Baltimore passed on him and Boston took him in the fourth round and later traded him to Houston where he's become a good-looking, power-hitting first baseman. In the olden days before the draft Leo would've been in the hunt for Bagwell and might have signed him for Baltimore and would have attracted a lot of attention from his bosses during the whole process.

"Our club didn't draft Bagwell and that's not Leo Labosiere's fault," says Hemond. "It's our fault. But in evaluating Leo as a scout, I, as a general manager, must always remember that he recommended a player who has become an all-star, so he obvi-ously knew what he was doing."

Baseball in general and scouts in particular need more leaders like Hemond who truly understand the limitations the draft places on the scouting profession. Far too many general managers today refuse to respect the skills of an outstanding scout, which explains why a lot of skilled scouts are leaving the profession. That's too bad for baseball because they aren't replaceable, and I hope the baseball establishment wakes up and realizes what it is losing before it's too late. Baseball, like any other business, simply doesn't improve by being manned by a preponderance of yes-men.

That sums up my feeling about the draft's impact on scouts, so let's learn something about how the draft is conducted. To understand the rudiments, we must first explain who is eligible.

High school seniors, once they've finished their high school eligibility, or seniors who have lost eligibility by failing school work may be drafted. Junior college players may be drafted at the end of each junior college season. A senior college player may not be drafted until he either finishes his junior season or turns twenty-one.

Three or four days before draft day each team gathers its field scouts, cross-checkers, and management for a predraft meeting. The gathering results in plenty of friendly rivalry between scouts from each region of the country. This is where scouts become salesmen, hawking the outstanding traits of their best ballplayers to club management. Everyone's comments are recorded.

Teams draft in inverted order from their finish in league standings the previous season. For instance, if the Mets finished last with the worst record in all of baseball, then the Mets are first in line on draft day.

Once the predraft meeting itself starts, the scouting director brings everyone to order by asking, Does anyone have a first-round draft choice in your region? If you do, name him now and let's talk about him.

In any given year only a few scouts have players they considered number-one choices. In fact even I've been known to say, "I don't have a number-one draft candidate this year," and each time I said that everyone else would laugh. "Yeah, right, Murff. You're going to trick us into thinking you have a number-one whether you really do or not." Sometimes they were right.

One of the most productive predraft meetings I ever attended took place when I was with the Montreal Expos. The 1977 meeting also resulted in one of the most dynamic drafts I ever participated in, which resulted in Montreal getting Gary Carter, Ellis Valentine, and Dan Schatzeder among others. It's some tale.

At the predraft meeting scouting director Mel Didier began his detailed inquisition about our ballplayers. West Coast scout Bob Zuk opened the propaganda session by talking about his two best players, Gary Carter and Ellis Valentine. He championed Carter and Valentine as definite first-round candidates, and he described them as outstanding, talented ballplayers.

Believe it or not, that year I felt left out of the competition. I had no first-round candidate, but I did have a pitcher I really liked, Dan Schatzeder, a left-hander from the University of Denver. My nephew, Ron Davis, first told me about Dan after the two had pitched together in the Alaskan summer semipro league. Even though I saw a report from the Major League Scouting Bureau that didn't grade him very high, Ron's favorable opinion piqued my interest enough to take a look at Dan myself.

Unfortunately, when I got to Denver, I learned Schatzeder's school had been placed on probation and would not be going to the college playoffs. Not to be denied, I arranged a workout so I could take a look at him, and I found out he would be pitching in a semipro game two days later.

It turned out that Schatzeder was far better than his previous grades indicated. Once Dan began his throwing workout, I saw him throw his fastball at more than ninety miles an hour, a live fastball that moved into or away from a right-handed hitter, a quality curve, and he was extremely accurate with all his pitches. To me he was a top-flight prospect.

At the predraft meeting, after Zuk had spoken, I told Mel Didier and all his scouts about Schatzeder. I said, "Now, I have a third-round draft choice. Name is Schatzeder. I never saw him in college competition, but I saw him work out, saw him in a semipro game, and I love his control, in fact his accuracy reminded me of Warren Spahn . . . that good."

When I uttered Spahn's name, the other scouts' eyes and ears perked up as I announced the Red Murff Master Plan for Developing Dan Schatzeder and Sending Him to the Big Leagues.

"We should draft him in the third round, we shouldn't gamble that he'll be around any later than that. If we draft him, we'll have to get him in condition in the rookie leagues and then assign him to a Double A ball club. Let him pitch in Double A from August until the end of the season. Next year, get him a full spring training, assign him to Double A, get him a couple of starts there, then move him up to Triple A within the first week to ten days of the season. Then, in August, we should take a long, close look at him and see if he's ready to move up to the big leagues. If he is, move him up in September and he automatically becomes a part of the forty-man roster. By the following season we'll have a productive big-league pitcher on our hands."

See, ballplayer development is simple if you follow Murff's easy-to-understand instructions. You don't even have to read the directions, just ask me. Of course, it helps when the ballplayer you're developing is as talented as Schatzeder. On that day the words of praise for Dan and my plan for his progress apparently carried some weight. My superiors and colleagues were impressed.

Zuk told me, "Well, heck, Red, Schatzeder's gotta be a first-rounder, then, because my two ballplayers can't get to the big leagues that quickly."

I said, "Bob, Dan is a potential first-rounder. But there's no way we draft him number one, because nobody else that I know of has looked at him or wants him." Here I go again, loving a ballplayer nobody likes or has heard of.

So we drafted Schatzeder in the third round behind Gary Carter and Ellis Valentine. For more than ten years Dan was the solid pitcher I thought he'd be, but my song and dance on his behalf turned out to be just the beginning of a wildly productive predraft meeting, which had the full and noisy complement of rivalry, competitiveness, and fire-in-the-gut determination.

THE SCOUT

My job was to look after the organization's best interest, and if that meant turning the session into a "my ballplayer is better than your ballplayer" free-for-all, so be it. Sometimes the politics, the arguments, the discussions turned nasty, but these crucial predraft meetings determine the course a team will take during the draft and are, in my mind, the spice of life for a scout. After all we're competitors, regardless of our age. Sometimes scouts lose the players they want. Sometimes feelings get hurt. But when the meeting ends, the scouts go to dinner and over the course of the evening become fast friends again. Once that happens, we get reenergized and we're off on the hunt once more.

A scout's life from January until June revolves around his club's preparation for the draft. Once the draft is over, there's no time to waste. We remain on the road and extremely busy. Major-league clubs must make contact with each drafted player's family within two weeks of the date of the draft, and scouts set up meetings between clubs and families. It doesn't happen like it once did when scouts made a turnkey deal with a young player. Today we get involved by meeting with the family and relaying the club's initial contract offer, meet again and take their counteroffer back to our club.

When the money gets into the hundreds of thousands of dollars, the club's general manager gets involved. In most cases the first-, second-, and third-round picks have been getting financial advice from an agent or lawyer, which isn't always a good idea. If the young man is a recent high school graduate, he'd better not have a signed agreement with an agent, because if he does and decides not to sign a major-league contract, college rules prevent him from accepting a scholarship.

If the young man is a college player with no eligibility remaining, we often find ourselves dealing with an agent, even though the young man has little contract leverage. Agents may overprice their players, which can backfire and result in vocational suicide. A big-league club may pass on signing the young man, retain his draft rights for a year, and then, if the young man or his agent have not lowered their asking price, the club may decide to let him go.

Many big-league clubs now don't make serious monetary offers to lower-round draft choices. They've adopted a policy they call "draft and follow." They draft a young man in the lower rounds, don't offer a sufficient amount of money to interest the young man or his parents, and then retain the player's draft rights for the year.

I don't like the "draft and follow" approach. To me it's a system instituted by clubs who don't have a lot of faith in their scouts. "Draft and follow" gives the team a year to make up its mind about a young player's potential, it doesn't challenge a club to make a decision and it doesn't hold a club's scouting department accountable for judging a ballplayer. It simply delays the whole process because no one can make up his mind.

In Red Murff World, if I think enough of a young player's ability to persuade my club to draft him, then I ought to do all I can within the rules to sign him to a professional baseball contract. I believed very strongly in doing business that way. Remember, my training under former Colt .45s general manager Gabe Paul taught me that I alone was accountable for my decisions regarding the players I scouted.

Once the signing process is finished, the scouts hit the road again during the midsummer months on "professional coverage." Each major-league club does its best to maintain an up-to-date working knowledge of every other club's talent, and each regional scout is responsible for knowing the personnel on all the professional clubs within his territory. For instance, I would spend a week in a city with a Single A, Double A, or Triple A club. The Double A Texas League is in my territory, so I'll head to Tulsa, Midland, San Antonio, or El Paso to look at each pitcher on both teams. I can usually accomplish that within one four-game series. While I'm watching pitchers, I'm also scrutinizing the other position players. I want to know if any player I'm scouting can help my big-league club. If he can, then I'll recommend a trade or contract purchase to my major-league bosses.

THE SCOUT

While I spent a preponderance of my time as a sleuth, I was also responsible for keeping an eye on ballplayers drafted by our team who had not signed contracts. This would happen when the club failed to come to an agreement with a drafted player and he'd go off to play in a Connie Mack or fast amateur summer league until the parties resolved the contractual situation. I'd always keep track of those players in limbo, watch their games, and maybe say hello to their folks for good measure.

Those Connie Mack leagues, college and semipro circuits were interesting for another reason. Any young man who finishes his high school eligibility, finishes his first or second year in junior college, or finishes his senior-college eligibility can be signed as a nondrafted free agent. In some cases a young man who wasn't drafted might be developing as a prospect and might deserve a chance to sign a pro contract. So if I saw a player like that, I'd make it a priority to see him in action and perhaps try to sign him.

A perfect example of that kind of ballplayer is Mike Stanton, currently a reliever for the Boston Red Sox. I signed him for the Braves after watching him pitch several years ago in Houston's Karl Young Collegiate League. Mike had just graduated from Midland High School and had signed a scholarship with Southwestern University in Georgetown, Texas. As I was passing through Houston on my way back from a Florida scouting trip, I saw the lights on at Delmar Stadium on the city's northwest side and stopped to stretch my legs and look for prospects. I can't tell you how many times I've done that.

I walked into the ballpark and watched this left-hander. I didn't know who he was, but he was throwing major-league average fastballs and challenging experienced college sophomores and juniors even though he had just graduated from high school. I talked to some fans in the stands who knew him and they filled me in. The fact that he had a college scholarship sort of surprised me, because I thought I knew most of the top-flight pitchers in Texas who had scholarships. Somehow Stanton had slipped by me.

Never being standoffish in situations like this, after the game I approached him, introduced myself, said I considered him a big-league prospect, and asked if he'd be willing to sign a free-agent contract with the Atlanta Braves. He told me he was excited about his scholarship, intended to honor it, and didn't believe he was ready to play professional ball.

He assured me he would call if his plans changed, but he seemed pretty intent on enrolling at Southwestern. Still I promised him I would be back to see him pitch again in the Karl Young League and I pledged I'd ask him one more time to sign before the end of the summer.

In August Mike again insisted he was going to college, but he lost his academic eligibility after his first semester and transferred to Alvin Junior College. Bingo. Within a year I had him signed, sealed, and delivered to the Atlanta organization and the rest is history. He's an excellent major-league reliever, discovered as an undrafted ballplayer by a scout who just happened to stop in to see some fast summer-league competition.

So once the summer ends you are probably thinking that my job is done for the season, right? Wrong. By the time the amateur-league seasons and the minor-league seasons wind down sometime in late August or early September, it's time to begin looking at fall league play. Some high schools in Oklahoma played lengthy fall league schedules, so if I know about a potential prospect playing in an Oklahoma high school, I head there for a look. Also junior colleges and some senior colleges play fall schedules, consisting sometimes of as many as thirty or forty games. These games allowed me to get an early read on promising ballplayers for next spring as I began to ready my prospect list.

The college fall seasons always wind up about the first or second week of November. That means I've been on the road for the past eleven months. By now I'm weary and ready for a few days at home to rest up, maybe work around the garden, maybe get in some deer hunting with Jerry Grote or one of my other buddies. Then there's the visiting I have to get in with friends and family who have missed having me around, and while that's going on we begin making plans for Thanksgiving and

Christmas, and I just settle into a role as a normal, average citizen of Brenham, Texas.

I do the concerned, friendly citizen job pretty well. I'm a gregarious, talkative personality, involved in Rotary Club and some other civic activities because, quite honestly, I love people. But about a month or six weeks after I come off the road, sometime just after Christmas and right before the New Year's Day bowl games, I'm getting that familiar itch again. It may be cold and icy outside, and there's no hint of green on any nearby tree. Like the greenery at this time of year, baseball lies dormant in the minds of most sports fans. All the newspapers and television sportscasts and radio sports talk shows and all my friends at the Rotary Club are talking about who's number one in college football and the NFL playoffs and college basketball. That's okay. When I stand outside, meditating in my own backyard, as I gaze at the heavens on a frosty, starry winter night, my senses come alive. I not only smell burning live oak or hickory from nearby fireplaces, I also vividly begin to feel the impending arrival of baseball in the icy air. All of a sudden, I'm reenergized and ready to go find some more ballplayers.

Red's Random Thought . . .

Players who run like jackrabbits excite me. They can play for Red Murff. Speed creates its own delights and problems for managers, but fast players win ball games; it says so right here.

Chapter 8

Speed and Power

Name me one truly great major-league ballplayer who didn't have excellent running speed. One. Okay, Nolan Ryan. That's not fair, he's a pitcher. I'm not talking about one-dimensional, home-run-hitting-only specialists who have evolved in baseball since the advent of the designated hitter. I'm talking about the true superstar and everyday ballplayers. You simply cannot name one who didn't have great running speed. Cobb, Speaker, Mays, Mantle, Aaron, Brock, Griffey Jr. From baseball's beginnings to the present, all the greats could run. You might argue that Ted Williams couldn't, but he was such a phenomenal hitter you could forgive that weakness. Yes, Babe Ruth was an excellent runner and much faster than his girth implied.

When Jackie Robinson came into the game in 1947 and when Willie Mays, Lou Brock, Hank Aaron, and other African Americans were allowed to play professional baseball, their presence changed the way managers played defense. They had to learn to adapt their game to defend against speed. For a while baseball found itself searching for more and more athletes with speed. Today the problem is that more and more clubs have moved away from speed and have been signing one-dimensional ballplayers who can't run. That factor has hurt the game and changed it from an all-around athlete's sport, to a sport that too often caters to a ballplayer who can hit and nothing else. If you think I'm talking just about the designated hitter rule, you're right. That rule has hurt the game in too many instances and taken away the speed factor. We need to get it back.

I always believed that if I found a young man who could really run, then I could teach him the few fundamentals that would qualify him for a shot in professional baseball. Maybe we could teach him to drag bunt for base hits, or to chop down on the ball and try to hit through the infield, anything so he could use his God-given talent for speed. It says right here in the semiofficial Murff scouting manual that fast runners impress me more than those who can't run.

Speed is so important in baseball. Speed on the base paths puts pressure on infielders, outfielders, the pitcher, and the catcher. A speed burner on first base is a threat to steal second and gives the pitcher and catcher an additional problem to think about besides just retiring the hitter at bat. A fast runner on the bases makes outfielders nervous, makes them worry that the runner could take an extra base once the ball is hit to the outfield.

On defense, fast-running infielders cover more ground and can cut off hard-hit ground balls headed through the infield. Fast-moving outfielders keep well-hit balls from rolling to the wall, and that keeps runners from advancing to extra bases or scoring. Speed allows an outfielder to get to the fence and grab a fly ball that's headed out of the park.

Running talent is so terribly critical and fundamental that everyday major leaguers simply have to have it as a basic tool. Too many today don't, and the overall excellence of the game of baseball has suffered as a result.

Scouts grade speed this way: After hitting the ball, the average right-handed major leaguer runs from home to first base in 4.3 seconds. Because the batter's box is a step closer, therefore a tenth of a second closer, the average left-handed major-league hitter must run from home to first base in 4.2 seconds.

THE SCOUT

We also grade a player on how fast he covers sixty yards. The sixty-yard distance is crucial in baseball because that is the distance between home and second, first and third, and the distance an outfielder usually has to run from his position to the fence to catch up with a fly ball that's headed for the stands. We want a major-league prospect to be able to run sixty yards in 6.7 seconds or better.

Speed is easy to judge. All it takes is a stopwatch. A player can run or he can't. It's that simple. Grading hitters, however, is a different problem altogether.

During the past fifteen to twenty years, judging and grading high school, junior college, and senior college hitters has become extremely difficult. Most of the difficulty is due to the use of aluminum bats by amateur players rather than traditional wooden bats. The aluminum bat has made a big difference in the game and in the way in which we scout young hitters. Before the advent of the aluminum bat, young pitchers learned to "saw off" the bat in a hitter's hands, which means that he threw the ball to the inside corner of the plate, trying to make the hitter hit the ball with the bat's weak, wooden handle. Many times a ball hit on the handle causes the bat to break, or to be "sawed off" in the batter's hands, and more often than not resulted in an easy out.

You don't see that in amateur ball anymore. The hard, unforgiving aluminum bat handle cannot be broken. If the pitcher tries to work the inside corner of the plate, the hitter can still get a base hit even if the ball is struck with the handle. Because the young pitcher no longer owns the inside part of the plate, he's forced to throw more breaking pitches to the outside corner in an effort to retire the hitter.

Aluminum bats also cause another problem for scouts. We cannot accurately judge a young hitter's true power potential anymore. The aluminum bat is much harder than the standard wooden bat. I have heard other scouts estimate, and I agree, that aluminum bats result in an increase in hitting distance by 10 to 20 percent greater than that of wood.

Another factor is that the average aluminum bat's weight can be as much as eight ounces or more less than that of a wooden bat of the same length. What does this mean to a young hitter? Well, think about it. Would you rather swing a hard-surfaced, unbreakable, light bat, or a softer-surfaced, breakable, heavier wooden bat? Would you rather hit the ball 350 feet with wood or 385–420 feet with aluminum? Well, that explains a few of the differences in the two bats. Let me clinch the sale this way: The "sweet spot" or hitting zone on the barrel of the bat—the part of the bat where ballplayers try to hit the ball—is only three inches on a wooden bat. The sweet spot on an aluminum bat is more than eighteen inches, more than six times greater than wood.

Colleges and high schools use aluminum bats because the durability of the bats allows them to save money. At the same time aluminum bats make the job of the scouts much more difficult. We simply cannot judge a young player's hitting ability as easily as we once did. We can look at his bat speed and his hitting mechanics and grade both of those, but we don't know how good a hitter he'll be. I have a standard rule that says it takes one to three years for an amateur hitter accustomed to an aluminum bat to adjust to wood.

Billy Capps tells the story of one exceptional player he signed a few years back who refused to use aluminum and for a very good reason. "The late Steve Macko, who played for the Cubs for a while, always used wood. I'm talking about in high school and at Baylor University. Steve's dad Joe played in the Texas League and American Association for years and was a great minor-league home-run hitter. The Mackos knew what scouts were looking for in a hitter, and they wanted us to be able to get a good reading on his hitting ability, without any complicating factors. Plus Steve himself didn't want to have to go through any kind of adjustment period, so once he started using wood in Little League, he never switched."

Unfortunately Steve's story is tragic. Right after he made it to the big leagues, he was diagnosed with cancer and never recovered. But Steve and his dad used the right judgment in letting the scouts see him swing a wooden bat. I wish other young prospects had the courage Steve Macko had to try it.

Red's Random Thought . . .

One of my friends asked me if scouts believe in luck. I can't speak for other scouts, but I told him I did. I think the harder I worked at this game of scouting, the luckier I got.

Chapter 9

Infielders with Grit

The first time I saw him at a Mets tryout camp in Rockdale, Texas, in 1964, I knew. This kid was a potential major-league infielder. He had that long, lean, sinewy look about him. Although he was about six feet tall and 150 pounds, I figured he'd fill out to about 175, plenty big enough.

He could run, could make that long throw from the hole between short and third, not quite as strong as I'd like to see, but more than good enough. He had an attitude that no ball would ever get by him. He dived for ground balls. He got his uniform dirty. His elbows bled sometimes. Kenny Boswell was a ballplayer.

When you hear someone say, "He can really stroke the ball," that's what this kid could do. Line drives coming off his bat cracked like a .30-06 rifle shot. As a schoolboy at Travis High in Austin he played shortstop. I figured him as a big-league second baseman.

Only a week or so after his high school graduation, young Kenny Boswell faced a dilemma. I had seen enough to know I wanted him to sign with the New York Mets, and he was convinced he knew exactly what he wanted to do.

"You wanna sign with us?" I asked the young prospect. "No, sir, I don't," he replied, almost apologetically. "My folks really want me to go to college, and I think I'm gonna sign a scholarship with Sam Houston State over in Huntsville."

I knew several other scouts were interested in young Boswell, including Al LaMachia from the Braves. LaMachia lost interest after Kenny told him he wouldn't sign with anyone until he first talked to Red Murff. LaMachia knew if I was after Boswell he stood to get into a bidding war and he didn't want that. Still, every scout in the Southwest knew Kenny Boswell was a player. Kenny and I both knew he really didn't want to be a student, but that's what he became.

I saw Kenny during the fall season of 1964, and he spent the afternoon impressing me by slamming home runs into the tall pine trees outside the fence at the Sam Houston ballpark.

By the spring of 1965 Kenny proved both to himself and to me he wasn't a student. He had been placed on academic probation and was ineligible to play baseball. I visited him one day at the Sam Houston ballpark. As we watched a game, Kenny lamented his situation.

"I don't want to be here anymore, Mr. Murff," he said. "I really want to sign with the Mets."

"I'm sorry, Kenny, the rules of baseball say you are bound to Sam Houston until you finish your sophomore year." (The rule now stipulates the end of the junior year or age twenty-one.)

"But, Mr. Murff," he argued, "I'm no student. I'm a ballplayer. It's not fair that I have to sit here when I could be out earning a living as a professional ballplayer. I *want* to sign, Mr. Murff!"

I tried my best to console him, but I wasn't having much luck. We left the park and headed downtown for dinner. On the way I asked him, "How badly do you want to sign, son?"

"In the worst way, sir. I really, really want to play professional baseball."

Once at the restaurant I told young Boswell the only way he would even have a remote chance of being drafted—the draft had just been instituted and the first one was set to take place three months from then—would be to write a letter to the commissioner of baseball and explain to him that the rules of baseball were made to allow a player to pursue his chosen profession, not to keep him out of it. "Tell him," I said, "that you have proven you are not a student, you have flunked out, and therefore cannot participate in college baseball. And past that, let him know how eager you are to get on with your professional career. Send it by certified mail. That way there will be a written record that his office received it and you can track it that way."

So Kenny Boswell went to work. He mailed the letter and received confirmation of its receipt from the commissioner's office. March passed, then April, then most of May. Still, Kenny had received no word.

In early May I was sitting in the Texas Lutheran College ballpark in Seguin, Texas, with several scouts, including Hugh Alexander of the Dodgers. Alexander stood up between innings, stretched and with no prompting announced, "I'll bet anyone here fifty bucks that Kenny Boswell won't be eligible for the draft."

Holy smokes, I thought. *Someone besides me knows Kenny has applied for a special draft status.* Alexander's off-the-cuff remark put even more pressure on me and on Kenny to get some definitive word from the commissioner.

When I left for the draft in New York, I still had no idea about Kenny Boswell's draft status. When I arrived at my hotel room, I had a message from him. When I returned his call, he told me that the commissioner's office had agreed that he should be eligible for the draft. I told Kenny I needed written proof of the conversation, and fortunately he received a follow-up letter that he sent to me via Western Union. I got the letter at 2:00 A.M. on the morning of the draft. At 6:30 A.M. I went to see Mets scouting director Bing Devine.

I told Devine about Boswell's letter and the part I played in it. "Bing, when the draft starts today, we need to draft this young man as soon as we can. He's a great ballplayer, has loads of talent, and I'm afraid other teams may be onto the fact that his is a special case, so we stand a good chance of losing him if we don't take him early."

Devine questioned my involvement in the letter-writing incident. "Why didn't you let me know about this, Red?"

"Well, Bing, I figured if only a few people knew about this the Mets ultimately would be better off. And I figured if I told you, then you might tell someone with another team and we'd have more competition on our hands," I said.

Shortly before the draft began, a spokesman from the commissioner's office announced that Kenny Boswell was a "special addition" that sent other teams scurrying for telephones, trying to find their Texas field scouts. Not everyone brought their field scouts in for the draft like the Mets did, so several teams had no information on Boswell because they couldn't find their scouts with the file on the young infielder. They lost out.

We drafted Kenny Boswell in the third round. Nolan Ryan came to us in the eighth round of the same draft. Kenny and Nolan played Rookie League ball together.

Toward the end of Kenny's first professional season, I, like the other Mets scouts, had been invited to be an instructor at the club's Rookie Instructional League camp in St. Petersburg, Florida. The camp was a reward for work well done, and it gave the scouts a chance to observe and tutor the organization's best prospects and help them fine-tune their games. So I got an up-close, everyday look at my man Kenny. As part of the routine during each day's ball game, I sat in the dugout with the other scouts and with Eddie Stanky, then the Mets director of player development, who was running the Instructional League.

On this particular day Kenny stunk up the joint. He looked miserable at the plate. He couldn't come close to getting a base hit. Plus he mishandled a couple of potential double-play balls and generally did not look like a big-league prospect.

After the game ended, players and scouts trudged into the locker room, heads down, following a dismal effort. Some players were in the showers, some were working on their equipment, and some just sat dejectedly wondering what had gone wrong. At that point Stanky came up to me and said, "Red, tell your boy Boswell to come see me."

I went down to Kenny's locker and told him to get his asbestos pants on because Stanky was going to really chew him out for his performance. I followed him into Stanky's office and shut the door.

Cold beads of sweat popped out on Kenny's forehead as he stood erect as a board, shifting his weight nervously from side to side. Stanky asked us both to sit down and then he began his speech to the young ballplayer.

"Kenny, you are going to play in the big leagues, and because you are, you are going to be on national television and you will be a role model for thousands of young players across the country," he pontificated.

"I noticed that when the national anthem was being played, you had your glove in your right hand, you didn't have your right hand over your heart, and you were scratching the seat of your pants with your left hand. If you plan to play in the major leagues for the New York Mets, young man, you'd best learn to stand at attention with that cap in your right hand over your heart and set a patriotic tone for the young people of this country."

Kenny assured Stanky that he too was a patriot and that he'd learn to stand at attention. Kenny also breathed a sigh of relief. He was convinced Stanky was going to read him the riot act, not for a lack of patriotism, but for his lousy play on the field. Eddie Stanky was right. Kenny did make the major leagues in a big way. By 1969 he was an integral part of the Mets world championship team, and I watched him closely before every game. Kenny Boswell always stood at attention during the national anthem.

• • • • • • • • • •

During my forty-three years in baseball I never ran across a better developer of young players than Eddie Stanky. Most folks don't know it, but he was also the most sophisticated ice cream connoisseur I ever met in the big leagues. During that same camp, in the middle of a conversation about Kenny Boswell's future, Eddie interrupted me, saying, "Say, Red, what's your favorite ice cream?"

I couldn't believe my ears. "Well, Eddie, I never thought about it too much, but I guess I like all thirty-one flavors!"

"Oh, no, Red. Breyer's. Breyer's is the best I've ever had anywhere!"

Flabbergasted, I shook my head in disbelief. "Okay, fine, Eddie, whatever."

Fifteen years later Eddie Stanky came to Houston as head baseball coach with the University of South Alabama. His club had three games scheduled with the University of Houston, and I went out to the park to see Eddie and to check out a couple of his ballplayers. Down on the field, just before batting practice, I asked him, "Say, you remember the ice cream question you asked me years ago? You know, which one is the best?"

"Oh, yeah, sure."

"Well, I have a new favorite, and it's a rage in this part of the country and it's made right where I live up in Brenham. It's called Blue Bell, and I never tasted anything close to it."

"Oh, really, where can I get some?"

"Well, any store in town will have it, but you're staying with your daughter here in Houston, aren't you?"

"Yep."

"Well, I guarantee she has some in the refrigerator, so you oughta try it out!"

The next day at the ballpark Stanky was screaming my name when he saw me walk in. "Get over here, get over here. You were right. That Blue Bell is absolutely incredible. Now I gotta find a way to get it to Alabama." Eventually, he got it there, but I never saw anything like Eddie Stanky, the connoisseur and purveyor of Kenny Boswell, of baseball talent in general, and ice cream, for crying out loud.

THE SCOUT

While I first discovered Kenny Boswell at a Mets tryout camp, I found most of my ballplayers at ballparks where I practiced one of my secret weapons in the endless competition for talent: I almost always showed up long before the game was scheduled to start. Why? I wanted to get a feel for the ballpark itself and what effects the surroundings might have on my targeted prospect.

For instance, if the fences appeared closer to home plate than the distances painted on them, then an alleged home-run hitter might not be as good as advertised. When I thought the fences were closer, I'd often go down on the field, before the players arrived there, and step off the distance.

One time I went to a small town in deep East Texas to have a look at a young man who was supposed to be a home-run hitting phenom. When I got to the ballpark, I understood why. The place was an absolute bandbox. It looked like a Little League park! I stepped off the right field distance at 233 feet, 70–90 feet shorter than most regular ballparks, and I stepped off the left field distance at about 280 feet, about 30–40 short. Subtle nuances like that often told me the story behind the story of a particular player. When I saw the young man hit, I knew he was getting loads of unwarranted attention because he was hitting bogus home runs. This kid got drafted as a first-round choice, but he never made it because, as I told my bosses, "He can't hit home runs, and he can't hit at all."

I also liked to get to the park early so I could visit with the coaches. I always believed they would give me all the input I needed on the players I was scouting, and I valued their judgment and insight.

Most importantly I wanted to be at the ballpark in plenty of time to watch batting practice and infield and outfield practice.

Most of my grading took place during these practices. Watching a young player in the batting cage before the game told the tale of his bat speed, how much power he had, and it allowed me to watch for any problems he might have with his swing.

Seeing infielders go through their drills gave me an opportunity to grade a player's arm strength, his ability to catch the ball, to turn the double play, and I could check his mobility and agility. I could do the same for outfielders.

Watching practice is critical, simply because the player you are there to see might not get a fielding chance during an entire ball game. If the scout is there to see a hitter, chances are he might be walked a couple of times during the course of the game.

It's always been self-evident to me that if a scout only sees the actual game, skipping practice altogether, he risks not getting a chance to grade the player he came to see accurately. Yet you would be surprised at how many scouts don't do something as elementary as arrive early at the ballpark.

So what am I there to look for in an infielder? Let's break it down in a couple of ways. First, we have the power infielders, the third basemen and the first basemen. We call them power infielders because in addition to their defensive abilities these players are expected to have some hitting power with home runs and runs batted in.

The first baseman should be the guy who leads or is second on the team in home runs. He should be either first or second on the team in runs batted in. Big-league team management believes it can sacrifice a small amount of defensive ability in a third baseman or a first baseman, if that player man can hit the ball hard and hit it out of the ballpark.

As far as defensive tools go, I want to see a first baseman demonstrate some agility to move quickly to his right or left, backward and forward. Foot speed is not an absolute necessity, but quickness is. If a first baseman has great running ability, he enhances his chances to field well and stretch doubles into triples.

For several reasons it's an advantage if the first baseman is left-handed. Because a left-hander wears his glove on his right, he doesn't have to reach across his body to help close the defensive hole between first and second. He can hold a runner on first more easily than a right-handed first baseman who has to reach across the bag to tag a runner coming back to the base.

A first baseman must have an average major-league throwing arm. In this context I mean his arm should be strong enough to allow him to be the relay man on a throw from the right fielder to home plate. This is a critical throw that often saves ball games, so he has to be fast, strong, and deadly accurate.

Size is also a critical factor. I think the ideal first baseman should be more than five-feet-ten so he's a good target for the other infielders to throw to, although there are notable exceptions. Jeff Bagwell of the Houston Astros is probably a little too short, but he makes up for it by being an extremely good hitter. I know Steve Garvey of the Dodgers and Padres was short too, but for the most part, give me a big, rangy guy with some quickness.

I have some personal experience on the field with top-rate first basemen. I played with Joe Adcock with the Milwaukee Braves and against Stan Musial during his first-base days with the Cardinals. Stan could really move around first and had an excellent throwing arm and fielding ability.

To me the prototypical first baseman in today's game is Will Clark. I first saw him as a junior in high school and then went back to see him as a senior. When I went to New Orleans and observed his workout, it was obvious he was trying to play with an injured leg. Before the game I had a chance to invite him to a Montreal Expos tryout camp I was hosting in Brenham, Texas, later that year. I told him I didn't want to grade him while he was injured. "I'd love to come," Will said.

Luck and timing have a lot to do with the scouting game. Will never did make that tryout camp because he hurt his leg again, which he obviously felt bad about. He wrote me a letter of apology, said he was sorry when I ran into him at Mississippi

State, and wanted to make amends yet again after he left the Giants for Texas.

I know Will Clark has taken a beating in the media and among fans for his stance in the 1994 players strike, but to me he is *the* prototypical major-league first baseman.

As for third basemen the requirements are basically the same with some exceptions. Like the first baseman, the third sacker should be a good home run and RBI man, but a great arm is absolutely necessary for success in this position because he must make two extremely difficult plays. The first is the ball hit hard right behind the third base bag. It takes a rifle arm to fire one across the diamond after fielding the ball hit to the third baseman's right. The second is that slow roller hit down the third-base line. Brooks Robinson made this play as well as anyone, and he was the only third baseman I ever saw who could make that play with an overhand peg instead of the one-handed, bare-handed "scoop and throw" so many third basemen try to execute.

The third baseman has to have other defensive abilities besides a cannon arm. He must be baseball smart, anticipating the next play, always alert, and he's got to have better foot speed than the first baseman.

As far as size goes, give me a third baseman who's at least five-feet-eleven and physically strong. I know longtime big leaguer Ron Cey who used to be with the Dodgers and Cubs was a couple of inches shorter than that, but players like him are few and far between.

The other two infield positions, shortstop and second base, are the ones I call defensive positions. If a ball club will give up a little defense to gain a great deal of offense from its first and third basemen, it will give up a little offense to get great defense from its second baseman and shortstop.

I love looking at shortstops. The ideal candidate is five-feet-nine to about six-one, with a long, lean physique that possesses the smooth quickness of a whippet rather than the plodding moves of a weightlifter. A shortstop also has to be rangy enough to field high popups into left field or down the foul line behind third. Obviously, since shortstops cement the middle of the infield, the man must have a powerful arm.

The acid test for judging a shortstop is the throw from the hole between short and third. To succeed, fast reflexes are required to get to a ball hit hard in the hole, and a rifle arm is absolutely necessary to make the long throw across the diamond. Either a young shortstop can get it there or he can't. If he doesn't have enough arm to make that throw, he doesn't have a chance of becoming a major-league shortstop. End of story.

It also helps if a shortstop has a little fire in his belly, like Johnny Logan of the Milwaukee Braves clubs in the middle 1950s. I played with Johnny, who fit the basic criteria for a great shortstop, but he was also feisty and aggressive and didn't mind mixing it up every now and then. Logan's spirit, not to mention that of Eddie Matthews, won us some ball games we probably should have lost.

I think Ernie Banks was the best shortstop I ever saw. Not only could he play defense like a fiend, he had tremendous power. Unfortunately Ernie was never surrounded with championship talent on the Cubs, but if you have a young man with great defensive skills at short and he can hit, well, you have a number-one draft choice.

Second basemen can get away with having slightly slower foot speed than a shortstop and his hands don't have to be as sure. He's closer to first, has a shorter throw to make, so he can knock the ball down and still throw out a runner. The shortstop doesn't have such a luxury.

An excellent second baseman has to be an extremely quick player, able to move to his right, left, backward, and forward, which makes it very difficult for the other team to hit the ball up the middle of the infield. Moving fast also helps to close the hole between first and second, or to pick up a slow roller past the pitcher and throw the runner out. He needs these skills in his bag of tricks.

Also he has to have the sense to position himself for each hitter, especially for a potential double play. For example, by "cheating" half a step toward the second-base bag, the smart second baseman will be able to cover his base better on a double play.

The second baseman can get away with having a slightly weaker arm than the shortstop, but on the double play he better have an extremely quick release and the ability to make the turn and throw.

Above all the second baseman must have the right attitude. He's gotta feel the ball will not get past him no matter what! which is the competitive edge that defined Kenny Boswell, Ryne Sandberg, Lou Whitaker, Bobby Richardson, Charlie Gehringer, and virtually all great second basemen.

Red's Random Thought . . .

The most difficult play in sports isn't hitting a major-league fastball. It's when an outfielder chases down a well-hit line drive that's headed straight for the seats, jumps high while trying not to crash into the fence, snatches the ball, turns, and hits the cutoff man. Try it some time. But before you do, make sure your insurance is up to date because it's a killer play.

Chapter 10

Angels in the Outfield

All the greats could do it. DiMaggio, Mays, and Mantle had it down. Pete Reiser, Duke Snider, Jim Piersall, and Jim Busby did it, too. Terry Moore, the old Cardinals center fielder from the 1930s and 1940s, and the amazingly talented Hank Aaron . . . these men could perform a dangerous and delicate feat that is the baseball equivalent of the Space Shuttle *Atlantis* linking up with the Mir space station while traveling at twenty-seven thousand miles an hour.

I'm talking about what happens when a hitter slams a high line drive between the outfielders and the ball is heading over the fence unless an outfielder can somehow run it down and make the catch. Heroic outfielders like the late Roberto Clemente, Bobby Tolan, and Ken Griffey Jr. must be blessed with their own "on-board computers" because there's no other explanation for this miraculous play.

As the play begins, the ball rockets off the bat at better than one hundred miles an hour more than three hundred feet from the spot where the outfielder is standing. Racing like a gazelle across the green tiff-bermuda carpet with eyes peering intently through the bright light at the tiny white sphere, the outfielder's natural radar has to help him judge the direction of the ball, its speed, and make corrections for the wind's effect on its flight.

Close to the outfield wall he senses the crunch of the cinder warning track underfoot, then he leaps like a deer, snatches the ball from just above the outfield barrier, and saves a home run, making an airborne pirouette and landing in position to fire a strike to the cutoff man at least two hundred feet away.

What physical dexterity, speed, and courage are needed to complete that mission? If any little thing goes wrong, he can seriously injure himself or even end his career. In fact young Ken Griffey broke his wrist early in the 1995 season trying to make the play.

That's why I think it's the single most difficult maneuver in sports. A successful hitter gets 150 to 200 base hits a year, but how many home-run saving plays are executed successfully each season? Maybe 25 or 30, tops.

Remember something else. The masters of this feat were not all signed by their big-league clubs as outfielders. Legendary Yankees scout Tom Greenwade signed Mickey Mantle as a shortstop. DiMaggio signed as a shortstop, as did Pete Reiser and Willie Mays.

These outfielders were and are complete ballplayers, and I think too many big-league scouts have gotten away from looking for that type of athlete. It's an all-too-typical big-league scouting mistake to put too much emphasis on an outfielder's hitting ability and not enough on his crucial defensive skills. Over the years I've listened to other scouts talk about an outfield prospect who can hit but can't field his position very well.

"Well, he can really hit the ball out of the ballpark," is a typical remark. "Yep, but he can't play defense," ol' Red says.

"He can really put a charge in it and knock it over the fence consistently," they reply. "Yep, and he's swinging an aluminum bat. We don't know how much power he really has," Red says.

"He's an RBI threat," is another argument. "He may be, but he makes meatheaded plays in the field and allows three runs in for every one he drives in at bat," Red observes.

Cross-checkers often sign off on the "more power, less defense" theory, too. Sometimes a cross-checker will show up, and a young outfielder will hit a home run and that's all it takes to be a prospect. Never mind if the outfielder can play defense, in fact, the cross-checker may never see him throw or run at all. Forget the fact that this alleged prospect is using an aluminum bat. Home run equals prospect, which is exactly the wrong way to scout a ballplayer, but that's the way too many of 'em are doing it these days.

Just look around at all the big-league clubs now and tell me how many truly good defensive outfields there are. How many have three solid defensive players or three legitimate major-league arms capable of throwing out base runners and keeping runners from taking an extra base on a base hit? How many out-fields have three real speed demons who can cut off a base hit before it hits the wall and keep a double from turning into a triple? Not many.

Pitchers' earned-run averages may have gone up because they aren't as good overall as they once were, but outfield play isn't as good either. Because of poor defense ERAs skyrocket. Just look at how many 8–5, 10–6, or 12–5 ball games there are now. Outfielders don't talk to each other once a fly ball is in the air, and as a result they crash into each other like the Three Stooges. Fly balls drop when they should be caught. I see big-league game after game where outfielders fail to hit the proper cutoff man. Good team play is becoming a rarity, and managers' hair turns gray prematurely.

I firmly believe that outfields made up of defensive players who can make the great catch with the game on the line, who hit the cutoff man, who talk to each other when the ball is in the air—those are the outfields that win championships year in and year out.

I want to see outfielders who run on the balls of their feet as they chase fly balls. Why? Well, running that way keeps their heads from bobbing up and down and turns a sprint into a literal glide across the grass. That enables the young outfielder to keep his eyes fixed on the ball from the time it leaves the bat until he catches it.

We don't always find potential major-league outfielders playing in amateur, high school, or college outfields, of course, but a young man whom we project to be a big-leaguer must be able to run extremely well. By that I mean better-than-major-league average. I want to see that sixty-yard dash speed in the 6.6 to 6.7 range, because that's just about the distance a good outfielder will have to run to chase down a well-hit fly ball headed out of the ballpark. My outfield prospects *must* be able to make the difficult throw from right field to third base with plenty of steam on it every single time.

Don Denbow from Corsicana, Texas, can play like that. So can Tom Grieve's young son, Ben, signed in 1994 as the number-one choice of the Oakland Athletics.

This kind of young potential big-league outfielder is a rare bird these days, but they're the ones major-league fans have come to expect to see whenever they go to the ballpark. Scouts should be expected to deliver them to the ball clubs. To me there are too many left fielders playing center field and right field in the big leagues. Left field is usually the position where the man with the weakest defensive outfield skills plays. The left fielder doesn't have to have as strong an arm as the right fielder or center fielder because he doesn't have to make the really long throws, like the one from right field to third base. In most ballparks left field usually has the least amount of territory to cover, so the left fielder doesn't have to run as well as the other two outfielders. But now too many outfielders with left-field tools are playing center and right. In my opinion that has hurt the game badly.

Another factor that has diminished a team's defensive skills has been the use of artificial turf over the past twenty-five years. The artificial stuff puts a greater premium on foot speed, but in my mind it helps the one-dimensional ballplayer who is a hitter only. The ball moves so fast on artificial turf, base hits have been made on balls that got by infielders that would've been caught had the infield been natural grass.

THE SCOUT

Fortunately things are changing back to the way they should be, so fans of old-fashioned, well-rounded ballplayers should take heart. New stadiums like Jacobs Field in Cleveland, The Ballpark at Arlington, Coors Field in Denver, and Camden Yards in Baltimore all have natural grass. Kansas City has a new grass carpet. They're going to put grass in Busch Stadium in St. Louis. Somebody in baseball is beginning to realize that natural grass is *the* natural playing surface for baseball, and it showcases fine all-around ballplayers, not the one-dimensional, designated hitters.

An outfielder for Red Murff must have offensive skills, but he doesn't always have to be a big home-run hitter. As long as an outfielder hits crisp line drives, possesses a little power, and has excellent defensive ability, he's a prospect to me. That's what potential is to Red Murff. Now if we can just get someone to do something about the designated hitter rule.

Red's Random Thought . . .

Baseball pays too much money to people who cannot play in the big leagues. Just go to a ballpark sometime and note the number of mistakes, missed cutoff men, base-running blunders, and mental errors that are made by these bogus big leaguers. Why? Well, even Red Murff makes mistakes.

Chapter 11

· · · · · · · · · · · · · · · · · · · ·

Sometimes We Miss

Scouts aren't infallible. We show up at ballparks every day of
the season to see ballplayers who aren't prospects and never
will be. We waste our time and the club's money. Sometimes a
kid's advance billing is a lot better than the reality, and sometimes a young man has been overlooked. But that's the beauty
and challenge of it. You gotta look for yourself, and, believe
me, I've made plenty of mistakes on the young ballplayers I was
scouting.

One time I heard some fellow scouts talking about a
prospect. "Can't miss," they said. "Another Carlton Fisk," one
insisted. "Fisk but faster," said another. "A sure-fire number-
one draft choice and worth unloading the bank for," was the
final pronouncement.

The subject of this overripe speculation was a young catcher
named Danny Goodwin, the Chicago White Sox number-one
draft choice in 1971. Goodwin was a fine, studious young man,
but instead of signing a contract with the White Sox, he decided
to sign on at a school in my territory, Southern University in
Baton Rouge, Louisiana.

Normally I try not to listen to the scouting grapevine. I
always pride myself on finding my own ballplayers and doing my

own research. But I heard so much about this young catcher, I had to go and take a look-see, since I never took anyone else's word as doctrine. I had long since learned my lesson about that.

I was in the ballpark less than fifteen minutes when I realized the rumor mill was dead wrong. Goodwin couldn't throw, he didn't have good footwork behind the plate, and he was never going to be a big-league hitter as far as I was concerned. In my estimation this youngster arrived at the ballpark each day with the "No Prospect" label firmly attached.

Like the gossip grapevine in every other walk of life, the one in baseball can be extremely stupid and mulish, and false rumors are extremely slow to die. So it should come as no surprise that another team made the same mistake four years later, when the California Angels drafted Goodwin in the first round again.

That year, 1975, right before the draft, I went back to Baton Rouge to take another look just to make sure nothing had changed. While he later spent parts of only a few seasons in the big leagues, it was apparent to me twenty years ago that Goodwin would never be mentioned in the same breath as Gabby Hartnett, Johnny Bench, or Jerry Grote and certainly was destined to fail to live up to his rumored potential.

Sometimes ego gets in the way of good judgment. In Goodwin's case a scout's stubbornness and his refusal to look closely and honestly at a ballplayer (not to mention the silliness of his scouting director) cost a club $125,000 in bonus money for a kid who never should have been drafted in the first place. While his managers saw the same shortcomings I had seen and finally released him, the blatant error resulted because a bunch of scouts started comparing notes. The more they talked, the better young Goodwin became. Next thing you know, to hear them tell it, he was baseball's Paul Bunyan. Problem was he played like Babe the Blue Ox.

• • • • • • • • • • •

Probably Murff's all-time greatest, most-tragic talent blunder took place when I was a rookie scout in 1961. I spent a lot of time watching a catcher I really liked at Sam Houston State in Huntsville, Texas. Gary Herrington's arm wasn't as good as Jerry Grote's, still he could throw well, could hit with some power, and he handled pitchers with authority.

One day as I sat at the Sam Houston ballpark with another scout, my colleague said, "Hey, Red, you like that catcher, don't you?"

"Sure do."

"Well, I liked him a lot, too, and wanted to sign him myself, but he's had a couple of operations on both his knees, so I'm not going to touch him."

Holy smokes. The other scout's words caught me off guard and all at once I was surprised and disappointed. I just knew I'd really found another potential big-league catcher to go along with Jerry Grote and John Bateman. So without talking to the kid himself about his knees, I immediately scratched him off my list and never gave it another thought until years later.

Gary and I remained friends through the years. He never signed a professional contract with anyone, but he stayed in base-ball because he loved it. Gary went on to become a very successful high school coach in Baytown, Texas, and twenty years after I'd scouted him, I ran into him at a coaches clinic. We got to talking, as coaches and I often did, about past playing experiences, and the conversation came around to high praise for Gary's ability.

"Gary, I have to tell you something. I thought you were going to catch in the big leagues. I was going to send you out myself, until I found out about your knees."

"What about my knees, Mr. Murff?"

"Well, I heard you'd had operations on both of them and I just didn't figure a catcher with a history of knee problems would hold up in professional baseball."

"Mr. Murff, I never had any knee problems. Where did you get that idea?"

What? I was shocked. Angry at myself. I apologized pro-fusely to Gary Herrington and at the same time cursed my own misjudgment. I had committed the scout's unpardonable sin. I had listened to another scout about a ballplayer and hadn't done my homework. As a result I had disqualified a young man who should have been given a chance, and I was heartbroken for him. I cost Gary Herrington a shot at professional baseball and maybe big-league stardom. To this day I have never forgiven myself for such a stupid mistake. Fortunately for me Gary did. Unfortunately there were more.

"Here, Red, here's a list of the only major-league prospects in the state of Texas in 1961," a scout for another club said as he showed me a scrap of paper with four names on it. This was my first year on the road as a scout for the Houston Colt .45s, and my friend appeared to be doing me a favor by showing me his list. In reality he was, most likely, trying to set me up and throw me off the trail of some really great talent. There was only one problem: I knew there were more than four big-league prospects in Texas that year.

"I swear, those are the only ones, Red," he said.

I was taken aback. "In a state as large as Texas, there's simply got to be more than that," I kept insisting.

Don't worry, there's not," he promised.

Well, I later proved my supposed well-intentioned friend as wrong as could be. In the first place my fellow scout hadn't even listed Jerry Grote, a prospect for sure, and all the major-league scouts in my territory knew about Jerry. Nor had he noticed Carroll Sembera, a young man we later signed for the Colt .45s who had an outstanding if short-lived career as a reliever in Houston and Montreal. He skipped over Darrell Brandon, a man I signed for Houston, who was later traded to the Boston Red Sox. Brandon's pitching talents, along with the talents of Jim Lonborg, Carl Yastrzemski, et al. led the Boston Red Sox to the 1967 World Series.

While the four on his list were legitimate major-league prospects, none ever made the big leagues, but I signed four other players that year who went on to terrific careers. My "friend" was not able to trick me into making the mistakes he ultimately made.

THE SCOUT

Unfortunately some of our biggest blunders even make it to the big leagues because clubs invest millions of dollars in bonuses to players who simply aren't qualified. When such a mistake occurs, club executives are loathe to 'fess up, and they end up giving those bonus babies every chance to play in the majors, sometimes to the detriment of the team.

In the end the truth wins out. Guys who can't play can't hide for long, and the club's mistake becomes blatantly obvious. While baseball too often ends up drafting the wrong players and paying them too much money, conversely, we sometimes draft players in the later rounds who turn out to be superstars.

Let's discuss an example of the former. I was with the Montreal Expos in 1985 when Pete Incaviglia was finishing his career at Oklahoma State. I followed Pete for three years at the school and sent in report after report insisting "Incaviglia's *not* a National League ballplayer!"

In my opinion Pete couldn't play defense well enough to project him as an everyday outfielder. I didn't think he ran well or had anywhere near a major-league-average arm. Too many college third-base coaches were yelling giddyup to base runners on balls hit to Incaviglia. In fact even the slowest college runners could go from first to third on a ground ball hit to this kid in left field. Pete didn't appear to have good enough eyesight, he couldn't follow the path of a batted ball, and as a result some routine fly balls hit to him ended up being Indiana Jones adventures—always plenty of action, you just never knew how they were going to turn out. Without good defensive skills I figured he'd give professional managers more than their share of gray hair. As far as hitting the ball, I judged him as having good power, but he didn't make sufficient contact, and I thought he struck out too much. I continually told my bosses in Montreal that if Incaviglia was going to play in the big leagues it would have to be as a designated hitter in the American League.

Well, they didn't agree. In fact they told me they were ready to ensure Incaviglia's status as a number-one draft choice—at least in *their* minds—by offering him a million-dollar signing bonus.

I went thermonuclear. How could they do that? After my unrelenting protests to scouting director Gary Hughes, I was shocked that any team I worked for would go against my advice and spend that kind of money for a player like Incaviglia. Time to say adios, I thought, and I parted ways with the Expos.

Later the Expos traded the draft rights to Incaviglia to the Rangers, and "Inky" got his million plus a couple of good home-run years in the big leagues, but he never was an all-around ballplayer or in my mind a top prospect. Now Pete Incaviglia's latest stop is in Japan, a brand of ball about the Class AAA level, and he's struggling.

Massive foul-ups are bound to happen when groups of scouts get together and begin jabbering. Pretty soon they've blown a player's abilities out of proportion, and the misinformation gets spread through the scouting grapevine, magnifying it even further. Sometimes an insecure scout will upgrade his report to reflect nothing he has seen in person. To me the only trustworthy scouting report is one founded on an eyewitness evaluation based totally and completely on experienced judgment and gut instinct.

It's also interesting to note here that sometimes rumors are circulated in an effort to upgrade a particular team's draft status. One scout may intentionally overrate a player, in effect, lie to another scout, hoping the scout he's misleading will make a mistake on a player both men have seen. This type of chicanery goes on all the time among those eager participants in the grapevine chatterbox.

Scouts often make grave errors by evaluating a young player too early in the season. Maybe a kid with a great reputation didn't have a good day because it was cold that afternoon, or he'd only had a couple of practices before the scout saw him, so he didn't show much talent. Scouts write him off and decide not to follow him during the year. It's tragic when such a young man improves dramatically, but no scout sees him play again. He mistakenly was judged lacking in February or March and that's that.

Then there's the prospect himself. Sometimes we make mistakes by not getting to know a youngster's personal life well enough. He gets drafted and no one realizes his girlfriend is pregnant or his mother recently died. So, of course, his concentration suffers and he's set up to fail before he's in a psychological position to realize his full potential. After all these are just kids we're talking about, and a stable home life is a lot less distracting.

In Texas, King Football has often cost us baseball prospects. Perhaps a high school coach forces a first baseman to decide between football and baseball on the basis of their relative "manliness." This football-loving coach pressures the kid, and it's not unusual for him to feel that he has to prove his manhood on the gridiron. Then he gets hurt and loses his baseball prospect status.

In fact, in 1974, one Dickinson, Texas, kid, Hal Dews, actually quit school because his female classmates called him Old Yeller when he chose "sissy" baseball over "macho" football. It wasn't just the girls who gave him grief. Football coaches continually stalked him in the school hallways and told him he was "gutless" and "chicken" and "yellow" for not playing the fall sport.

Hal was six-four and weighed 190 and had been groomed to be the school's star quarterback, but he wanted to play baseball more than football. With his size and strength the football coaches, of course, salivated over the prospects of having him play for them, but they went about it in an ignorant, short-sighted way and didn't think about the diminished value of having a kid who really didn't want to play. Still the football coaches kept up the harangue. After weeks of this nonsense, Hal just couldn't take the constant harassment and dropped out of school.

I first saw Hal at an American Legion tournament just after what should have been his senior year. He had the size I always looked for and he had a good, live fastball that I had clocked in the low nineties and a good breaking pitch. Hal was almost apologetic when I asked him how he did in high school.

He said, "Mr. Murff, I just couldn't take being called a sissy and yellow just because I wanted to specialize in baseball, so I quit."

I couldn't believe my ears when I heard this story, but I promised Hal he'd get a chance to make those people sorry. Did he ever! Within three years of my signing him, Hal was pitching in the big leagues with the Montreal Expos. Although an arm injury ultimately took him out of the game, Hal courageously overcame king football, stuck to his guns, played baseball, and made it much further than he ever would have gone as a football player.

Some of the most notorious scouting miscalculations involve young players taken late in the draft who turn out to be front-line major-league talent. You never know if on a given afternoon, a kid is showing you his best stuff or if he's having an off day. Sometimes you barely get a glimpse of a possible major-league talent, so some really great prospects don't get drafted until the thirtieth round and then sign for a minimal or no bonus. But some of the late-drafted ones who go to the Rookie Leagues then come into their own, excel far past expectations, and climb the minor-league ladder. These are the surprising ones to watch as they improve and dominate every step of the way to the big leagues.

One such ballplayer is Ellis Burks. Burks came out of Everman High School, near Fort Worth, Texas, with absolutely no credentials except tons of talent that the scouts initially missed. He had played on a high school team that featured a right-handed pitcher who became a number-one draft choice, but no one spotted Ellis, including me.

In fact he received a college scholarship circuitously through a player showcase put on by the Dallas-Fort Worth ex-professional baseball players association. Each year high school coaches in that area choose the best young men on their ball clubs without scholarships to play in the Showcase, which is a series of games played at the Texas Rangers Ballpark in Arlington. College coaches from all over the Southwest watch the games and end up picking a number of promising players for their programs. The Showcase is a great idea that came from an incredibly active ninety-six-year-old former minor-league owner named George Schepps.

Noticed only by a very perceptive coach from Ranger Junior College, Burks went on to school on scholarship and was later drafted in a low round. The next thing you know, there's Ellis playing center field for the Red Sox and then the Rockies. How's that for initially missing a top-flight ballplayer?

Then there's Fred Patek. He was an infielder from Seguin, Texas, near San Antonio. He was only five-four and weighed maybe 160 pounds soaking wet. In my mind, and I've told Fred this, he's as good a major-league player, pound for pound, as ever played the game, but quite honestly only a few scouts in Texas knew much about this young man when he signed with the Pirates in the mid-1960s and began a very successful fourteen-year career with the Pirates, Kansas City, and the California Angels. Freddie Patek's diminutive stature scared lots of scouts away, and even my own San Antonio-based subscout in that area never told me about him. Boy could he play! Fred could really run, and he had a cannon for an arm. He could make that long throw from the hole at shortstop. Most of all Freddie Patek possessed major-league desire. He *wanted* to play baseball, and lack of size was not going to keep him away.

When discussions about such out-of-the-ordinary ballplayers come up among scouts in the stands, someone always says, "Yep, I knew he could do it all along. I knew he could make it to the big leagues."

I always reply, "The heck you did! If you really thought he was that good, you'd have made sure your club drafted him in a higher round." The truth is, we all miss.

Players like Ellis Burks, Pete Rose, and Freddie Patek, those atypical ballplayers who don't fit our cookie-cutter mold, who don't initially appear to have the great talent but make up for it with a "never say die" attitude will always cause the scouts to err. Surprises always happen, and that's what makes this crazy game so cotton-picking much fun. Remember this: No scout bats a thousand, not even Red Murff.

Red's Random Thought . . .

I lost the last baseball job I had because a young, inexperienced executive would not listen to me about a ballplayer no one else but me liked. I made a career out of loving players like that, but I absolutely refused to surrender my honor, and it cost me my job.

Chapter 12

Scout's Honor

I guess I'd still be working in baseball if I'd learned to be a politician. Apparently it's a much more important role than I ever thought. By nature I have always said what I thought, and for the most part during my scouting career my up-front, no-nonsense attitude played well. Most scouting directors I worked for always encouraged field scouts to say what we thought about ballplayers, and we never had to worry about being punished for airing our feelings.

As baseball becomes overrun with what I call the MBA bean counters, unfortunately, mastery of the art of politics has become a crucial part of a scout's survival skills. My friend Buzzy Keller, a veteran baseball man and now a field scout with the Chicago Cubs, says the problem is that these guys have little if any baseball experience and have never done it on the field.

Ever since baseball scouts came to exist they've had to lobby management to get their ballplayers signed. I learned early in my scouting career to sell my ballplayers hard. I did it with Nolan and pestered enough people to get him drafted finally. I did that countless other times in the years that followed. The problems that ultimately led to my early "retirement" from baseball developed during the last year I spent as a full-time scout with the Atlanta Braves.

All full-time scouts have a lot of input in meetings that take place before draft day. For this particular predraft meeting I went to Atlanta with several players on my list, but one player burned brightly in my mind. Don Denbow Jr. Six-four, 195 pounds of extremely talented baseball potential. He was an out-fielder from Corsicana, Texas, about fifty miles south of Dallas. Young Denbow could do it all.

He certainly had the genetics for it. His dad had played football and baseball at Corsicana High. The elder Denbow signed a football-baseball scholarship at SMU, where he starred in both sports. When he was twenty-two, Denbow could hit, but I judged him a marginal talent. Still he signed a contract with the Los Angeles Dodgers. Don Sr. got as high as Class A, then gave up baseball and finally became a top-flight high school football coach and now athletic director at Corsicana.

This man marked his son with excellent athletic talent. Don Jr. had tremendous foot speed, especially for a young man his size. The younger Denbow simply was a natural. His dad had trained him to be a college quarterback, but baseball and Red Murff got in the way.

I first saw the youngster during his sophomore year in high school at a tournament in Waxahachie, Texas. He hit two long home runs that day, but home-run power was not what drew my attention to Denbow—it was his running speed that impressed me the most.

Other scouts attended the tournament that day. They were there looking at a catcher from Waxahachie, and they all took off because he was having a bad day. I loved opportunities like that. I didn't like the catcher, but I kept hanging around because I knew young Denbow would be playing. Once he was done with his two home runs and his stolen bases, I knew I'd be following this young man for the next two years.

THE SCOUT

In my mind he was a sure bet. He could run from home to first three-tenths of a second faster than the average major leaguer. That's a bunch! I knew he would get stronger and faster as he matured, and I was right.

At the beginning of young Denbow's senior season, I began writing glowing reports about him to the Braves. I continually emphasized that I believed Denbow was at least a second-round pick, and I told my bosses he was worth a bonus of about $150,000.

The Don Denbow Jr.'s of the world make scouting really easy. Not only did he have tremendous talent, but he was a fine young man, not in any kind of trouble because his parents raised him right. After each game I saw him play, I always made a point to let him know I had been watching, that baseball was watching, and that Red Murff believed in him. I told young Don if he continued to improve, he could be worth a lot of money. The youngster had an All-American boy smile and he always told me how much he appreciated my attention.

As I followed young Denbow, I noticed he received little attention from the other scouts. Again, like so many other players I pursued through the years, I was surprised I had so little competition.

As draft day drew near, I invited a Braves cross-checker in for a look. Unfortunately it wasn't Don's best performance. My prospect ran and swung the bat well, but during the course of the game he dropped a couple of fly balls. The cross-checker was unimpressed and recommended to the Braves management that Denbow be drafted in the low rounds at a minimal salary and bonus.

I was incensed. I had already told the Braves I had tremendous faith in Denbow and believed he was worth drafting in the second round with a more significant dollar bonus. In my heart I knew I would be in for a battle with management at our predraft meeting, and I also suspected the price I might end up paying for trying to win that battle would be my job. Knowing that, I planned my tactics at great length and prayed about it constantly, asking for fortitude and inspiration. I have always been one will-ing to go toe to toe for what I believe in—and I was convinced that Don Denbow Jr. was worth every penny I said he was.

As the scouts sat down in Atlanta for our get-together, I felt a definite air of animosity directed toward me. I admit that at this time in my career I had tired of trying to train scouting directors to understand just what it is we field scouts are supposed to do. So many times scouting directors have not spent a lot of time, if any, looking for ballplayers, and in many instances young men who are on baseball's fast track get scouting directors' jobs while looking forward to becoming general managers. That's okay, I guess, but it upset me that in too many instances the Peter Principle was a well-established fact of life.

It is a well-known fact within the scouting profession that I did not get along with a few scouting directors, and the young man who was the scouting boss for the Braves in those days and I simply did not see eye to eye on ballplayers, which is fine. I also knew that when the subject of Don Denbow Jr. came up at out predraft meeting, my boss and I would get into a heated discus-sion. Going into that meeting, I was fired up about Don Denbow, but no sooner had I said his name than trouble began. I outlined Denbow's strengths. I noted his size, his speed, his athletic ability, and his bat speed. As I spoke, my boss acted bored, but I went ahead with my presentation about young Denbow's talents.

In the midst of my Denbow speech trouble began. My boss played devil's advocate, questioning the wisdom of setting a $150,000 price tag on a young ballplayer who no one but Red Murff liked.

My blood boiled. I tried to cool down, but I just couldn't. I kept thinking about how angry I always got when field scouts pooled their resources, talked among themselves, and shared looks at each other's draft lists. I simply never operated like that, and then I thought about all the times in previous years that I had been the lone scout to like a ballplayer. I had been right about Ryan, Koosman, Boswell, Grote, Schatzeder, Stanton, and more than four dozen others. Weren't they all proof that I had a knack for finding gems among stones? Who cares if these other motor-mouthed scouts didn't agree?

My skin turned beet red, and I lost my temper. "That's the reason," I growled, "the Atlanta Braves hired me in the first place, to find ballplayers like that, ballplayers nobody else knows or cares about. I made a long, successful career being that kind of scout!"

My boss wouldn't let up. He just couldn't understand paying that much money for a youngster nobody liked but me.

I told him that's the amount I thought young Denbow was worth, not what we could get him for, which I believed was about $20,000 plus some college money. I thought it was a great deal for Atlanta because we could get a young ballplayer I was totally convinced would play in the big leagues for a relatively minor amount of money up front.

Still, he adamantly disagreed. He was not about to budge.

By this time I had lost all control of my temper. I felt I was being shown no respect and I guess Don Denbow became my line in the sand with the Braves and my boss. Enough was enough, and I was about to blow. My cheeks were flushed. My voice trembled.

"Let's go on and talk about my next prospect, but you remember one thing. Nobody, *nobody* liked Nolan Ryan either."

As it turned out, the Braves drafted Don Denbow in the thirty-first round. He was about the eight hundredth player chosen. Before contract negotiations I was authorized to offer the family a contract specifying nine hundred dollars a month salary and nothing more. No bonus, no college, nothing past the paltry salary. I argued that we would have to offer at least four semesters of college expenses, but the Braves were adamant. Nine hundred dollars a month for Denbow. Period.

I can tell you honestly and emphatically I was heartbroken. I knew that would be my last draft day for the Atlanta Braves, and

I feared that at my age, seventy-one at the time, it might be my last draft in baseball. My honor and principles had been compromised, and no job anywhere was worth that kind of humiliation.

I also believed that if young Denbow signed with the Braves, given the problems I'd had with my bosses, then at some point in his career they would release him just to spite me. Don Denbow and his family did not deserve to be caught in such a cross fire, so I volunteered my services as counselor as well as scout. I knew that the young man had a junior college scholarship offer, and I told him and his family I believed he should take it.

So Don accepted a scholarship with Blinn Junior College in my hometown of Brenham, Texas. I told him the Braves would retain his draft rights for one year, and at the end of his freshman season he could sign with Atlanta if he wished. But he didn't, and no one from Atlanta ever mentioned his name to me again. For the next two seasons Denbow terrorized Texas junior college pitchers. He developed even more power, more strength, and more speed. As a freshman he became a home-run threat and made the All-Conference team that year. As a sophomore he made Junior College All America, and became "Baseball America" Junior College Player of the Year in 1993.

At the end of Don's sophomore year, the San Francisco Giants turned me into a prophet once again. They drafted him and signed him to a contract that included a $160,000 bonus. Now, despite some struggles, Denbow is continuing his climb to the big leagues.

Just as I had predicted to friends and fellow scouts, I received a letter a short time after draft day from the Braves informing me that my services would no longer be needed and that my contract would not be renewed. I'm officially retired after thirty-three years in the scouting game. Sometimes I miss it, but too much has changed since I started. Gone are the days when a club listened to a lone scout who relied on himself, his knowledge and his instincts. Scouting has become some kind of popularity contest and money match. I'm lucky to have come along during the days when kids signed up to play baseball for the right reason: for the love of the game. Deals in those days ended with a handshake and a pat on the back, and, most importantly, people said "Thank you."

Red's Random Thought . . .

In 1961 a couple of veteran scouts with the Baltimore Orioles played hardball with me. I was a novice scout then and I promised I'd repay their courtesy. I did too. With the help of the FBI.

Chapter 13

Hardball and the FBI

The old 1940s radio drama would begin with an eerie question: "What evil lurks in the hearts of men? The Shadow knoooows!" I can relate to that. I've always seen myself as baseball's version of that character, The Shadow, a man of suspense and intrigue. A spy on a rainy night, standing at the end of a dark alley, dressed in a snap-brim hat, with part of my face covered by the right corner of my overcoat collar. I'm a man at his optimum, operating best in the darkest recesses of life, shedding light on the subject and succeeding handsomely. A man drawn away from crowds toward the secretive. Just call me the Lamont Cranston of scouting. My profession was a lot more fun back in the days of subterfuge, the days before the free-agent draft.

In those days a good scout usually had only three or four really top-flight ballplayers he wanted to sign. So, in an effort to win the scout's game of "sign the best ballplayer away from your competitor," it was kind of business as usual to hide a ballplayer. We'd have his parents tell other scouts he wasn't home, or we'd put him and his folks up in a motel in another town for a few days at the club's expense until we had a chance to make an offer away from the prying eyes, the loudmouths, and the open checkbooks of our competitors. Sometimes this derring-do would work. Sometimes it crashed and burned for reasons that deserve an explanation.

Here's a good one that provoked me to no end. My first year as a big-league scout was in 1961 with the Houston Colt .45s. At the end of the 1961 college baseball season, I invited Texas A&M coach Tom Chandler and his star freshman shortstop David Johnson to dinner at the Gunter Hotel in San Antonio. Besides his job as A&M's coach, Chandler was working as a subscout for the Colt .45s.

I made no secret that I liked what I saw in David Johnson, and I wanted to sign him for the Colt .45s. In 1961 scouts could sign college players at any time during their careers. A player did not have to wait until his sophomore or junior year or his twenty-first birthday to sign a professional baseball contract. But I had a little problem.

"Mr. Murff, I've decided not to sign right now. I plan to spend this coming summer playing in the Basin League up in the Dakotas. They've got some pretty salty competition there. Then I'll come back to A&M and sign a contract at the end of my sophomore year," the young Johnson told me decisively.

"Well," I said, "there will be plenty of scouts watching that Basin League and some of them are going to think they've discovered you. I think I'm the scout who found you, so I would appreciate it if you and I could have a handshake agreement. Promise me if any one of those scouts offers you a contract, you will call me immediately. I guarantee I'll make a counteroffer that will be better than anyone else's. Do we have a deal?"

"Yes sir, Mr. Murff. I promise I'll call you if anything like that happens."

Two days later I was on the road to New Mexico to watch some games in a newly formed professional league catering to second-year players, called appropriately enough the Sophomore League. Along the way I stopped at a coffee shop and picked up a San Antonio paper. In big bold type the headline said, "San Antonio's Johnson Signs with Baltimore Orioles." My heart sank, and I never got a phone call.

THE SCOUT

Later that winter I invited David to a Boys Club banquet in San Antonio and he accepted the invitation. During a lull in the proceedings I took him aside.

"David, didn't you and I agree that if another scout offered you a contract that you would call me immediately?"

"Yes sir. Yes sir, oh, I'm sorry, Mr. Murff. But here's what happened. Before I left San Antonio, two Baltimore scouts, Dee Phillips and Jimmy Russo, had me and my dad in a hotel room with thirty thousand dollars cash bonus written into a contract, and they wanted me to sign on the spot. I told them I promised I would call you before I signed a contract and they said if that's what I wanted, fine, but if I did, they would pull the deal off the table. I tell you, Mr. Murff, I couldn't afford to turn them down. I needed that money and so did my family, so I signed," he lamented.

"That's okay," I told him. "I just wanted to know how they operated, what kind of hardball they play. I'll know how to handle them next time, I promise you that."

"I'm really sorry, Mr. Murff. I know I didn't live up to our agreement, but I just couldn't turn down that money, there were too many people depending on me."

"David, that's not your fault. I don't blame you. That's a lot of temptation and a lot of money to wave in front of a young man's face. I don't know that I'd have conducted myself any differently, so don't you worry about it one bit," I told him.

David Johnson went on to an all-star career as a second baseman with the Orioles, made a few World Series appearances, and has managed successfully in the big leagues, and that's all well and good for him. I must admit to you up-front, I was not full of Christian charity when I thought about the Orioles scouts who pulled that stunt—Dee Phillips and Jimmy Russo. I spent a lot of time dreaming up some friendly paybacks for my "buddies," and I promised myself that somewhere down the line there would be retribution. Unfortunately it took a few years before those measures were carried out to my satisfaction.

In 1965, I think, I became interested in a right-handed pitcher named Ron Taylor. He was only seventeen the first time I saw him, but his fastball would blast through a brick wall. His only problem was he needed some seasoning.

Ron's dad and I talked it over and decided it would be a good idea for the young pitcher to enroll at the University of Houston. I asked only for the same consideration that I asked David Johnson. "If any scout offers you a contract, would you please, please give me a call before you sign it?"

Both Ron and his dad agreed, and the young pitcher went off to Houston. For the next several months I called Ron and his dad from time to time, and occasionally I went to see Ron pitch. Each time we talked, I reminded them to call me if any scouts came around, and each time both Taylors promised they'd call if that happened.

Late one spring afternoon, just after Ron's college season ended, I received a panicked phone call from his dad. "Mr. Murff, I have a problem, a *big* problem," Mr. Taylor said. "It's Ron, Mr. Murff. A couple of scouts, a Jimmy Russo and a Dee Phillips with the Baltimore Orioles, have Ron holed up in a motel room here in Houston, and they say they won't let him out until he signs a contract with them. Can you help me, Mr. Murff? I've told them we have to call you before we sign a contract and they still say they won't let him go 'til he signs with them."

I felt my blood boil. My skin turned beet red. My eyes glazed over. Déjà vu!

Russo and Phillips, is it, I thought. *Up to their old tricks again, are they?* I guess those yahoos thought I was going to roll over and play dead for another one of their shady shenanigans. Once I settled down, I began to lick my chops thinking about the opportunity I had. "Paybacks will be more than you boys bargained for," I mumbled to myself as I launched my diabolical plot of revenge.

"Mr. Taylor, is your son in that motel room without his consent or your consent?"

"Yes sir, he is. Neither he nor I want him there," Ron's father said.

"Sir, you call them back and you tell them if Ron doesn't call you within the next fifteen minutes and tell you he's left that motel without signing a contract, then your next call will be to the FBI. You tell them your son is being held against your will and against your son's will and in the United States, Mr. Taylor, we call that kidnapping. That's a federal offense. You tell them you'll call the FBI and will file kidnapping charges against them if they don't turn Ron loose!"

"Can I do that, Mr. Murff? Is that legal?"

"Of course, you can," I answered.

How dare they pull such a stunt, especially after they did essentially the same thing to David Johnson? Especially to Red Murff!

I don't think the federal joint, striped shirts, and the chain gang were exactly what these boys had in mind. They turned Ron loose and I signed him for the New York Mets. As it turned out, a year or so later the Baltimore Orioles acquired his contract rights, so I guess Russo and Phillips really did like Ron Taylor.

I never forgot this little misadventure, and I always kept my back covered in anticipation of further repayment stunts my Baltimore "buddies" might decide to pull. Several years later, while sitting in the stands with a group of scouts, I reminded Dee Phillips about his little charade, a memory he conveniently tried not to recall. Red being Red, I kept needling him, but Dee only laughed nervously and changed the subject. Even though some years had passed, I think Dee could still see himself busting rocks at high noon in a blazing sun, and the thought made him shudder! I think my nemesis had learned his lesson though. Don't play Hide the Prospect with Red Murff . . . or with the FBI.

Red's Random Thought . . .

As a kid I didn't think much about organized crime except for a George Raft or Jimmy Cagney gangster movie I'd see at the theater. Growing up in Burlington, Texas, I'd never even heard of a mob boss, but I also never really dreamed I'd play in the big leagues either. Sometimes a country boy can only dream about what's past the horizon, and most in my community never thought little Red Murff would travel way, way past Oz.

Chapter 14

Softshoe with the Mob

This great game of baseball places its participants in any number of unusual situations during a career. Sometimes those events test the very fabric of your upbringing. No matter whether you're a player, a coach, a manager, or a scout, you cross paths with peculiar people. Including, in this case, gangsters.

No, I never gambled on baseball games, carried out a contract hit, ran a numbers racket, or participated in any kind of crime. That is, other than to say it was a crime the way I pitched on some nights. I did have inadvertent brushes with the Mob during my lengthy career, and it just goes to show you that dangerous men lurk around the brightest corners and sometimes don't look that much different from you and me.

In 1955 I was going great guns with the Dallas Eagles in the Texas League. I led the league in victories that year—twenty-seven—the fourth highest total number of wins in a season in Texas League history. I was a celebrity in town then, and being red-headed and six-three I tended to attract attention. Being a natural-born ham, I never shunned the spotlight. If people will listen, Red's got an opinion and is always ready for a friendly discussion.

Before my family moved to Dallas for the summer, I stayed in a hotel called the St. Lawrence. Every morning, whether I'd pitched the night before or not, I'd wake up hungry and in dire need of a cup of java. So about 8:30 or 9:00 I'd head down to the coffee shop to read the paper and eat breakfast. Every morning I'd see the same beautiful blonde having breakfast there, too.

We said polite hellos for a couple of weeks, and then she recognized me, presumably from my picture in the sports sections of *The Dallas Morning News* and *The Dallas Times Herald*. She would come over to my table every morning and ask how the Eagles had done the night before. Although this pretty lady and I regularly exchanged small talk, there was nothing else between us—believe me.

A waitress took me aside one morning after this lady—I didn't even know her name and had never formally introduced myself—and I had had a particularly enjoyable chat.

"Mr. Murff, stay away from that woman."

I was taken aback. "What do you mean?"

"That woman," she said, "she belongs to a Mob boss who comes here to Dallas frequently to see her."

"So who is she?" I inquired.

"She's a well-known stripper here in Dallas and around the country," the waitress informed me like the ignoramus I was. "And you'd better leave her alone if you know what I mean," she warned.

I never had any intention of doing anything other than leave her alone after that breakfast. Mob bosses! Strippers! That woke up this country boy in a big hurry. The world and the town I was now living in was much different, unfortunately, than the church-centered, friendly community where I was brought up.

I made a silent vow to stay alert and away from potential trouble like that, but as a baseball personality you sometimes become involved in situations over which you have no control. That brings us to the next frightening incident.

Early in 1956 in my rookie major-league season, I pitched in relief and lost a twelve-inning ball game in Brooklyn. Gene Conley, the six-eight Milwaukee Braves pitcher who also played pro basketball for the Boston Celtics, and I had become good friends. As consolation to me Gene decided to go out for dinner after the game, but the place we planned to go was jammed with people. So we headed in another direction.

Gene said, "Hey, let's go to a little Italian place I know," and we hailed a cab and headed off. Once there we began to relax and forget about the disappointing loss we'd just suffered. After a great meal Gene looked out the window and spotted a dapper but tough-looking guy beating and kicking a woman outside the restaurant. He leaped from his seat and raced toward the door.

The maître d' tried to stop him. "Mr. Conley, you'd better sit down and mind your own business," he counseled.

"Listen," Gene interrupted, "I'm a country boy and in the country we don't treat women like that, and I'm gonna put a stop to it."

Gene opened the door and yelled at the man, making such a ruckus that the assailant turned the woman loose. She ran screaming and crying into the night, and Gene ambled back to our table.

Less than a minute later Mr. Tough Guy stormed into the restaurant, followed by a thick-chested, six-foot hulk of a man who moved and looked like a professional wrestler. Both men were followed by a short, slender fellow who stood about fifteen feet behind them.

Mr. Tough Guy hovered over the table, leaned right in and growled in a Brooklyn brogue at Gene, "Ya jes' stuck ya nose inta sumthin' thet wuz nun uh ya biznes, Mr. Conley."

Gene stood up slowly, stretching like a monolith, almost to the ceiling of this tiny Italian joint. He towered over his accuser and stared down into his beady little eyes. Conley appeared poised to take this guy apart.

"You shouldn't beat up a woman," he drawled menacingly.

About that time I noticed the slender guy putting his hands in his pockets. I decided these three were gangsters and fingered the smallest one as the group's hired gun. So being the brash country boy I am, I walked over to the supposed triggerman as

Conley and Mr. Tough Guy continued their less than amiable conversation.

I quietly growled at the small guy, "I guess you and I get to dance this dance, huh? I don't want you involved in that discussion over there, you hear me?"

"I ain't involved," he answered.

"Oh, yes, you are," I said forcefully. "And if you make a move with either of your hands, I'm gonna knock you out cold on the deck, you got it? You are not going to participate in this argument, understand? So, keep 'em both out in the open so I can see 'em, or you're gonna get a bloody nose and a bad headache, mister."

"I'm gonna do what my boss says," he said quietly.

"Don't get yourself hurt."

About that time Gene Conley and Mr. Tough Guy reached some kind of uneasy understanding, and all three thugs withdrew from the restaurant.

"Hey, thanks for taking care of the big guy," Conley said sarcastically.

"Gene, did you realize the smaller guy was the pistol and knife packer in the group?"

"Are you kidding me? Are you serious? My gracious, I didn't know we were that close to serious trouble," Conley sighed.

"Yes, you were," said the maître d' who had stood there, frozen in place during the confrontation. "I told you not to mess with him. That was Johnny D, one of the biggest enforcers in this town."

Conley and I stared blankly at each other, our faces drained of color.

Three years later Johnny D was gunned down by some other gangsters as he made a telephone call from a phone booth near the restaurant where we had our little meeting. From that day forward Gene Conley and I tried real hard to stay out of other people's business when we were on the road. Most of the time.

The third incident happened while I was working for the Montreal Expos. I was sitting at home twiddling my thumbs, making some travel plans and just relaxing in Texas City on a Wednesday morning. During baseball season Wednesdays are almost always slow because few high school or college teams schedule to play on that day. I was making plans to head to New Orleans to watch a pitcher at Tulane University, and I needed to spend some time with a subscout of mine, Bill Dossey. He and I planned to spend the weekend looking at prospects in South Louisiana, and that meant we'd probably be seeing fifteen ball games during my three-day visit. As I finalized my plans, my phone rang.

"Hello, this Red Murff?"

"Yes sir, it sure is."

"This Red Murff, the baseball scout?"

"Yes sir, and might I ask who is inquiring?"

"My name's Marcello," the voice replied. "Carlos Marcello from New Orleans."

"Hmm," I responded. "Name's familiar, but I can't seem to place you."

"Well, you don't know me, Mr. Murff, but I've been told you are the best baseball scout in the business. Here's my problem. My friend's son plays high school ball here in New Orleans, and she thinks he's a big-league prospect. Would you come down here as a special favor to me and tell me what you think of him?"

It never crossed my mind that this "special favor" was almost a command.

"Well, it just so happens I'm seeing a pitcher at Tulane tomorrow at one o'clock. When does this young man play," I asked?

"He plays at four tomorrow afternoon at a ballpark a couple of miles from Tulane. Can you be there?" Mr. Marcello asked.

"Yes sir, I'll be there," I promised.

"Listen, Mr. Murff, go buy yourself a round-trip airline ticket. I'll pay for it. I'll have one of my men pick you up at the airport and bring you to the ballpark," he offered.

"Oh, no sir, I couldn't do that. I need my car and I'm on a per diem, so I take care of all of my expenses, but thanks just the same."

The next day I left Texas City before dawn and made it into New Orleans just in time to head to the Tulane ballpark. The pitcher I planned to see was not impressive, so I told a few scouts sitting with me that I was going to see the "big fellow." In scout's parlance that simply means, "I've had enough, this guy's no prospect, and I gotta go find someone who can play!" So off I went for the high school park and my planned visit with Marcello. At the front gate of the high school park, a surly, burly guy dressed in a snap brim hat, black suit, dark glasses, and talking in a gruff voice was waiting for me.

"You Murff?"

"Yes sir, I am."

"Follow me. Marcello is seated by himself, four rows in back of the third-base dugout. He's waitin' for you."

Two men also looking like the Blues Brothers stood at the end of the fourth row of the stands, near a man seated by himself. I assumed he was the man I had spoken with on the phone. It was obvious he had "friends" along for protection, although from what I didn't know.

I introduced myself and Marcello told me his friend's son was a second baseman, as he pointed to the "big fellow" I had come to see: a five-six kid weighing about 135 pounds. I noticed he had good movements around second base. It was obvious the young man had been to a few instructional camps. Problem was he couldn't run fast at all, he didn't throw well, and he had little strength or bat speed. Clearly, this young man was not and never would be a big-league prospect.

I relayed my thoughts to Mr. Marcello and said, "I have to be honest with you. I don't know what this young man's future holds, what his talents are, or what his life's work will be, but I can tell you quite frankly his future is not in baseball. I hope this doesn't hurt your feelings."

"Oh, no, Mr. Murff, not at all. I was told by friends that you were the best in the business, that you tell it like it is, and that's all I wanted. I knew after seeing him play that he would never be able to play at any level higher than high school. I just wanted it confirmed for my peace of mind and so my girlfriend could hear it from a real baseball man."

"Be specific," I advised. "Tell your friend he just doesn't run well enough, isn't strong enough, and I would be afraid that at his size if he tried to play at a higher level, he'd get hurt, and I don't want to see that happen to any young man, especially your girlfriend's son."

"I'll do that, Mr. Murff. Thank you so much for your time. I appreciate you coming and wasting your time with me. Thanks again."

"Mr. Marcello, sitting at a ballpark and talking baseball with friendly people is never a waste of my time. Heck, sometimes in conversations like the one we just had, I've often turned up names of a prospective ballplayer or two, so my time's never wasted. By the way, what do you do for a living?"

Marcello stuttered and stammered and cleared his throat.

"Ahem, well, Mr. Murff, I'm in the shipping business. Have been for years. Thanks again for coming to New Orleans. See you later." With that our conversation ended, and I marched out of the ballpark and headed off to meet my subscout, Bill Dossey.

Bill and I met at a dark, smoke-filled restaurant near the Mississippi River bridge. We sat down at a table and quickly ordered something to drink. As we sat there, Bill and I made small talk about our weekend plans, and then he asked me what I had done that day.

"Well, I just scouted a player for a fellow named Carlos Marcello."

All talk inside the restaurant stopped and two dozen sets of eyes were riveted on the two of us.

Bill grabbed me by the collar and said hoarsely, "Red, get back over here in the corner and keep your mouth shut."

"Why, what's the matter with you, Bill?"

"Shut up, Red, don't say another word and follow me."

Bill pulled me over to a corner, whipped out a napkin, tore off a corner and wrote on it the word Mafia and then, like a stoolie, swallowed the small piece of paper. Finally, it dawned on me where I'd heard that name before.

"Oh, yeah," said Red the dunderhead. "That Carlos Marcello. The Mob boss from Brownsville to Miami. Fortunately, he liked me," I chuckled, ignoring my frightened friend and fellow scout.

I've often wondered what I would've done if Marcello had asked me to sign his girlfriend's son. Knowing old "Tell It Like It Is Murff," I'd have said no and then been fitted for my first and only pair of cement spikes.

Red's Random Thought . . .

Ballplayers come in all shapes and sizes. I guess there have been some fat ballplayers, but darned few who were really successful. Anytime I ever saw a fat ballplayer I thought was a prospect, I always told him he was taking money out of my pocket and his. Most who were worth anything listened and lost weight.

Chapter 15

Outside the Cookie Cutter

I've told you in detail what qualities we look for in ballplayers. I often refer to size requirements as baseball's Cookie Cutter Mold. One of the secrets of my scouting success has always been that when I spotted unmistakable talent, ability that I knew beyond a shadow of a doubt was major-league quality, I didn't mind stepping outside that mold to sign a ballplayer no one else seemed to like. Certainly it was that way with Nolan Ryan, but I can name several other really fine players who went on to play in the big leagues who no one but Red Murff really wanted any part of.

Besides Nolan, the ballplayer who sticks out in my mind in this category is Jerry Koosman. Jerry pitched on all those great New York Mets teams in the late sixties and early seventies. He was a main cog and won nineteen games during the Mets 1969 world championship effort. In a great ten-year career, he won 168 ball games. Not bad for a young man who looked like he should have been working in a slaughterhouse or driving a beer truck instead of trying to strike out big-league hitters for a living.

I got wind of Jerry Koosman in a weird sort of way, and I basically had to get fired to land him. I was attending a U.S. Army tournament in Killeen, Texas, at Fort Hood while I was working for the Houston Colt .45s in September 1962. In those days, army baseball turned out some fiercely competitive clubs and occasionally we'd turn up a good prospect from among those ranks. As I was leaving the stands to grab a sandwich, I noticed a left-hander warming up for the next game. He was really throwing the heck out of the ball. I made a mental note to check him out, but I got sidetracked on some Colt .45s business while I was out on my sandwich run. Once I returned to the park to watch this left-hander, his game had already ended. I failed in my scouting assignment that day because I did not get this young man's name, but I learned that he had pitched for Fort Bliss. Even so, no one in the stands knew his name.

At the time, I was having trouble with my Houston superiors. I had a run-in with Tal Smith, a man who would later become general manager of the Houston Astros. In 1962 he was director of scouting for the Colt .45s. Tal and I had a basic disagreement over ballplayers. He saw them as a nuisance. I saw them as baseball's bread and butter. Don't get me wrong, Tal was and still is a solid baseball man. We just held to radically different philosophies.

After our first run-in, Tal told me that my scouting contract would not be renewed, which was just fine by me. I had enough experience to know I was a good scout, I knew I had plenty of contacts in baseball and that I would not have trouble finding another job. Besides finding that other job, I listed as my top priority finding out the name of that left-hander from Fort Bliss.

As fate would have it, my old friend Wid Mathews with the Mets hired me to scout the Southwest only a few days after the Colt .45s told me I was out of a job. As soon as the Mets signed me to a contract, I headed for El Paso and Fort Bliss, but I called the base before I left to find out where the ball club worked out. Once I found the place, I contacted the coach and told him I had heard he had a left-handed pitcher who might have big-league potential.

He trotted out a small, slender *right*-hander who was marginal at best. I was getting discouraged. I went back to the coach and asked him if he had anyone else who could throw hard. He replied, "Yep, if old Jerry out there in right field *feels* like it, he can really throw."

At the top of his voice the coach screamed, "Hey, Jerry, you feel like throwing for a New York Mets scout?" I looked at "old" Jerry and thought, *You gotta be kidding, coach. Are you talking about that fat guy? Him?*

"Yeah, I guess I feel like throwing for him," the fat man lazily answered as he lumbered in from the outfield.

Old Jerry Koosman told me that he was from Minnesota. As I watched him loosen up, I asked, "How can you throw like that being so fat?" I clearly upset him, but, no kidding, he was a whale at six-three and 240 badly distributed pounds. Despite the blubber, he could throw! He had nice, easy mechanics, and he turned loose an average major-league fastball with little or no effort.

Once he had warmed up, some teammates stepped up to the plate for a little batting practice. They never came close. Jerry handcuffed them with that fastball and a sharp, biting curve, way too much stuff for army hitters to handle.

After practice I took Koosman aside and asked if he'd be interested in signing a contract with the Mets. I also wanted to know what kind of bonus money it would take to get his name on the dotted line. Koosman told me he would be interested, but he had no idea how much he wanted to complete the deal.

I took a different approach. I asked if he had a car or any unpaid bills. He said he owed six hundred dollars on his car and that he had a problem with a Minnesota junior college he attended before entering the army.

When I asked about the problem, he said, "Well, Mr. Murff, I got upset with the coach. He and I didn't see eye to eye on any-thing, so I took off for the army. The coach and the school claim I owe them their scholarship money."

The bills added up to about two thousand dollars. So to keep the deal going, I suggested we go have some hamburgers and talk it over at the post exchange. I offered to sign him up for a two thousand dollar bonus, but he replied angrily, "No sir. I am worth a lot more money than that."

I looked at him and said, "No, Jerry, you aren't. Hear me out. You are not worth more than two thousand dollars. You went all the way through high school and junior college and no professional team ever expressed any interest in you. Only a few scouts have seen you pitch, and no one but me has ponied up any money at all. And I'll tell you one other thing, I am not about to gamble any more than two thousand dollars on anyone as fat as you are, even though you throw well."

I was rough on Koosman. Jerry told me that he wanted to play baseball once he had finished his stint in the army in about six months. I wanted him to play *if* he'd lose some weight and prove to me he was willing to make the sacrifice to do that and provided he would sign for a two thousand dollar bonus.

Of course, I was not through dealing with Jerry. As I got up to leave I told him I had a handshake deal in mind if he did not want to sign right then. I offered to have him write down my offer if it would make him feel better.

"Jerry," I said, "we'll sign you for two thousand dollars that will be paid after you get your discharge. If you don't sign now, I'll come back to watch you pitch in September at the army tournament. If you're in shape and if you look like you're worth more than two thousand, then I'll pay you more, depending on a figure we can agree on. But if you cannot convince me you're worth more, *you* have to pay my scouting expenses for coming to see you again. I get eight cents a mile plus a hotel room. Do we have a deal?"

The fat boy didn't exactly take this lying down. "We've got a deal," he replied tersely. "But I'll tell you one thing: you show up at that tournament and I'm going to be in shape and *prove* to you I'm worth a lot more than two crummy thousand dollars. I'll show you I can pitch, Mr. Murff."

One other stipulation we agreed on was that Jerry would not sign with anyone else before I returned to the tournament.

Just like I promised, I showed up at the army tournament in San Antonio and was watching Jerry Koosman and his Fort Bliss teammates. But this time I had a little company. Fifteen other scouts were there with me to see him pitch, but for some unknown reason, nobody there liked him—but me. And I really liked him! He had it all. He had the same, easy motion I'd seen before, and he blew the ball by hitters just as smooth as you please. Plus Jerry fulfilled his promise by coming to the tournament in excellent physical shape. He'd lost at least twenty-five pounds and appeared deadly serious about baseball. Koosman was beginning to look like a major-league ballplayer as well as pitch like one.

I sent a message to Jerry that I wanted to meet him for dinner at the Gunter Hotel in San Antonio at 6 P.M. Once he arrived, our contract talks became serious very quickly, at about 6:03, I think.

I got a tip to my competition in July when Minnesota Twins scout Eddie Stevens called about six weeks before the fall tournament. He asked me if I knew anything about a big, fat pitcher from El Paso. I told Stevens I had seen the young man he was talking about, but I volunteered little information past that.

As it turned out, Stevens told me that Jerry's father had written a letter to the Twins and told them his son was a great pitcher for Fort Bliss and some scouts were interested in signing him. The elder Koosman told the Twins he thought they should sign Jerry because he was from Minnesota and wanted to pitch for his home-state team. Pretty soon, Mr. Koosman let loose a barrage of communication so unrelenting and so adamant that the Twins figured they'd better send Eddie Stevens to El Paso for a look.

When I later saw the Minnesota scout in San Antonio, he was ranting and raving about his trek to Fort Bliss. He screamed and cursed, absolutely livid about Koosman: "I spent my time and the Twins money to go there, and I don't think this kid can pitch. He's so fat he can barely walk, let alone pitch."

After our conversation, I knew I could sign Jerry Koosman by using a little psychology. I reminded him of the Mets previous bonus offer of two thousand dollars. I told him it still stood and that I had not seen any justification for anything any higher. The look on his face told me this kid was convinced he'd pitched better than that. The more he thought about it, the madder he got.

"Based on our previous deal," I reminded him, "I wrote out a contract calling for a bonus of $1,540. That's the $2,000 less my expenses."

By this time, Jerry was so angry and so upset I didn't know if he would explode at me, get up and walk out, or punch me out. Enraged beyond reason, Jerry told me another scout would be glad to pay him more. I knew he was talking about Eddie Stevens with the Twins, and I also knew Koosman was bluffing.

I flipped Jerry a dime and told him to go call Stevens collect. I said to the red-faced, steaming young pitcher, "Go, go on, call him."

Eight minutes later, looking like a whipped dog, Jerry returned dejectedly to the table. He said that Stevens not only refused to accept his collect call but he shouted, "And I'm not playing Red Murff's game either!" Then he slammed the phone down in Jerry's ear.

Jerry Koosman signed his contract with the New York Mets that evening for my price. He later told reporters in New York he figured he'd better go ahead and sign because he was afraid he would end up *owing* money to Red Murff, the scout who signed him. But that's far from the end of the Jerry Koosman saga.

Three years into his professional career, while still in the minor leagues, Jerry became something of a discipline problem. He simply forgot all manner of responsible conduct he had learned in the army. He couldn't make curfew and often failed to show up on time for the long bus rides to out-of-town games.

These problems did not sit well with his manager and the Mets director of player development. The breaking point for the Mets officials came when Jerry missed a bus ride to an afternoon game in Florida. The minor-league camp director finally had had enough, and he ordered Koosman's release. The organization's bookkeeper drew up the paperwork, packed Koosman's belongings, and ordered him out of camp.

Just as the Mets officials were getting ready to put Jerry on a bus, someone discovered he owed a hundred dollars in spring training advances. The Mets decided there was no way they could release anyone indebted to them.

In the midst of the crisis, the manager of another Mets farm club just happened to be around, overheard the discussion, and offered to take Koosman for his club. So Koosman's hide was saved just in the nick of time for himself and the Mets organization, and it was a good thing. That summer Jerry Koosman led his league in victories and strikeouts and had the lowest earned run average of any starting pitcher in the Mets minor league organization. By September 1, Jerry Koosman was in the big leagues to finish the season. The following season he made it to the major leagues for good.

I guess some people have to hang by their fingernails from disaster's edge to get fired up enough to realize their full potential. Jerry Koosman became an all-star starter on the Mets 1969 club that won the world championship. Once again success came to an unknown ballplayer no one but Red Murff had any use for.

RIGHT: *A dapper young country boy dressed in my Sunday Go-to-Meeting attire. I left a short time later for the military and World War II.*

BELOW:
Aviation cadet, John Murff, 1944.

I pitched in the first major-league game I ever saw, against the Cincinnati Reds in relief in 1956. With me on the mound are all-star first baseman Joe Adcock and all-star catcher Del Crandall.

LEFT: *I finished my playing career at the Triple A level with the Wichita Braves in 1958, and then in Louisville in 1959. Here, second baseman Casey Wise is congratulating me on a victory.*

BELOW: *Eager Braves rookie pitchers Taylor Phillips, Red Murff, and Bob Trowbridge looking forward to a big 1956.*

In this sequence of photos, Jacksonville Braves manager Red Murff explains to the umpire what a swinging strike is, what a bunt strike is, and in the last frame the ump explains that his hand in this position means he's kicking me out of the game!

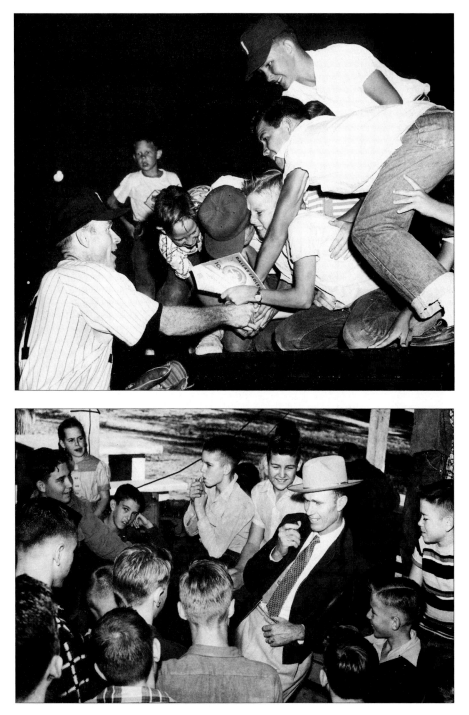

TOP: *I loved celebrating with the kids, loved it when they climbed all over each other for my autograph or to talk to me.*
BOTTOM: *Up-and-coming ballplayers get a dose of Murff wisdom at a Boys Club Meeting in 1961.*

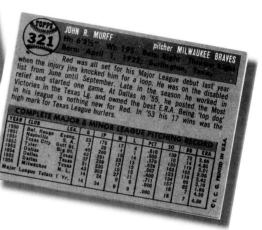

LEFT: *Every young ballplayer in my day dreamed of having his own baseball card. This is mine from 1957, the year my big league dream ended because of a back injury.*

BELOW: *Smile. It's Media Day in 1956 at the Milwaukee Braves spring training camp. The Topps Chewing Gum folks are taking my picture for a baseball card.*

DALLAS EAGLES - 1953

ABOVE: *Dixie Series Champion Dallas Eagles in 1953. We won the Texas League Championship under manager Little Dutch Meyer, and went on to defeat Nashville for the Dixie Championship.*

RIGHT: *Congratulating Dallas Eagles first baseman Bill White who'd just hit a home run to help me win one of 27 ballgames for the '55 Dallas club. He later became a National League All-Star and president of the National League.*

RIGHT: *Pitching drills in spring training 1956 with Gene Conley (on my right), a great all-around athlete and professional basketball player with the Boston Celtics. Gene always told people he was "Five feet, twenty inches tall."*

BELOW: *Players had more fun in my day. Dallas Eagles catcher Ray Murray, pitcher Pete Burnside, and shortstop Lee Tate watch me rack 'em up and break open the 1955 Texas League season.*

One of the greatest sports cartoonists of all time was the late Bill McClanahan of The Dallas Morning News. *Bill captured my athletic career on two separate occasions when I pitched for the Dallas Eagles.*

I spotted Jerry Koosman in 1962. Possessing a great fastball and wicked curve, he was an all-star and an integral member of the 1969 Mets World Championship pitching staff.

Mets draft choice, Kenny Boswell, became an excellent major-league infielder, and played a key role on the '69 World Championship team.

Even though I miss the game, I have so many wonderfully joyous memories of players, fellow scouts, and fans throughout my forty-three-year career. What better life could any man have lived?

Cather Jerry Grote was the heart and soul of the 1969 World Champion New York Mets. I've never seen a better arm on a catcher, nor have I ever known a more intensely determined competitor.

I should've worn an army helmet and flack jacket whenever I faced Stan Musial. All I could do was duck in-line drives. He got sixteen straight hits off me, (including his 2600th lifetime base hit) but somehow I got him out the seventeenth time I faced him.

RIGHT: *I found pitcher Mike Stanton the same way I did dozens of other ballplayers—a chance stop at a ballpark in Houston. Mike's fastball and bulldog determination sold me, and I signed him for Atlanta. The Braves later traded him to the Red Sox.*

BELOW: *It's nice to be recognized by your peers for all the miles you drive, reports you fill out, and ballplayers you sign. Expos Scouting Director, Jim Fanning, presents me with the Montreal Scout of the Year Award in 1975.*

ABOVE: *Three baseball generations. Milwaukee scout Earl Halstead recommended that the Braves buy my contract from the Dallas Eagles in 1955. And, of course, I lobbied hard for the Mets to draft and sign the legendary pitcher in the middle. Thank goodness Earl Halstead is a great gin rummy player.*

RIGHT: *In my element. Sitting in the stands at a ballpark anywhere in the world with my stopwatch, notebook, and radar gun, represented home for me for thirty-four years.*

RIGHT: *One of the proudest moments of my baseball career—induction into the Texas Baseball Hall of Fame in 1989.*

BELOW: *You'll never catch me at a loss for words. I always love talking to television, radio, and newspaper reporters. Here Mark Holtz from Home Sports Entertainment interviews me at the Texas High School state baseball tournament in the early 1980s.*

Grandson Ben and Papa Red at Ben's first tryout camp. This one was a Braves camp in 1991, just before Ben climbed down and ran the bases. I couldn't catch him.

What baseball man wouldn't love to have a field named after him? I helped begin the baseball program at Mary Hardin Baylor University in Belton, Texas. In 1972, they named their ballpark Red Murff Field—a real honor.

Red's Random Thought . . .

I always thought the days of lynch mobs ended back in the Old West with Marshall Dillon or Wild Bill Hickok or Roy Rogers. I never thought I'd have to face down a lynch mob to sign a ballplayer. But I did in the Caribbean.

Chapter 16

Beyond the Call

Among the people I admire most in this life are those public servants who regularly go above and beyond the call of duty in helping their fellowman. Police and firemen do it every day. Doctors, nurses, and emergency medical technicians handle similar situations. You expect that at some point in their lives they'll be in peril.

I never thought a profession as low-key as scouting ballplayers would ever require a risk of life and limb, but it sure happened to me in Latin America. Before we get into that story, let's do a brief synopsis of scouting south of the border.

Major League Baseball began mining Latin talent in the 1940s and 1950s. In those days few scouts regularly ventured into the Latin countries. A scout might take an occasional trip there to look at a prospect, but wholesale scouting didn't begin there until the 1960s, and I helped lead the way. The old Washington Senators, however, took advantage of one entrepreneurial businessman named Carnavales who had discovered and developed dozens of Latin ballplayers and sold their contracts to the big-league clubs.

Major-league clubs also began sending managers from their Double A and Triple A clubs to manage in the Puerto Rican,

Dominican, and Venezuelan leagues, ostensibly to lend their expertise to Latin baseball, but more importantly to file reports with their parent clubs about their best Latin ballplayers. The clubs then sent some scouts to take a second look and sign the cream of the crop. Sometimes big-league clubs would invite a few Latin players to spring training. If those players proved themselves, they would be put under contract and start playing their way up the minor-league ladder to the big leagues.

During my professional career I played and managed winter ball in Puerto Rico, the Dominican Republic, and Venezuela and became very much aware of what a ballplayer gold mine Latin America was. I managed the legendary Pittsburgh Pirates Hall of Famer Roberto Clemente and longtime Cleveland Indians home-run-hitting first baseman Vic Power. I played in Venezuela with Luis Aparicio, the incredibly gifted all-star shortstop with the White Sox, and Felix Mantilla, another smooth-fielding shortstop whom I was also teamed with on the Braves, and another tremendous infielder, Chico Carrasquel. In fact so many good infielders have come from the Latin leagues that scouts now refer to any infielder displaying excellent, "soft" hands as having "Latin hands."

Having known all those ballplayers, having observed their talent, and knowing there were plenty more players in Latin America and the Caribbean, when I became a scout I started telling my bosses—first at Houston and then in New York—that they should spend some time and money scouring Latin America for top-flight ballplayers. Finally I convinced the Mets to hire former minor leaguer Nino Escalara as their full-time scout in Puerto Rico, and the Mets helped lead Major League Baseball into "beefing up" in Latin America. Now every club places great emphasis on watching the ballplayers in those countries. Scores of players from Puerto Rico, the Dominican Republic, and other Latin countries occupy spots on major-league rosters and many have become all-star performers. The Houston Astros have been operating an instructional camp in Venezuela that has turned out a couple of prospects. There is also increased scouting emphasis in Mexico, Australia, Canada, and, with the recent success of Dodgers pitcher Hideo Nomo, Japan. Baseball is becoming a truly worldwide game.

Why are these Latin American countries so fruitful for major-league scouts year in and year out? Well, that part of the world has a climate conducive to playing baseball eleven months out of the year. The more baseball you play, the better you play. There's also an economic factor. Players there have, in many instances, more ambition and drive than young ballplayers in the United States, and they get that way because, for them, baseball is the only way to escape poverty. Having enough to eat can be an incredible motivator.

Latinos have played so much baseball at such a high competitive level that their talents can be evaluated and projected by professional scouts at an earlier age than many youngsters here. Ballplayers from Latin America also seem to be blessed in almost every instance with tremendous reflexes and incredible speed and quickness. I've always said speed and quickness make great players.

Historical lessons aside, let's get back to my story about going above and beyond in scouting ballplayers. In early 1966 the New York Mets received a letter from a Puerto Rican doctor in San Sebastian. The Mets, of course, from a public relations and talent standpoint were extremely interested in acquiring Hispanic talent since vast numbers of New York's fans were Puerto Rican.

This doctor, Dr. Melendez, told us about a ballplayer he had been following for the past couple of years. The young man's name was Chico Rios, and Chico, according to the doctor, was the best shortstop in Puerto Rico and scouts from five other big-league teams had been looking at him. The problem was that no scout from the Mets had ever seen the young man. Chico's team would be playing a doubleheader in two days, so the Mets telegrammed instructions to me to contact Dr. Melendez as soon as possible. Arrangements were made for me to scout Chico Rios in San Sebastian.

Dr. Melendez and his driver picked me up at the airport when I arrived in Puerto Rico and took me directly to the ballpark. Once I was there and took a look at young Chico, I agreed with the doctor. This young man displayed the fluid grace, catlike quickness, and lightning foot speed of a star big-league infielder. He was six-one and weighed about 180 and he could throw! During the first game of the doubleheader, he also put on a hitting exhibition. I figured Rios could be the kind of ballplayer who would help the Mets for the next ten years.

The second game of the doubleheader was rained out. Team officials met with the league president and decided they would reschedule the game for the next Sunday. I couldn't believe it! I had flown all the way to Puerto Rico to try to sign this guy and the rainout meant he wouldn't be eligible to sign with the Mets for at least another week!

Just after the rainout was announced, the doctor and I went to the dugout and he began telling Chico about the Mets' intentions. Some boisterous, rabble-rousing, *cerveza*-swilling fans overheard bits of the conversation and something really important got lost in the translation: the word *eligible*. I wanted the doctor to inform Chico that the Mets were interested as soon has he became *eligible* to be signed, but these fans apparently heard something entirely different. They thought the Mets wanted Rios *right now!* As soon as the words left my mouth, they started grumbling among themselves, and the ugly rumor spread like a lava down a mountain, igniting their nationalistic pride and twisting it into some kind of crazed paranoia. Things got more and more out of hand as the bitter pill was washed down with more and more beer and they scrutinized the conversation between the *Yanquis* and their hero.

What they didn't know and did not understand was that I would never have signed Chico before his team's season was finished. I believed in honoring commitments, and I wanted Chico to honor his. I knew that Chico was a national idol and that, without him, San Sebastian would never win. If San Sebastian didn't win, the town's self-image would be damaged. I knew my limitations going into the situation, but I never expected my very presence would be so provocative and turn happy, celebrating fans into a threatening lynch mob. I also knew there were many more ballplayers in Puerto Rico that I would be interested in one day. So there was no way I'd do anything to upset the league officials and especially not this group of fans.

We were facing at least a fight that could at any moment spontaneously become a lynch mob or worse. So I looked quickly at Dr. Melendez and another Mets scout, Julian Morgan, who had joined me at the park that day, and yelled, "Let's get out of here!"

As I began to make my way through about five hundred fans, I saw some brandishing broken beer bottles. While I saw no knives, I was convinced several in the crowd were packing them. They were bellowing a thunder roll of threats at me. Cold beads of sweat popped out on my forehead. I was walking in rhythm with my heart, now steadily pounding in my throat.

I kept an angry, determined, steely-eyed look on my face as I moved through the menacing crowd, trying my best to disguise my fear. I believed the only way to diffuse the situation was to project my own forceful, macho image, and I dared not show any fear. I guess those upset fans sensed I was not going to put up with any grief, so the throng parted as I made my way toward our car.

As my anxious walk took me through a hundred yards of ankle-deep mud, I had assumed Julian and Dr. Melendez were behind me. I was still being followed by about fifteen yelling and screaming fans. Just as I opened the car door to get in, I turned and said, "Gee, Julian that was a close one. I didn't know we'd be putting our lives on the line to sign a ballplayer!" There was only one problem: Julian and Dr. Melendez were nowhere to be seen.

I went on and sat in the car and locked the door. Angry San

Sebastian fans milled around, yelling and screaming and slamming their fists against the car. Fortunately, that's as ugly as it got. Ten or fifteen minutes later, Julian and Dr. Melendez walked up.

"Julian, I thought you were right behind me!"

"Sorry, Red," he responded, "I thought they were going to kill you, and I didn't want any part of it."

"Gee, thanks for the support, Julian."

"Come on, Red." Julian was trying to placate me now. "You know the Mets are sticklers for filing reports. If the crowd had killed you, they would've been outraged at me for not staying and making a good report."

Well, there's absolutely nothing like facing a near riot to sign a ballplayer. That is, unless you're facing a near riot without any support.

I went back to San Sebastian the next Sunday and signed Chico *after* his team had won the Puerto Rican championship. Chico played some in the big leagues but never turned out to be a major star.

That's not all. During some of our downtime in Puerto Rico, Dr. Melendez helped me and a former Class AAA ballplayer Nino Escalara set up some instructional camps. Puerto Rican rules did not allow for tryout camps. Nino told me he knew of several promising ballplayers that had major-league potential. So, in an effort to see these young men, we sidestepped the rules and staged instructional gatherings.

We held four such camps and turned up some pretty good ballplayers. You might remember a pitcher named Ed Figueroa. He pitched several years in the big leagues. We found him in one of our instructional endeavors, as we did outfielder Jerry Morales. Morales was signed by the Mets at the age of sixteen after our camp. We also signed a right-handed pitcher named Juan Vientedos that way. We'd never have come across those ballplayers, however, had we not faced down a mob that day in San Sebastian.

THE SCOUT

That's been thirty years ago, and for the life of me I still can't figure out if the rewards were worth the danger, but Julian Morgan, Dr. Melendez, Nino Escalara, and I helped pave the way for the Mets to Latin America.

Red's Random Thought . . .

I always figured it was nobody's business but my own where I was when I went looking for ballplayers. Secrecy was paramount. In fact I fired a subscout once. I was in a small Texas town looking at a young prospect, and he made the mistake of telling other scouts where I was.

Chapter 17

Loose Lips Sink Scouts

During World War II our commanders continually warned us about the treachery of discussing military secrets with fellow soldiers. "Loose Lips Sink Ships" was the motto of the day, and it was a good slogan because no matter what a man's rank was, we *all* knew things that could endanger a mission. Our superiors simply didn't want us running our mouths about battle plans or any other secret information.

That's the way I always conducted my business as a scout. Keeping my mouth shut and tending to my own affairs worked as well in the scouting game as it did in military matters, although I have always been surprised by how many other scouts aired out their company secrets. Some scouting directors were often the worst at keeping secrets and often traded inside player information, as unbelievable as that may seem. Imagine a vice president at General Motors calling up Ford and reading him the plans and specifications for a new line of automobiles. Well, that's what happens too much in baseball. On more than one occasion, loose lips sank my scouting ship and the ship of more than one of my rivals.

During the early part of the 1971 high school season, a friend of mine in Palestine, Texas, told me about a young outfielder from Chapel Hill High School in Tyler. He said that this kid was the fastest runner he'd ever seen on a baseball field or anywhere else for that matter. "You really gotta take a look at this one, Red, you won't believe him," he promised.

So I called the Chapel Hill coach for the team's schedule and drove to Tyler to take a look. Jerry Mumphrey would've fit Hollywood's central casting "look" for a major-league baseball prospect. Whippet-lean at six-two and about 175 pounds, he made me double-check my stopwatch the first time he hit the ball and ran to first base. He ran an astounding 3.6 seconds after swinging the bat as a right-handed hitter. That's seven-tenths of a second faster than the average major leaguer! He looked like Halley's comet streaking down the line to first base. He had rockets in his pockets his second time up, stretching what should have been a single into a double, running the sixty yards in 6.35, or about half a second faster than the major league average! As I've said before, speed in position players excites me like no other tool a player exhibits. Jerry Mumphrey had me flipping mental cartwheels! I filed a report with the Expos that night and made sure to underline in red ink Jerry's running speed.

I saw Jerry play three more times during his senior season, and luckily for me—or so I thought—I never saw another scout. I was convinced I was the only one on his trail. I was excited each time I headed for the ballpark to see him play. I never saw another scout until the final game of Jerry's senior season.

I arrived at the ballpark as I normally do, about ninety minutes before game time on a hot, sticky Tuesday evening, to observe batting and fielding practice. Unfortunately one of the first people I spotted that day was a subscout with the Giants. He and I nodded, but I never spoke to him. Just knowing he was there gave me an awful, sick feeling in the pit of my stomach.

Just before Jerry's team came on the field for practice, the skies opened up and what we call in Texas "a three-inch gully washer" deluged the Chapel Hill ballpark. Umpires postponed the game until the next day, and I left the park more than disappointed. I just had to get one more look at this speedy ballplayer. I spent a restless night in Tyler before heading back to the ballpark the next day.

When I got there, I couldn't believe my eyes. As I gazed at the stands, I spotted more scouts than fans and parents! There must've been at least twenty teams represented in the bleachers. It looked as if someone had called an emergency scouts reunion and designated the site as the front four rows of the Chapel Hill ballpark! Scouts from all over Texas, Oklahoma, Louisiana, and New Mexico were there. Every one of my competitors showed up as well as a few I didn't know, and every single one had a stopwatch dangling from his neck. Guess who they were there to see? Drat and double drat!

As I stood beside an old friend from Tyler, I dejectedly remarked, "Hey, the gang's all here! We might as well call Kentucky Fried Chicken, find out if they deliver, and tell 'em to bring over several buckets of extra crispy and a couple dozen cokes so we can just have ourselves a picnic while we watch Jerry Mumphrey. Even if the Colonel doesn't deliver, we got plenty of guys here who could truck on over and bring some back before the game starts." So much for trying to hide a ballplayer in the days of the draft.

Apparently the Giants subscout called his supervisors and told them that Red Murff was in Tyler looking at the outfielder at Chapel Hill High. One supervisor told another scout who told another who told another, and the next thing you know, "Look out, here comes the herd!" Loose lips sank my plans.

Jerry Mumphrey didn't disappoint the throng. He staged his own personal version of the Indy 500 on the base paths that night. Each time he ran, all my buddies checked their stopwatches then looked at each other in disbelief. They too had now seen one of the fastest high school players ever.

Even though I now knew that at least twenty major-league clubs were acquainted with him—and I knew that my club, the Expos, most likely would never get a chance to draft him—I spoke with Jerry after the game and invited him to a Montreal tryout camp in Brenham three days later. When he showed up, Jerry staged an Olympic performance. No one came close to matching his speed during any of the running tests. In high school, he had played shortstop. While he was okay there, he was not a big-league prospect at an infield position. He had a good arm, but not a shortstop-style arm. I pictured him as a center fielder—a switch-hitting, speed-burning center fielder.

I explained to him I thought he could use his speed to greater advantage if we could teach him to switch-hit. If he could learn to hit from the left, he would be one step closer to first base. If he could learn to drag bunt and to chop down at the ball, he could beat out a lot of ground balls for base hits. On defense, if he switched to the outfield, I knew he'd be able to make that one spectacular play to thwart potential home runs.

Jerry said it made sense to him, so he went to work modifying his game. Three days later, by the end of the camp, he'd made tremendous progress with his switch-hitting, and he was excited about it and promised to stick with it. I promised him I would do all I could to draft him for the Expos, but I also told him that as talented as he was I'd be surprised if he were still on the board when it came our turn to pick.

I lobbied hard. I made dozens of phone calls to the Expos scouting director about Jerry, but we lost him. The St. Louis Cardinals picked Jerry Mumphrey in the 1971 draft and by 1974 he was in the big leagues as a regular center fielder.

Jerry Mumphrey went on to a sterling, fifteen-year major-league career. He hit a lifetime .289, was a constant base-stealing threat, and a terrific center fielder. Believe me, as competitive as I am, it was tough knowing I might have had him if not for the scouting grapevine.

Much more painful was the distressing dilemma experienced by my friend, former manager and scouting rival Billy Capps. During Billy's thirty-five-year career with the Cubs, he signed some terrific ballplayers, including pitcher Burt Hooton who won 151 games in a fifteen-year career with the Cubs, Dodgers, and Rangers. He signed Roger Metzger, a terrific shortstop, traded by the Cubs to the Astros, who was having a brilliant career in Houston until an unfortunate accident with a saw severed some fingers.

In 1965 Billy was just about to score what would have been one of the game's most unbelievable scouting coups. For the better part of a year he was the only big-league scout following a young catcher from Binger, Oklahoma, named Johnny Bench. Billy loved him! He saw game after game and filed dozens of glowing reports on the young catcher. "Great arm, great movements behind the plate, great hitter," Capps wrote to his Chicago bosses.

As the only scout in the stands, Billy was overwhelmed by what he saw during a three-day fall tournament when Johnny was only sixteen years old. The kid had thirteen base hits, including four home runs, and twenty runs batted in! Bench played three positions during that tournament—third base, pitcher, and, of course, catcher. Billy never saw such an offensive or defensive display by a young prospect. Billy's like I am in that he simply doesn't get overly excited about ballplayers, but Johnny Bench's ability made his pulse race. Capps literally licked his chops when he envisioned Bench's home-run swing, tailor-made for the friendly confines of Wrigley Field. Could you imagine the barrage of home runs Bench would've unleashed onto Waveland Avenue playing there eighty-one times a year, especially on days when the wind blows out? Billy Capps could. He was convinced Bench could lead the Chicago Cubs to the National League pennant with his hitting, catching, and throwing. He desperately coveted the young ballplayer.

One fateful day Billy's scouting director happened to read one of the glowing reports on Johnny Bench and then make an incredibly ludicrous call to a friend—the Cincinnati Reds scouting director! The Cubs executive asked his Cincinnati counterpart what he knew about the young catcher from

Oklahoma. The Reds had no information on Bench, that is, until the Cubs called. Within hours Cincinnati dispatched scout Tony Robello to Binger to take a look.

"Do all you can," his scouting director told him, "to find out everything as quickly as possible about this young catcher Bench." That's what Tony did. Once he began showing up regularly in Binger, the scouting grapevine lit up. Everyone in the Southwest found out about Johnny Bench. When I overheard the talk, I gave my Mets bosses a call, and they sent an Oklahoma subscout in for a look.

Scouts for Cincinnati, Chicago, and the Mets showed up together one night for an American Legion doubleheader in Binger. It was a Johnny Bench show. Four home runs, eight RBIs, and two runners thrown out trying to steal second base sent three scouts home with their mouths gaping. Billy's hard, diligent work went for naught. His coveted secret became public knowledge, but more importantly to baseball: a scout had been betrayed by his own boss.

Despite the fact that Billy Capps had kept Bench under wraps to everyone but his scouting director, he lost the scouting find of a lifetime. He went about his business, confidentially filing reports on a prospect that by rights he should have drafted and signed, yet he came up empty-handed. Imagine how you'd feel if your boss betrayed you that way and you lost an important account, or your boss handed someone else a promotion that you deserved and by rights should have had. Imagine how Billy must have felt, especially after Bench became an all-star, led his team to championships, and ultimately ended up in the Hall of Fame?

Johnny Bench, as baseball fans know, was drafted by the Cincinnati Reds before the Cubs ever had a chance. The next time Billy saw Johnny was a couple years into the catcher's big-league career. Billy was attending a Reds game in Houston. Right after batting practice, Johnny walked over to Billy, who was sitting with a group of scouts behind home plate. They shook hands and Johnny patted Billy on the shoulder and said,

THE SCOUT

"Billy, I thought for sure you were going to draft me and sign me for the Cubs."

All my friend could say was, "I thought so too, Johnny. I thought so too."

Red's Random Thought . . .

The intensity it takes to play the game of baseball cannot be passed along from father to son any other way
than genetically. You cannot make your son want to
play. He has to want it and want it badly. The desire
must come from within. It definitely is a gift, this need
to play baseball.

Chapter 18

Can My Son Play?

If I had a dollar for each time over the last forty years a father has come up to me and asked me, "Can my son play?" I'd be the Daddy Warbucks of Brenham, Texas. That's understandably one of the most asked questions of professional baseball people since Abner Doubleday or whoever invented this great game. Practically as soon as his son takes his first step, many a proud, hopeful dad wants to know if the boy has what it takes. Those dads love the game and their sons, so I can sure understand their curiosity.

In the early 1970s I was sitting in the stands at a ballpark in College Station, Texas, looking at a big first baseman from Austin who could really hit the baseball. As was so often the case, I got to talking to the young hitter's dad, and he introduced me to another man, a Mr. Crenshaw, whose son was playing right field.

As the conversation progressed, the Austin right fielder's dad was perplexed. "Mr. Murff, would you please give my son a pep talk? He doesn't act like he wants to play baseball at all, and I really want him to," the disappointed father asked. Mr. Crenshaw told me that he had played some college ball, and he wanted his son to follow in his footsteps.

"Mr. Crenshaw, I hate to tell you this, but your boy isn't a very good ballplayer," I said hesitatingly. "Are you sure I ought to talk to him?"

"Well," he continued, "I don't understand it. He's a great golfer, regularly shoots under seventy and he's easily the best golfer in Austin. In fact, he just won the city pro-am at age seventeen, and that's the first time anyone so young has won that tournament. But I just think he ought to be a baseball player."

"If I were you, I'd tell Ben to stick with golf," I advised.

Ben Crenshaw's dad wanted his son to be a baseball player. Can you imagine the game of golf without the great Ben Crenshaw? Golf without Ben Crenshaw would be just about the same as baseball without Nolan Ryan. What if his dad had made him stick with baseball and forced him away from golf? Sometimes fathers try too hard to relive their missed glory days through their sons.

What do you want *your* son to be? If the answer is a professional baseball player, then the next question should be, Does the boy himself want to play baseball? Does he really want to play? Like Mr. Crenshaw, misdiagnosing this desire can ultimately cause unnecessary anxiety between fathers and sons.

There is no harm in a kid not wanting to play baseball. Nowadays there are so many noble, honorable, and wonderful physical activities a child can be involved in outside this sport. Of course I wish every kid in the world wanted to play baseball. But they don't, and that's okay.

Those fathers who seem bent on reliving failed athletic careers through their sons need to understand that it will do nothing but ruin the sheer fun of the game for the youngster. You see it happen time and time and time again. Baseball suffers for it. Kids suffer for it. In the long run the parents suffer for it too.

You can always spot a kid who has the true heart and soul of a baseball player. These internal characteristics are what you need to look for, because they're every bit as important as a great arm, speed, or endurance.

THE SCOUT

I guess my family has always craved the baseball diamond, and to understand the following story is to understand why I'm blessed with the "have to be there" genetics for the game. My grandfather, John Andrew Jackson Bell of Burlington, Texas, was a justice of the peace. He loved going to the ballpark, not to play, but to umpire. It was a "civic duty" he told the other family members—plus he really loved it. Poor Grandfather was umpiring a ball game between the local semipro team and another club one summer Sunday in 1919. After a close play at the plate, one of the ballplayers bumped into him. My grandfather shoved him back and told him he'd better learn to respect the umpire. That ballplayer's brother grabbed a baseball bat and struck my grandfather in the head. Unfortunately he died three months later. Every member of my family who knew him swore that Grandpa may have regretted getting hit in the head, but they reveled in the fact that he died close to a place he loved—the ballpark. Now no one should take the game that seriously, but my grandfather's genes have been passed along quite handsomely.

As a case in point, let me tell you a story about an incredible young man. I have an eight-year-old nephew named Ike Davis. In all my days on this earth and in all the time I have been around the game, I have never seen anyone who wanted to play baseball any more than Ike. From sunup till sundown, seven days a week, Ike talks about baseball and reads about it and thinks about it, but most of all he'd rather be outside playing the game.

When Ike was six, he and I hooked up in a game of strikes at a family reunion. In strikes the players stand on the mound and try to throw as many strikes as they can to the catcher. I pitched from the standard sixty feet six inches and Ike from the forty-five foot Little League distance. Ike matched me strike for strike. He showed no quarter. He competed as if his life depended on it, all the while taunting and boasting, "Uncle Red, I'm gonna out-throw you. I'm gonna beat you, Uncle Red. You better watch out, here I come." Ike would *not* let himself be defeated. At six years old!

Ike's dad, Ron, had pitched in the big leagues and Ike knows that, but Ron has never put any pressure on his son to play baseball. Ike *wants* to play baseball, *lives* to play baseball. He possesses a desire for the game that parents simply cannot buy, teach, or force their son to have. Ike is one of the lucky ones.

I can relate easily to Ike because I was one of those kids who wanted to play so badly it ached. Growing up in Burlington, Texas, with a population of twelve hundred, I had few friends or relatives who wanted to play as badly as me. Things became so desperate, I had to learn to box in order to play catch. Box? Well, let me tell you the story.

I have a cousin, Russell Bell. If you're a fight fan, you may have heard of him. Forty-some years ago he fought the legendary Jake "Raging Bull" LaMotta. LaMotta beat him, but not badly. Russell, or Red as he was known in the ring, had a brilliant future as a fighter ahead of him had his hands not suffered shrapnel wounds during World War II.

Anyway, when we were kids, Cousin Red and his family would come over to our place on the weekends. If I wanted him to play catch with me, I had to box with him. He wounded me too. I still have a scar above my eye where he opened up a nice, oozing cut during one of our "friendly" matches. But what the heck, I needed someone to catch for me, and Red was one of the only ones anywhere around who could. I figured baseball was worth getting knocked around a little—that's how badly I wanted to play.

I'm not saying a youngster has to take a punch to learn how to pitch, catch, or field. Nor does he have to have the same burning desire young Ike has to enjoy Little League. But the answer to the burning question, "Can my son play?" so often lies in the heart of the young man who is blessed with this unquenchable thirst for the game of baseball—a thirst no one can teach and a thirst not all scouts can spot.

Can your son play college or professional ball? The answer is maybe, if—and this is an extremely big *if*—he really, truly has it in his heart. What I am about to ask you to do now is terribly difficult, especially if you've always dreamed your son someday would be a big-league ballplayer. You'll know the answer immediately if you make a thorough, truly honest assessment and divorce your personal feelings and love for the game from the equation. If you want the question answered, you must take it upon yourself to find out. If you have a boy who is T-ball, pee-wee, or Little League age and you'd like him to play the sport you love, sit down with him and ask if *he's* interested. Chances are pretty good that you already know. He and his friends will have been talking about it incessantly, asking for gloves and balls and pleading with you to come outside and play catch.

If he doesn't have baseball on his mind, then casually mention it and let him take the next steps. If he's not interested, you can try buying a couple of gloves and a ball and casually see if he's interested in going outside and playing catch. If he doesn't get too excited about that, back off and find another sport or activity to do together. If that's what has happened, then you now know that your son simply wasn't born with a baseball player's spirit, just like a tone-deaf child will never enjoy piano lessons. Remember Ben Crenshaw. The biggest mistake a parent can make is to force a child to play baseball.

There are thousands of Little League parents, coaches, and players who are having fun while they're learning teamwork and enjoying the game. We in baseball desperately need those dedicated, fun-seeking teachers and positive-attitude purveyors to supply us continually with youngsters who know how to play and have learned to love it. That's terrific for the kids and good for baseball and, ultimately, for those friends who keep the game healthy and alive past all the greed and selfishness we've seen in the ranks of major-league players and owners over the past few years.

Unfortunately, in my opinion, there are too many "coaches" trying to emulate major-league managers by putting pressure on kids, trying to turn them into "winners" instead of players and lovers of the game. Playing for coaches like that damages kids.

Kids don't learn the game, they don't learn to love it, and they don't appreciate it. The sad fact is that these folks turn kids away from the game forever. Baseball cannot afford to lose any more potential players or fans!

Our job as baseball protagonists should be to teach the *fun*damentals and let children play the game without parents screaming and making fools of themselves—and in the process upsetting umpires and ruining what should be a great time in the sunshine. Don't our children deserve a chance to enjoy kid's games without such rancorous parental interference? Of course they do!

My five-year-old grandson, Ben, is in a T-Ball league in Tulsa that does it the right way. Everybody gets in the game. Everybody has fun. Most importantly no one keeps score! Believe it or not, these guys are incredibly fun to watch. They don't really know how to play the game at Ben's age, and they are far too young to be taught fundamentals, but they do know they want to be involved and they are bent on having a great time. Every time the ball is hit, no matter where it goes and no matter what position each kid is playing, everyone takes off after the ball! The sight looks like a cattle stampede. They all storm after the ball as if their very lives depended on it. They're not really sure what to do once they pick it up, but it's fun to watch them having fun like that! The no-score philosophy adds to the frivolity. This is an extremely important factor, especially for youngsters who are just starting out. No score means no competition. That means parents can't put additional pressure on these young children to win at all costs. You might argue that these kids are not learning teamwork in a league like this, but they are.

Go to most any Little League park and sit for a while. If you watch closely enough, you will see some things that may disturb you. All those things that upset you will most likely be the fault of the parents in the stands. You will see three distinct groups of youngsters on the playing field.

The first group is made up of the youngsters whose eyes are on fire as they run to their positions. They and their zeal for the game are so marvelously obvious that no amount of interference, failure, or meddling will dampen their spirits. In fact they are out there aching to learn the game because they want to be on a ball field more than anywhere else in the world. These are the kids with spirit.

The second group has fear written all over them. They are in Little League to please someone else, yet they are scared to death of making a mistake and disappointing a parent. These kids may start out liking the game, really wanting to have fun, but after being subjected to parental criticism or a loud-mouthed coach trying to win his own version of the World Series, they learn to loathe rather than learn the rudiments of baseball.

The third group are those kids who don't want to be out there at all. Perhaps a well-meaning, overeager parent forced them into baseball. These guys are the ones who pay little, if any, attention to the game. Perhaps they are goofing around with a lizard or a butterfly or simply daydreaming. Obviously baseball isn't the game for them. It's important to recognize that it's okay not to want to play baseball.

Again, at the risk of being repetitive, all parents should evaluate why their children are playing on a team! Is it your child's idea or is it your idea?

Enough of my soapbox. Let's say this youngster of yours has a positive Little League experience with good coaching, and he's progressing and loving the game. Let's say he has some talent, or you think he does, and he wants to improve. What should a supportive parent do?

If you're in a community that places great emphasis on baseball, then your son will have ample chances to play and progress. If you live in a city or town that doesn't, never fear. Red Murff has never been accused of not having answers for questions. Here are my suggestions.

I am and always have been a big believer in exposing young players to the best professional instruction possible at the time in a youngster's life when he and his game are begging for it. I think usually by the ages of twelve, thirteen, or fourteen a youngster has advanced far enough physically to benefit from professional training.

By professional instruction I mean camps or clinics that run for a week or two and offer intense instruction—preferably by former professional ballplayers—for six to eight hours a day. You want a camp or school that offers instruction in the four baseball basics—hitting, throwing, running, and catching. If you don't know how to find one of these camps, look in any publication like *Baseball Weekly* or *Baseball America*. Camps are regularly advertised in the back pages of these newspapers. That's one place to start.

Talk to the local high school baseball coach. Be careful here, because some high school coaches run their own camps, and if you don't know the coach and don't know much about his program, you cannot always be sure your son will receive the best instruction. That's not a knock on high school coaches, because there are some truly fine ones around who have played in college or professionally and really know how to teach. Do your homework and research a coach's camp carefully. Ask a lot of questions before making a firm monetary commitment.

You can also try to find a professional scout in your area. Talk to him and pick his brain before you make a choice on a good camp. He knows the baseball people in your area, and he'll have some ideas. I'll bet a thousand dads came up to me and asked me about camps over the years. I never minded being interrupted during a game by a well-meaning father wanting to know how to help his son improve his game. I figured it was my way of giving something back to the game of baseball. If you cannot find a big-league scout at a local high school or semiprofessional game, then call or write to the public relations director at minor-league or major-league baseball clubs in your area and ask for advice.

A few big-league clubs offer a day camp with instruction by some of the club's players. These are okay. They're good public relations tools for the teams, but they are not the really intense, day in and day out, repetitive instructional camps that young players need.

Some camps allow eight-, nine-, and ten-year-olds in for training, but I think that's too young. A youngster should be to the point where he has played three or four years and has some idea what the game is all about before his parents enroll him in a professional camp or school. In addition the youngster has to have some degree of maturity in his musculature and bone development before he can begin to benefit from intense baseball training.

Above all ask plenty of questions! Find out who is doing the teaching. Find out their baseball backgrounds, where they played, how long, and what position they played. Ask the camp owner or manager for references and if he offers specialized teaching for each position. Talk to other parents who have sent their sons to the camp, and ask them if their sons enjoyed the camp and if their play improved as a result of the instruction they received. Good recommendations for a specific program are an excellent endorsement for that camp.

Just make sure before your son heads off to a camp that he is in great physical shape. A steady diet of television and junk food instead of running, throwing, playing, and good nutrition won't allow a youngster to keep up once he gets there. Most of these camps really work the young men hard, so they really should be preconditioned to handle the rigorous schedule.

Okay, we've advanced your son into his early teenage years and he's having some success. He's probably in some pretty fast summer-league competition against other boys his age, progressing well, and looking forward to making the varsity high school team.

Be careful not to burn out the youngster on the game—you won't be able to if he really loves it—and make sure to offer him every opportunity to attend instructional camps. Without being overbearing, encourage him to believe in himself and his baseball playing abilities. This mental part of the game is extremely important. Knowing that you are or can be the best among your peers is essential. Challenging yourself mentally to become a better ballplayer than you already are can do nothing but make you better. Accentuate the positive and work on improving the negative.

Once your son has made the high school varsity, he still needs instructional help. He'll most likely be showing some tools that scouts can see and evaluate, so let's make sure he's continually honing those valuable skills. No matter how talented he is at this age, he is by no means a finished ballplayer. At this time in your son's ball-playing adventure, if you can find a former professional player in your area to work with him and help him spot his flaws and smooth them out, then you'll be helping him immensely. Thoroughly interview the former professional ballplayer, ask for references, and talk to other parents who may have used him to help their sons. Another thing, make sure he and your son are a good fit. Don't just allow a former professional to work with your kid because the man has played for money. Professional instruction, one on one from a former pro, someone who has been in the trenches, can really be advantageous.

At this point you want your kid to have every advantage because as he continues his high school varsity career, he is competing against other extremely competitive boys who are a year or two older. Also at this time, positive mental aspects of the game really come into play.

Let's say your son is a sophomore and he's an accomplished hitter competing for the center field job against an experienced senior ballplayer. It won't be enough for your son to be good. He's going to have to be extremely good—clearly better than the senior—to be given the regular job. From a high school coach's point of view, the senior has been around a year or two and will provide a sure, steady hand. The sophomore must dominate if he is to win the job, and to do that he has to be convinced in his own mind and heart that he's worthy.

Once your son has established himself as a varsity player and once you can see he has the ability to go farther than high school, proceed with caution, tact, and wisdom. At this point you do not want to be anything other than a supporter and a source of encouragement. You should never get in his coach's face with suggestions or try to tell the coach how he should and should not be handling your son. Your son does not need that added pressure. It's simply not fair to anyone involved.

At this point he should be playing in the fastest summer league he can find. He should be doing well on his varsity team, even dominating. If he has what it takes, you will notice that he's an extremely fast runner—faster than everyone else on the team, has a strong, accurate throwing arm, and hits the ball hard and with power. If this boy has the potential to advance, those innate tools will appear to be appreciably better than the others on the field. Other fans will notice and you will hear them talking about him. If he can really play, you'll begin to see major-league scouts in the stands, and they just may introduce themselves to you.

That's exciting but don't let it turn your head or your son's. At this point in his life your son should not be in the mode of believing in his own press clippings. He has too far to go as a ballplayer. Reading the stories of his accomplishments is okay. Believing them is naive.

Encourage your son to compete mentally with players far past those at the high school district level if he intends to get a college scholarship or a pro contract. He must be targeting that center fielder in California, or the pitcher in Oklahoma, or that catcher in Puerto Rico, Australia, or wherever as his top competition.

At this point in his life a truly gifted young man will want to become a world-class ballplayer, and he'll begin to make personal sacrifices such as swinging a leaded bat a couple hundred times a day, running, doing exercises and eating properly. If all of the above things are happening, more specialized instruction may be in order. You may want to continue working with the former professional player you used before. You may find a major-league scout who will work quietly with your son. I stepped in to help Nolan Ryan and several other young men, and I can vouch for this tactic's benefits to the up-and-coming young ballplayer—and it can build an extra layer of confidence he'll need to advance.

One other thing should be mentioned here: jealousy. If your son becomes an outstanding, dominating ballplayer, expect the other players, their parents, and sometimes their coaches to be a little jealous. My advice in these situations always is for both of you to practice ignoring jibes, pettiness, and simply being adult about it and continue on, confident in your ability to parent and your son's ability to play. I have seen too many parents get too involved emotionally and end up putting needless pressure on their sons. Just let the negativity slide and encourage your son to prove his point between the lines on the field. Dealing with jealousy is great character-building practice and a tool your son will need to handle the world of college or professional sports if he continues to play well.

Past the negativity, a talented teenager's mental attitude at this point in his life should be, "I'm a quality high school baseball player, but I'm going to be an even better college or professional player." As he takes each sequential step up the ladder, providing his ability allows him to get that far, his mental attitude should be a constant challenge to make himself run faster, throw farther and more accurately, hit better, and field the ball better.

When we find young players with that kind of stout, determined mental attitude as well as the physical ability to play, then we begin to say good things about them to our bosses and we start to lobby our teams to pick that type of young man when draft day rolls around.

For the sake of discussion, let's say a scout approaches your son. My attitude in making the initial move in letting a kid know I am interested went something like this.

"I'm Red Murff with the New York Mets. I think you have a chance to be a really good ballplayer. Is this something you're interested in—becoming a professional ballplayer?"

With this straightforward approach, I always found out right away if the kid wanted to continue in baseball. Believe me, some have told me up front that they were not interested, and that's okay. Knowing that kept me from wasting my time pursuing someone who doesn't want it. For those who said they were interested, I would say something like, "Just because you have been approached by a major-league scout does not mean you are a major-league player. It doesn't improve your ability, nor does it make you better than a lot of others. It just means I am interested in watching your development and perhaps pursuing you seriously at a later date."

What I try to do is open a door for this young man and ease his journey down the road to success. I felt that as a major-league scout, that was part of my job—making it easy for the young man to chart his course.

I also warned the kid not to begin imitating his favorite big leaguer, nor did I want him to do anything differently as a player. I just wanted him to know I expected to see him continue working hard and continue showing me his extraordinary talent.

I also cautioned parents not to brag too much nor become overprotective. I would warn them to avoid talking to a lot of different friends and family members. Talking to seemingly well-meaning people can often times do nothing but confuse and complicate a delicate situation. A scout's words are merely a first step and in no way guarantee that the youngster will become a professional ballplayer.

It's natural that a lot of friends and family members will want to be involved and celebrate your good news. Before you talk to those people about what the scout had to say, you'd best ask that talented son of yours, "Is this professional baseball idea what you really want?" So many times I have encountered parents who got so caught up in their own moment celebrating their son's success that they forgot to ask him that important question.

I caution parents to remember at this point in their son's life that his emotions are probably as overabundant as his talent. A misspoken word from you could set him on the wrong path, and we don't want any abrupt changes. So go slowly, move deliberately, and keep him on the same course that got him to this point. Remember, above all else, the process of your son's becoming a professional ballplayer is far from over. He is no better baseball player than he was the day before a scout talked to him for the first time.

As long as I've been around baseball, seeing boys progress from Little League infant to a mature, draftable ballplayer has been one of the richest rewards of my scouting career.

Of course, every young man can't make it that far. If your son's ability tops out in Pony League, that's okay. Rejoice in the good times you had together playing catch, watching his games, and talking about them later. If he makes it to high school varsity or the college level, that's great! Just remember to enjoy the successes, forget the failures, and revel in the fact that your son played the game and played it well, no matter how far his natural ability and drive takes him.

One other thing: Because you and your son have learned the game and had some success together, you share a strong common bond through baseball. Even if he never makes the major leagues—which 99.99 percent never will—you and he can attend ball games together as fans. You'll be great fans and great supporters of the game because you loved it together, you lived it together, and you still enjoy it for the great game it is.

Red's Random Thought . . .

A Bible verse says something to the effect that many are called but few are chosen. It's that way in Major League Baseball. The way I have it figured, when a young man is chosen by a big-league club, he has only one option.

Chapter 19

Should My Son Sign?

Early each June, just as sure as golden brown suntans, cherry snow cones, and steamy summertime are right around the corner, about a thousand families in the United States face a perplexing problem. "My son has just been drafted by a major-league club. He's worked from dawn until dusk for more than a decade to achieve this moment. Only a few young men in the world possess his level of talent for a sport he dearly loves. What should we do? Do we allow him to sign with the big-league team or do we insist he go to college first?"

My initial gut reaction as a veteran professional baseball player, manager, and scout is simple: sign the professional contract. In the interest of all concerned, however, let's go through the deliberations. This is a difficult decision and a decision that deserves careful, prayerful thought and attention.

Thousands of dads and moms have asked me which is better for their son, a pro contract or college? Let me say up-front that I believe in education—my wife is a schoolteacher—and for thirty-five years I've spent hours trying to come up with the best possible answer. Although I never had a son and been faced with this decision, I now have a sixteen-year-old grandson who is showing some skills and I may soon be called upon to help him make the right choice.

Parents play a key role in this decision and can either help or hinder, simplify or complicate matters. I believe it's up to the parents to clarify the choice and ensure that a young man thoroughly thinks through all of his options. I cannot tell you how many parents have said to me on my first visit, "We've committed to making sure our Johnny gets a good education. Our son must have a college education!" My reply was always, "Well, fine. What's he majoring in?" In almost every instance neither the parents nor the kid had any idea. So I pushed the idea of a baseball "major" with the understanding that there's no harm done in having academics take a back seat for a while if the young man makes the commitment to get an education as soon as it's feasible. Of course a degree and a profession are important hedges for the future, but the young man can always go to college. He can't always play baseball for a living.

Two stories come to mind in dealing with parents bent on their son attending college. A first baseman from the Houston area was an incredible prospect. He's now playing at the AAA level and he may or may not be able to take the big step to the majors. On my first visit to his home, his father, the kid, and I were having a great discussion about the young man's future and what his ambitions were. He told me he wanted to play baseball in the worst way, but once his mother entered the room the tone of the conversation changed drastically. She insisted that her son was college material. She was adamant that he had a fine mind—he had a 4.0-plus grade point average—and she let me know in no uncertain terms that a college education would take priority over baseball. And it did despite his protestations. The young man signed a scholarship agreement with a prestigious university on the West Coast. Three years later he signed a professional contract, which not everybody is able to do. College for him was a big risk, and his development as a ballplayer lagged behind because of the three years he spent in a college and not in a professional baseball setting. We have yet to see if his college experience was worth it.

Another story along those same lines involves a young pitcher from Texas who once was a certain first-round draft choice coming out of high school. In his day his signing bonus would have been four hundred to five hundred thousand dollars. He also had an opportunity to sign a scholarship at the university that his father had attended, so the father became involved.

"I'll pay my son four hundred thousand dollars *not* to sign a pro contract," the young man's stubborn father bragged. The kid listened to his dad's ranting and declined to sign the contract. To make a long story short, he went to college and accomplished nothing toward developing his enormous talent. Yes, he pitched for his college team and won some games, but he did not progress the way he should have had he signed right out of high school. When he became eligible for the draft three years later, he was picked in a lower round and the major-league club that drafted him assigned him to a club in Class A ball. Given his talent level, had he signed right out of high school and followed a normal progression path, the young man would've been in Class AAA baseball or the big leagues within a couple of years. He lost years of valuable professional ground to college baseball.

What's so bad about losing time? It means two things: training and experience. The young man gave up at least two years' intense, thorough professional instruction for a chance to play for old State U., but more importantly he lost two years of valuable earning power in professional baseball. That means he lost 15 percent of a potential fourteen-year major-league career, assuming he was able to make the major leagues. A good, productive major-league pitcher makes about three to five million dollars a year. So this homage to dad's alma mater cost this player somewhere in the neighborhood of six million dollars. Money he most likely will never be able to make up over the course of his career in either professional baseball or in corporate America.

"Okay, Murff," you say, "this kid has an education, and you can't put a price tag on that, so it was time well spent."

That's right, but let me argue my point by pondering one crucial point. Given rapidly changing technology and information, by the time a prospect gets a chance to use his education, his knowledge may be outdated and irrelevant. So how can you gauge its worth? My advice is that a talented player should do both. No matter how academically gifted a young man may be, he should sign a professional baseball contract as soon as he's offered one. As a part of the deal with the major-league club, take the cash bonus and demand a college scholarship of at least eight semesters at the college or university of your choice and make sure the scholarship provision is written into the contract. This is not a scholarship to play ball in college. This is a scholarship to pay all the college costs for a professional ballplayer.

I find several problems with a player signing a college scholarship to play baseball. The first is a really sore point because a lot of players and parents don't understand what a scholarship is. College recruiting talk of four-year "full ride" scholarships for baseball is baloney. The rules governing athletic scholarships for all NCAA colleges and universities limits any scholarship agreement to only *two* semesters. Any coach or recruiter who promises more than two semesters is misrepresenting what can be done legitimately under the rules that govern collegiate baseball. In my opinion any school or recruiter trying to sell a young man or woman on a four-year scholarship is being deceptive and should be fired on the spot.

Mixing a professional baseball career with college puts your son on a definite career path. If for some reason he doesn't make it in baseball, he's already got the financial wherewithal for a college education and can earn a degree and move forward with his life.

There's something else that needs to be considered as well. Professional baseball clubs emphasize talent development above all else. When your son signs with a professional club, he'll receive intense, one-on-one instruction, the likes of which he would never see anywhere else. Major-league clubs have made an investment in your son. They want to win, and to win they must develop the talent they acquire. They have the most skillful development people in the business. This way your son has the opportunity to see really how far his God-given talent can take him.

I don't have the same faith in college programs. In my opinion a college coach's emphasis, livelihood, and ambition revolve around winning ball games now, not on developing a young player's skills. Consequently we often see young players—especially pitchers—abused by coaches who are more interested in winning than in the long-term well-being of a gifted but inexperienced athlete. It's also not unheard of for a college coach to sign a young ballplayer to a scholarship agreement just to keep another school from getting him and then never giving the young man a chance to play. At age eighteen or nineteen, a talented kid needs to be on the field honing his talent, not sitting around wasting away. Coaches who recruit kids and don't give them a chance are immoral and should be run out of the business.

The coach benefits, of course, but what about the young player who has devoted a huge portion of his life to baseball and stands to lose a career at the hands of an abusive coach? How many good young pitchers go into senior college programs only to come away damaged at the end of three seasons? Even one is one too many, and there have been dozens. Doesn't each player deserve a chance to develop his skills and succeed as much as his coach?

Junior college is a good alternative. The rules of baseball allow a junior college player to keep his talents on display, readily available to a major-league scout. A young man who signs with a junior college program is eligible to be signed by a professional baseball club after the end of his freshman season and again at the end of his sophomore year. Many junior colleges play more games than the NCAA allows senior colleges to play. Should a young man have a sensational freshman year, he may move up and become a top-flight prospect, eligible to sign on with a professional club, unlike a fellow freshman at a senior college.

This college-contract question has upset me, puzzled me, and confused me for decades. Why can't there be a way for everyone to get what they want, including the parents who have their hearts set on their son starting college immediately after high school? My friend Roland Hemond has pondered this too.

"I've always had a grave concern for younger players in professional baseball who were not pursuing their college educations," Roland says. "It always seemed to me that they had a lot of free time in the off-season—time that could have been, but was not being used to further their college studies. Red and I began to work about ten years ago on a plan that would allow young men to pursue their educations while still playing professional baseball."

Under our plan baseball would sponsor a professional winter league at one or several colleges. The professional baseball signee would be expected to enroll in this program voluntarily. We'd offer a business education program, including some baseball-related leadership courses. Business courses would teach the rudiments of handling and investing money. The baseball courses would include how to scout or become a general manager or how to run a farm system. The courses would be taught by regular college professors and experts in the game of baseball. Since the program would be run through accredited universities and colleges, the player gains credits that would count toward a degree. The volunteer nature of the plan is intended to encourage young men interested in the game beyond hitting or pitching or fielding and to give them an opportunity to make baseball their life's work even if they don't have long playing careers. Roland and I are convinced this plan would attract the smartest, most ambitious, and competitive minds and would eventually result in turning out young people to run ball clubs who truly love and appreciate the game.

Under this program the college for ballplayers would coordinate the start of its fall semester sometime in October and run through the end of February, just before the beginning of spring training. During the semester a student-player would take a full load of classes and earn college credit hours while playing professional-level baseball, supervised in a fall league by professional instructors.

With baseball's talent pool being continually drained by expansion, this idea would be the ticket to restocking the big leagues and improving the educational requirements for the young men who might not make it to the majors. This is the best program yet, and I think professional baseball needs to act on this idea as quickly as possible.

Buzzy Keller, an old friend and scouting competitor, once was director of the Kansas City Royals well-publicized Baseball Academy that operated from 1970 to 1974 in Sarasota, Florida. The Royals gave it up because they said it lost too much money, but Buzzy thinks the monetary investment in a college plan like ours could save baseball money in the long run and turn out terrific ballplayers.

"We came up with some innovative training and player grading techniques that were scoffed at by the old-line baseball people, but it's thinking that is now standard operating procedure," Buzzy claims. "Our academy idea worked. Of the eighty-four players who came through there, seventeen of them played in the big leagues. That means 20 percent made it. That's five times better than the success rate for all the youngsters we sign. And don't forget, the players from the academy all came from tryout camps. Think of what could be done if we took the cream of the crop, all drafted ballplayers, and placed them in a major-league baseball-style college setting. Baseball needs to adopt this idea again. The teams that do will dominate the game for decades."

I am convinced that if all Major League Baseball teams adopted our idea, the quality of baseball would rise dramatically. With the worldwide population explosion, the number of talented players would increase as would the need for more leaders. Those leaders should be developed in a professional baseball college development program like the one we are proposing.

The original academy's success rate is open for debate. I personally think, for the amount of money that was spent on it, it was unsuccessful. The fact remains, however, that baseball must take an aggressive approach to player development with a college emphasis if the sport expects to attract top-flight athletes during the years to come.

Now that we've discussed the pros and cons of signing, let's do a little step-by-step primer on how you should react should a major-league club draft your son. Since I'm a veteran scout and have signed more than two hundred ballplayers, I feel more than confident in guiding you through this process.

Remember that a major-league baseball club has paid your son the finest compliment in his life when it announces his name during this international process. The club has made a statement: We think this young man is talented. We want to own the rights to his services. We want to play a major role in his development. We are willing to pay to do all of that. What it also means is that you and your son, as a family, are now facing what is possibly the most critical decision of a young man's life. Just as important you need to consider that this may be the last decision you make as a family while he's living at home. Take your time and ask the scout you're dealing with any questions you want, the more the better. If he doesn't have a satisfactory answer, have him ask his bosses. I always found that a lot of parents entered contract negotiations full of fear and trepidation simply because they didn't understand the process. Once they had their questions answered, more often than not, the rest of the negotiation was smooth sailing.

Shortly after you find out your son has been drafted, a scout from the drafting club will be calling to set up a meeting between your family and the team. Usually this first meeting takes place in the family home, but you can have it anywhere you want, anywhere you are comfortable. During the initial meeting with a family, I always tried to make everyone feel at ease with the negotiation process and with professional baseball in general. I always dealt truthfully with each family, especially when salary discussions commenced. I carried a chart that showed the average salaries for players in each round of the draft over the past twenty-five years. It explained quite clearly the pecking order from first-round choice all the way through the thirtieth round. Once the family saw the chart, they could decide if the monetary offer was fair.

Some parents said, "Well, my son is special, he deserves more than the average player in that round."

My response was, "Yes, your son is special, but no more so than the son who set the standard for this particular round in the draft." Furthermore, my attitude was, "I want your son to sign a contract with my team. I believe in him, in his ability, and that he will be an asset to the game of baseball. If for some reason we cannot reach an agreement, I want you to know I want to still be friends. I honor these negotiations, and I promise not to play games with you. I hope you won't play games with me."

I also counseled parents to speak with an attorney or an accountant at any time, but I cautioned them not to sign a contract with an agent because once they did, and if the professional negotiations broke off for some reason, NCAA rules prevent anyone who was represented by an agent from receiving a scholarship. You see this happening in college football more than baseball, and it has caused some programs to be placed on probation. Still, it doesn't make any difference what sport we're talking about, no agents are allowed. It's fine to talk to someone like that, but don't sign or verbally agree to representation.

Past that, be patient and understand the process takes time. I have been around families who wanted their son to accept the club's initial offer. I've had mothers and fathers who simply said, "Mr. Murff, please do whatever it takes to get my kid into professional ball. He wants it so badly." At the other end of the scale, I've had folks who wanted no part of my act or baseball. Don't be surprised if the negotiations take several meetings, but please deal truthfully with the scout and with the club and they'll do the same for you.

If the scout you're dealing with is any good, he'll have said to you what I always said to each young man I signed: "I will always be your scout. Call me if you need help."

Three years after I retired from scouting, the players I signed are still calling on me. I must have done something right.

Red's Random Thought . . .

Sometimes our kids don't fulfill the dreams we have for them. They have their own dreams. Sometimes it's hard for parents to understand that, but those who do, those who let go, learn a whole new meaning for the word *love*.

Chapter 20

Turning Them Loose

Our children, God bless them, are our Maker's richest blessing to us. They provide rich sources of human emotions for parents. As they grow and mature, trusting them and allowing them the freedom to express themselves can be one of life's greatest challenges for a father and a mother.

When my third daughter, Melinda, turned three, she begged us for a nurse's kit. It might have been just a silly toy to her mother and me, but to this earnest little girl this was what she needed to do a good job of playing. "I wanna be a nurse, that's what I wanna be, that's what I'm going to be," she insisted in her tiny, determined voice.

Being a nurse was all she ever really wanted to do, and I'm proud to say for the past quarter of a century she has cared for hundreds of sick and recovering people. Melinda made the family extremely proud simply because she pursued her dream, persevered, and reached a goal I believed she would've achieved with or without support of her parents. Sometimes it's not all that easy for a parent to let go.

Robbie Schleider graduated from A&M Consolidated High School in College Station, Texas, in the spring of 1969. Brother, he could really throw a baseball. He was a right-handed pitcher, and his fastball was in the low-ninety-miles-an-hour range when I drafted him that June for the Montreal Expos after he made an incredible showing at my tryout camp in Brenham, Texas.

I knew young Schleider would be tough to sign. He came from a home that placed great emphasis on college and on advanced learning. Robbie's dad, Bob, worked as an engineer with the Texas Highway Department and was an engineering professor at Texas A&M University. I figured the Schleider family really had no need for baseball. I pegged Robbie as a college man through and through.

I called the Schleider home shortly after the draft to set up a meeting with the family so they could get to know me and the Montreal Expos. I didn't want his folks to feel any pressure to sign; I just wanted them to have some kind of friendly introduction to professional baseball.

Bob Schleider was a gentleman, extremely cordial on the telephone and receptive to meeting me. He promised me the royal treatment and offered to have me over to his home for breakfast at my earliest convenience. I figured the royal treatment meant we'd eat breakfast and he'd politely tell me his son was going to college.

When I got there, I was met by a friendly, smiling, talkative family, but something was obviously awry. Love notes had been pasted on the refrigerator, on the top of the kitchen table, on the bathroom door, the telephone, everywhere.

"I love you, this will all work out," said one note. "I love you, whatever happens will be for the best," said another.

I figured one parent was trying to convince the other to keep Robbie from signing a professional baseball contract. I assumed this highly educated man obviously wanted the same thing for his son. I kept thinking, *Murff, you're wasting your time.*

I made my pitch anyway. I told the Schleiders I simply wanted them to know that because Montreal had drafted their son, the Expos really wanted him to play professional baseball. When I looked at Robbie and told him how good he was and how much potential I thought he had, his face lit up like the White House Christmas tree. I could tell the young man really wanted to play baseball. But what about his dad and mom? What about those love notes?

They had kindly set an incredible table with eggs, sausage, and toast, served with all the coffee and juice I could drink, but the feed may as well have been bread and water. My breakfast had no taste because I believed I was fighting a losing battle.

Finally, when I ended my spiel, the brushed-cut, sturdily built father stood up from the table and very matter of factly said, "Mr. Murff, I have something I want to say to you."

I had a desert-dry lump in my throat. My palms were sweaty. Mentally I had lined myself up in front of the firing squad, put on the blindfold, said my prayers, and made ready for the execution.

"Mr. Murff, when Robbie was born, I was the proudest engineer you ever heard tell about on the face of this earth. I mean I had a *son*, a child whom I intended to turn into the world's best engineer. Robbie Schleider literally cut his teeth on a slide rule," his father began.

Murff, you're dead meat.

Bob Schleider continued his dissertation, "Yes sir, I brainwashed him to be an engineer, Mr. Murff. Robbie was a good son. He took advanced math classes, trigonometry, geometry, and calculus in junior high. I used to bring engineering problems home, and he'd solve them. I just knew Schleider & Son, Engineers, would become a reality," he said.

That's all she wrote, Red, old buddy.

"But, I tell you something, Mr. Murff," Bob Schleider continued. "When Robbie was fifteen years old he tried out for the varsity baseball team at A&M Consolidated High and he made it. Since then all *he's* talked about, dreamed about, or thought about has been becoming a major-league baseball player. I lost my engineer, Mr. Murff, but you gained a baseball player. I have to let him sign. I have to let him go. He's got it in his heart and soul."

Talk about a rally in the bottom of the ninth! You have to admire a father like that. I looked at this generous man, breathed a sigh of relief, and felt an unbelievable glow inside, a joyfulness in being in the company of something as incredible as a truly loving parent.

I have dealt with some wonderful fathers and mothers through the years. Lynn and Martha, Nolan Ryan's parents, were great. Jerry Grote's dad was a fine, fine man. Bob Schleider, however, was the classiest, most understanding, most compassionate father I have ever dealt with. The unconditional love and support he showed for his son is a prime example of the proper role of a prospect's father. But Bob Schleider is not by himself. I also admired fathers who took bad news with grace and fortitude. This one isn't so easy.

Del Baker had spent three decades in baseball. He caught for the Boston Red Sox. At one time he managed the Red Sox and later the Detroit Tigers, and he also scouted for the Boston club. Del Baker was a player's player, a manager's manager, and a scout's scout. Del Baker was a baseball man through and through, and he really looked the part—weathered skin, wide shoulders, thick forearms. I also called him my friend.

Del's son, Smoky, played in the outfield for Trinity University in San Antonio. Smoky could really run and throw, but in my estimation Smoky could not hit the ball well enough to merit a chance as a professional ballplayer.

Del Baker, however, desperately wanted to get his son a job in professional baseball. I told Del what I thought about Smoky's lack of hitting ability, and I told him I really questioned whether he would ever be able to make it. Then I thought of something.

"Del, has Smoky ever played the infield? With his speed we might be able to teach him to hit and bunt enough to merit a professional chance if you think he can play the infield."

"Well, Red, Smoky's never played there, but I'll bet he'd like to give 'er a try," Baker answered.

"Have Smoky come to my tryout camp in Rockdale in a couple weeks, and I'll see if he can play enough second base to give him a chance in the rookie league," I promised.

Smoky appeared at the tryout camp and we went to work. I tried him as a switch-hitter, thinking hitting from the left side of the plate would put him a half-step closer to first. We could teach him to drag bunt for base hits. Smoky had good hands and quickness. During the first day of the tryout camp it appeared that he might be able to play a little bit at second base.

On the second day, during infield practice, I hit Smoky a ground ball that rolled between his legs. When he showed no remorse and no expression on his face for having committed the blunder and then walked after it, I blew my stack.

"Smoky, if you're too tired to run after that ball, you're too tired to play for me," I screamed.

"Hold on, hold on a minute, Mr. Murff," Smoky said as he jogged toward me at home plate.

"Mr. Murff, I got something to tell you," he said sadly. "Mr. Murff, I know you're trying your best to get me a job in baseball because you and my dad are friends. And I know I'm here just because of my father. But I got to tell you, I really don't care anything about baseball. I only play baseball to please my dad."

"Well, Smoky, there's only one thing you can do, son. You have to go tell your dad about your decision," I told him firmly.

"Oh, no, Mr. Murff, I couldn't do that. I just couldn't disappoint him that way."

"Smoky, you don't have a choice. Now, promise me you'll go home and tell him. Okay?"

"Okay, Mr. Murff. You're right. I will."

A couple of days later I walked into a ballpark and was met by several scouts. One of them said, "Red, Del Baker's sitting in the stands and he's really upset at you."

"Why," I asked. "What's his problem?"

"You know what the problem is. You promised Del you'd sign

Smoky and he came back from your tryout camp without a contract. That's what Del is upset about."

Well, well, well. Smoky had chickened out and hadn't talked with his dad after all.

"I'll go over and talk to Del and tell him what happened," I told the other scouts.

One warned, "Gee, I don't know if I would do that if I were you, Red. He's mighty upset and he might knock your head off."

I wasn't too worried about that. So I walked on into the ballpark, followed by the other scouts. I spotted Del Baker sitting in the stands with a couple of other scouts, and I walked over and stuck out my hand.

"Hello, Del, how ya doin'?" I asked.

He refused to look me in the eye, even though he shook my hand.

"Del," I asked, "Did Smoky tell you what happened at the tryout camp. Did he tell you why I didn't sign him to a contract?"

Apparently not. Del grunted no.

"Is Smoky here?"

"Yep," he responded, "Sittin' with his girlfriend right down there behind the third-base dugout."

"Excuse me, Del. We can clear this up in just a minute. No problem."

Off I marched after the younger Baker. As I approached Smoky, it appeared he was trying to hide. He didn't want me to spot him. But he had made a commitment and he needed to own up to it.

"Excuse me, Smoky, can you come here for a moment?"

"You mean me?"

"Yes sir, I mean you. Get over here for a second, please." I had him by the arm now and I wasn't going to let him off the hook.

"Smoky, didn't you promise me you were going to talk to your dad and tell him you don't really want to play baseball anymore? Didn't you tell me you would do that?"

"Oh, Mr. Murff," he whined. "I just couldn't do that. That news would break his heart."

"I don't care, Smoky. You and I had a deal. Now your dad is really upset with me and I'm about to lose a good friend because you wouldn't honor your promise to me. Now get on over there and tell him you don't wanna play."

The slump-shouldered young man slowly ambled up to his dad and in front of several major-league scouts he began his story.

"Dad, I have something I need to talk to you about."

"What is it, Smoky?"

"Dad, Mr. Murff tried his best to get me a job in baseball. But I just couldn't let him do it. I finally told him I really didn't want to play baseball and that I only play it to please you."

Someone could've hit Del Baker in the head with an axe and he would not have been more surprised. But he quickly regained his composure and reached out a darkly tanned, gnarled hand and touched his son's cheek.

"Smoky, ever since you were born, you've been the center of my life, the thing I lived for. Son, you don't have to play baseball to please me, you please me just being you. I love you, son."

This isn't supposed to happen to crusty old baseball scouts. I had just introduced a son to his father for the first time. My emotions overcame me. I ducked behind the stands and had myself a good cry. We curmudgeons have feelings too, you know.

Robbie Schleider played professionally for a couple of years, but he developed arm problems and had to leave the game. Now he's a successful owner of several restaurants in central Texas. Smoky Baker now builds homes in San Antonio.

Although they came from vastly different backgrounds, Bob Schleider and Del Baker approached parenting the same way. They dreamed a dream their sons really didn't want for themselves, but both men learned through this marvelous game of baseball to appreciate their sons for the excellent young men they are rather than the young men their fathers dreamed they would be.

Red's Random Thought . . .

When you look closely at their faces, you know each one is convinced in his heart and soul he is the player you're looking for. Unfortunately most of them aren't, but try telling that to anyone who comes to a big-league tryout camp.

Chapter 21

Tryout Camps

They come by themselves, in pairs, or in groups. They've driven perhaps as far as five hundred miles and arrive in every condition from revved up to sleepy-eyed. They show up with their mothers, fathers, girlfriends, or maybe even their high school coaches. They all carry with them the one thing that has brought them this far—determination.

Early on a muggy late-May Saturday morning, only hours before the major-league draft, they amble out of their cars and into the ballpark wearing their uniforms, carrying gloves and mitts and perhaps a favorite bat. Deadly serious looks line their young tanned faces. For some it's the last real shot they'll ever have, and they know it's now or never.

Supercharged with equal shots of adrenaline and testosterone, they come to the camp to prove something to me, or more likely to themselves. They want to show someone in major-league baseball that they can play professionally, that they'll slide and get dirty and skin their elbows and get sweaty and give it all they've got for a chance to play with the best. Deep down inside they know if they don't have the tools the scouts are looking for, at least they'll be able to tell their children and their grandchildren that they had a tryout with a major-league club, that Red Murff, the scout who signed Nolan Ryan, had given them a look. That's why this yearly ritual was so much fun to watch. Like a personnel director at a major corporation, these young men were applying for a job with me. When I saw them play, their ability filled out their résumés, and I was anxious to see what skills they could bring to my party—a spring ritual uniquely American and baseball.

It hasn't always been so here in Texas. Only after major-league baseball announced its expansion in 1960 would include Houston did interest in baseball in Texas rise dramatically. After the Houston club opened for operation late that same year, executives began receiving letters from Texas high school and college players asking for a chance to play for their home-state team.

Houston scouting director Bobby Bragan received more than forty-five letters from those players. As a fledgling ball club in a state that had never been home to big-league baseball, we decided to go looking for Texas talent. What better attraction, we asked ourselves, could we have than some home-grown ballplayers starring in Houston? A tryout camp, we believed, was just the ticket to finding out if any of the wannabes could actually play.

On January 28, 1961, we held the first Houston Colt .45s tryout camp in Texas City, Texas. We notified every all-district player we knew. We asked sportswriters from local newspapers to write small articles about the camp. We also relied on word of mouth. I guess we must have had about sixty young men show up.

Among a dozen or so letters I sent about six weeks before the January camp was one to a young man named Gary McBride from Killeen, Texas, who had been released recently from the Pittsburgh Pirates organization. I had seen him play before, and I thought he might have a chance to fill a role in the .45s minor-league system.

In December I received a letter from another young man named John Bateman. He described himself as six feet tall, weighing 243 pounds and "ready to play baseball." Like his friend Gary McBride, Bateman was also from Killeen, and he wanted to know if he could accompany his buddy to the camp.

I must say I wasn't thrilled about Bateman's size, so I wrote a very terse letter back. I brusquely told him the camp we planned was for baseball, not football, and I didn't believe anyone with his bulk belonged there. I ventured a guess that the Houston Oilers would be holding a tryout camp soon, and I recommended he spend his time there.

To my surprise on January 28, the determined Mr. Bateman changed his physique rather than his attitude and showed up at the camp having shed twenty-five pounds in less than a month. When this young man stepped up to the plate, he hit several line-drive home runs over the left-center-field tower outside the Texas City ballpark. Not only that, this kid was a catcher who could really throw and was as quick as a cat behind home plate. John Bateman was by himself as a prospect in this camp. No one else had anywhere near his talent, and I wanted to sign him to a Colt .45s contract.

Helping me run this camp was a man named Louis Schaper, former owner of the Texas City club in the Class B Gulf Coast League. Schaper and I had some terrific verbal battles through the years and didn't agree on much of anything except the talent of a few ballplayers or the lack thereof.

After spending about three and a half hours assessing the talent at the camp, Louis, for once in his life, agreed with me. He knew, for instance, that I had invited Gary McBride to the camp, and he just couldn't resist jabbing me about it. So he started his incessant mouthing.

"McBride can't play," Louis spat.

"Yeah, I know it."

"Know the only one who'll make it?"

"Bateman, the heavyset catcher."

"Right."

At that point neither Louis nor I had any idea if John Bateman had a contact with another club, so I cooked up a scheme. I didn't want Bateman to get away, so I used his room-mate, Gary McBride, as bait.

Early on the morning of the second day of the camp I called their room. "Hello, Gary, that you? This is Red Murff."

"Yes sir, Mr. Murff."

"Gary, how you feeling today, son?"

"Well, we're a little sore, Mr. Murff."

"Say, Gary, you and your roommate going to be back at the camp, aren't you?"

"Yes sir, we are, Mr. Murff."

"Well, Gary, why don't you and your buddy come on down to the coffee shop at your motel, and Louis and I will buy you breakfast."

"Oh, okay, Mr. Murff. We'll be there as quick as we can."

Louis Schaper looked at me with a raised eyebrow. "What are you doing, Red?"

"It's just a little plan, Louis. Stand by."

They showed up a few minutes later, a little stiff-legged but eager to talk to us. We had a good get-to-know-you visit over breakfast and by the time we all headed over to the ballpark, Louis and I were really excited. While both young men were impressive, Bateman was by far the best ballplayer in camp.

On the third morning of the camp, I told Louis it was time for another breakfast with the boys.

"Why do you keep calling McBride, Red. He can't play, so you're not going to sign him, are you?"

"Hold your horses, Louis. There's method to my madness. "You're right, McBride can't play. But that Bateman, he's a great prospect. I'm just making sure McBride keeps Bateman here until the end of the camp."

So we made the call again, and during the second breakfast I let John Bateman know I was interested in him and I hoped he would talk to me about signing a contract. Bateman said he would, so I called Tal Smith, then assistant scouting director for the Houston club.

"Tal, I have one ballplayer at this tryout camp we really need to sign. He's a catcher. He can hit and run and throw. I have no idea how much money it will take to sign him, but we ought to do it, Tal."

According to the baseball rules of the day, if a free agent or amateur ballplayer in his first year of professional ball was not protected on the forty-man roster of the team that signed him, another club could come along and draft him for eight thousand dollars. While I didn't have a fixed price in my mind, I figured an eight thousand dollar bonus would be a good business deal. Tal vehemently disagreed.

"Red, let me tell you something. If this young man was any good, he wouldn't be in your tryout camp. We'd already know about him."

"What do *you* know, Tal," I yelled as I slammed down the phone. Front-office politics was never my strong suit, and this and several other confrontations with Tal Smith ultimately led to my leaving the Houston club. But I stuck to my guns. I believed in John Bateman. He was a ballplayer.

Luckily I was able to sign Bateman to a contract for a salary of about five hundred dollars a month plus an incentive bonus of seventy five hundred dollars if he ever made the big leagues, which he did one year later. That was pretty decent money back then.

I told John, "Listen, son, you're going to see a lot of young men at your rookie league destination driving fancy sports cars and wearing nice suits and ties. So I'm going to throw in a cash gift of three hundred dollars so you can buy some nice clothes to wear."

"Oh, Mr. Murff, I don't need a bonus, I just want to play," he protested.

Can you imagine any kid saying that today? I love telling this story because I had a bargain in John Bateman. He went on to a ten-year major-league career as a catcher, sporting a .250 lifetime batting average with the Colt .45s, the Montreal Expos, and Philadelphia Phillies. He turned out to be an excellent defensive catcher as well and was named Canadian athlete of the year for two consecutive years. And he came from a try-out camp.

That early tryout camp for the Colt .45s evolved from other camps I had seen; however, I didn't like the way most tryout camps were run. The first one I ever attended was in the Dominican Republic in 1957. I was pitching for a club in the Dominican that winter, and Milwaukee Braves scout Ted McGrew asked me to help run a tryout for about seventy young men.

It wasn't organized well, so the experience was a real disappointment. Only about four youngsters had a chance to hit, and I don't think anyone there really showed us what he could do, thus defeating the whole purpose of the camp.

In 1960 I helped another Braves scout with a camp in Florida that ran along the same lines as the one in the Dominican. Although the process really frustrated me, the experience helped me form a plan for how to run one the right way.

After I had my first scouting job with the Colt .45s in 1961, I was able to put my plan into action and camp operation became practically a science after a few years. By the time baseball instituted the draft in 1965, we were conducting tryout camps that gave players a fair chance to show the scouts what they had.

We ran our tryout camp on three consecutive days just before the draft. We did this for a couple of reasons. First, I wanted to have one last shot at observing promising seniors in high school or junior-college players or twenty-one-year-old major-college youngsters who might be draftable. Second, it gave me a chance to have a look at high school juniors and sophomores against stiffer competition. The theory behind watching the juniors and sophomores closely follows that of a farmer: You have to put something in the ground if you want a yield next year. I figured if I could take a look at those kids for three days, I could decide which ones were good enough to follow the next spring.

The camps made sense too. Even though I worked with four or five subscouts in my territory, it was impossible to see every ballplayer who deserved professional scrutiny. The tryout camp was the perfect vehicle to allow us to see anyone we might have missed during the season.

The camps also became an experimental lab to find out if favored players could play another position, like Ernie McAnally. You might remember Ernie as a starter and reliever for the Montreal Expos. The Montreal club drafted Ernie off the Mets forty-man roster but he initially came to us as a catcher when I was working for the Mets at a tryout camp in 1968. He could move well behind the plate, but I just never thought he'd be able to hit enough to play every day in the big leagues.

With all the hubbub and goings-on at this particular camp, I hadn't seen Ernie throw very well and probably never would have given him a second look if Del Baker hadn't said something to me during an infield drill. While Ernie was nonchalantly throwing the ball to second base, Del said, "Red, that catcher can throw much, much better than he's showing."

I sidled up to McAnally. "Are you throwing as good as you can?"

"Oh, no sir, Mr. Murff. I don't want to show off in front of these other guys," he said almost apologetically. It sounded like some twisted sort of reverse peer pressure to me.

"Well, let me tell you something, son. Now is the time for you to show off. There won't be any other times. If you don't show me more than you have, you can't stay in the camp!"

Next thing I knew, Ernie McAnally was throwing lasers to second base. Then we watched him make the difficult throw from right field to third base, well above major-league average.

Once we put him on the mound, we found out Ernie could throw in the low nineties, which made him above big-league average, so we signed him as a pitcher and away he went as another prodigy from our tryout camp.

We were able to get a lot of these kids to come to camp by talking to their coaches. We issued personal invitations to all-district high school players and anyone eligible we thought could play. Our camps were so popular we'd usually have 150 to 200 players show up for the first day, all with intensity in their eyes. It was obvious that each and every one of them truly believed he was the one we were searching for. They certainly intended to show us all they had.

To give every young man (and we had one young woman one year) his (or her) best shot, we instituted a numbering system that allowed us to track each player by position. On the first day of camp, we spent the first hour or hour and a half registering players according to position. Pitchers were numbered between 100 and 199, catchers between 200 and 299, first basemen between 300 and 399, second basemen between 400 and 499, third basemen between 500 and 599, shortstops between 600 and 699, left fielders between 700 and 799, center fielders between 800 and 899, and right fielders between 900 and 999.

I recruited a group of secretaries to handle the registration process. Each secretary was responsible for a position. The secretaries made sure each player's name and position number was on his registration card. This registration card was used as a player's grading card. We graded running speed, throwing ability, fielding ability, and hitting ability against a major-league average. For an example, refer to the facing page.

With so many players involved, this numbering system became extremely valuable because it was much easier to track a player by number than by name.

We also made each player sign a statement indicating that he understood that he complied with school and major-league eligibility rules. For instance, if a high school player's school wasn't officially out for the year, he wasn't eligible to participate in the camp until it was. Even if he was graduating that Saturday, he couldn't be a party to the camp until Sunday. If the young man was part of the American Legion baseball program, we made him bring a letter of permission signed by the post commander.

My subscouts and volunteer camp assistants helped me immensely and were given logical and specific areas of responsibility. For instance, I had a subscout who had played college ball

THE SCOUT

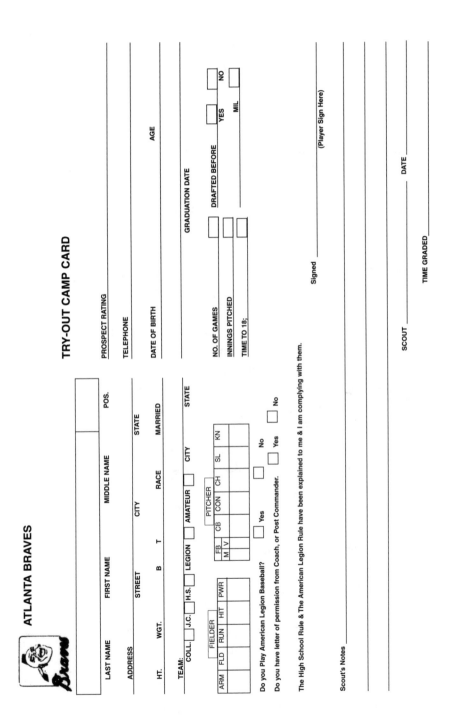

ATLANTA BRAVES

TRY-OUT CAMP CARD

PROSPECT RATING

TELEPHONE

LAST NAME   FIRST NAME   MIDDLE NAME   POS.

ADDRESS   STREET   CITY   STATE

HT.   WGT.   B   T   RACE   MARRIED   AGE

DATE OF BIRTH

TEAM:
COLL   J.C.   H.S.   LEGION   AMATEUR   CITY   STATE

GRADUATION DATE

FIELDER
ARM   FLD   RUN   HIT   PWR

PITCHER
FB   CB   CON   CH   SL   KN
M   V

NO. OF GAMES   DRAFTED BEFORE   YES   NO

INNINGS PITCHED

TIME TO 18:   MIL.

Do you Play American Legion Baseball?   Yes   No

Do you have letter of permission from Coach, or Post Commander.   Yes   No

The High School Rule & The American Legion Rule have been explained to me & I am complying with them.

Signed _____ (Player Sign Here)

Scout's Notes _____

_____

SCOUT _____ DATE _____

TIME GRADED _____

261

as an infielder and enjoyed working with aspiring infielders. So I made him responsible for tracking, grading, and recording the grades of each infielder on the individual registration-grading cards.

After camp registration we gathered the group and told them what we expected. We made it clear that they were to give their supreme effort at all times. We wanted to see their very best skills on display so we could grade their talents accurately against a major-league average.

In earlier years I wore the uniform of the team I worked for, but as I got older I began to make allowances for the hot weather. I always dressed in a wide-brimmed straw hat, long-sleeved shirt, and slacks that kept the sun off my light skin. As I spoke to the youngsters, my spiel went something like this: "More than likely you're a good ballplayer or think you are, otherwise, you wouldn't be here. You may be all-district, all-state, perhaps junior college all-conference, or maybe even all-conference at a major college. That's all well and good. As good as you may be, you may not be a big-league prospect. That's what we're here to find out. We want to know if you're better than everybody here. If you are, you may be a prospect. Now let's go out and have fun and see how good we really are."

The players were assigned to positional groups so they could begin loosening up for running speed tests. During the more than thirty years we ran tryout camps, these races turned out to be some of the most competitive, most hotly contested events. Since I always put tremendous emphasis on a player's running speed, and fast players rate extra consideration in my book, the tests were one of my favorite parts of the tryout camp.

We wanted to know each player's speed from home to first as well as a sixty-yard dash time. Major-league average speed from home to first for a right-handed hitter is 4.3 seconds while swinging the bat and 3.8 seconds while bunting. For left-handers the average was 4.2 seconds swinging the bat and 3.7

while bunting. The league average was 6.7 seconds for the sixty-yard dash.

Once we recorded everyone's running speed, we kept the players in their groups and began having them loosen up for infield and outfield drills. These exercises allowed us to grade arm strength, quickness, mobility, and fielding ability.

Each subscout ran the drills for the positions he'd been assigned. Each player had at least three and perhaps as many as nine or ten chances to field and throw the ball.

This took a while when you consider we were trying to see and grade as many as two hundred ballplayers. I always got in the middle of everything, yelling, screaming, encouraging, and in general making sure every drill was being run properly and each player was performing at his best. I wanted everyone on his toes, including the subscouts and volunteer assistants. I wanted those young men to have every chance to prove themselves to me.

While infield drills were under way, we had pitchers working in the bull pen. They warmed up first under the supervision of a subscout before throwing for a grade.

Once we finished the drills, which often ran more than two hours, we gave the players a chance to grab some water and cool off. Then we began scrimmage games, grading each player's hitting ability, and we gave each pitcher an additional look for another grade. After everybody hit twice I had a meeting with the subscouts and volunteer assistants and we looked over the grades and determined which players would be asked to stay for more scrimmage games. This was the beginning of the weeding-out process. Nobody likes to think they can't play, but in fairness to everyone we had to make cuts so we could give the best talent plenty of chances to impress us.

We weren't infallible in our judgments. I believe it was back in the late sixties when we cut a young man from camp and he got disgusted. That's not unusual. But this young man went in, took a shower, came out, and sat down in the stands in his street clothes. That was out of the ordinary since most kids are so understandably embarrassed, disappointed, and upset that they just take off and we never see them again. But this one was different. Once the scrimmage game began, I heard him yelling, "Hey, I can hit better than these guys!"

I heard him say it again and again, getting louder each time. Well, that got my attention, and I hollered, "Okay, young man, I believe you *are* a better hitter. So get your butt down here right now. You're the next hitter in the lineup."

Well, he stammered and stuttered that he'd have to get his uniform on. I told him to do it on the double and come on back. It turned out this young man had a broken ankle during the season and it had healed slowly, so he didn't run very well. But he could hit! In fact he may have been one of the best hitters we ever had at a camp. Unfortunately he didn't have enough other tools to become a professional ballplayer, but he received every opportunity to show me his stuff and he rose to the occasion. I respect that kind of gumption in a young man.

Late May in Texas is blistering, so after the first cut we stopped play and got everyone out of the midday heat. We usually started up again late in the afternoon and ran the scrimmage games until about ten at night. So a player who came to camp at 8 A.M. on a Saturday normally got in about eight or nine hours of baseball on the first day of camp.

We began the second day before 9 A.M., and if any new players showed up, we put them through drills and hitting. Once that was done, we continued the scrimmage games. They went on all day Sunday, picked up again on Monday morning, and the camp ended early Monday afternoon.

Three hard days of tryout camp really wore me out, but they were probably one of the most rewarding activities of my scouting career. We always had a hospitality suite with food and soft drinks for subscouts, volunteer assistants, secretaries, and high school and college coaches. Of course stories during the bull sessions flew furiously, which only added to the fun.

As a matter of fact, this book came about during one of our

tryout camp scouts bull sessions. Mike Capps and I were sitting around with a few other scouts and the stories were getting bigger, wilder, and louder when Mike stopped me in the midst of one of my tales and said, "Red, I hear you talkin', but we have to put these stories down in a book." That's why you're reading ol' Red's ramblings now.

The camps were extremely productive. Before 1965 we would always sign three to five players from each camp. After the draft we would usually turn up a surprise player who we thought should be drafted, and there would be a good college player or two who showed up looking for a baseball job. We were able to sign some as undrafted free agents and send them out to fill rookie league rosters. A few of those undrafted kids even made it as far as AA ball. All our work was well worth the time and effort and tons of fun to boot.

For most participants, admittedly, it's the last hope they have of impressing someone in baseball, but they still give it everything they have. In our camps I witnessed more than one youngster show blood and guts and extraordinary physical effort, even if he had less-than-average talent. Some of those kids refused to believe they didn't have what it took.

In my career I never shied away from a confrontation with the front office, but the hardest words I ever had to deliver were the heartbreaking ones that made it blatantly clear to a young man that he just was not good enough. That's awfully difficult for a kid to hear from a pro scout, but giving him an honest assessment is the most humane, most respectful way to treat someone who, for the past ten to fifteen years has given his heart and soul to the game. I always tried to be understanding in those circumstances because I have been there myself. Giving up your life's dream is traumatic and very, very touching. That's why I was always committed to giving every youngster who showed up every opportunity to impress me. Those kids never stopped coming, and I admired every one. As in all walks of life, sometimes the dream is just not meant to be.

Even though I often bore bad news, I valued getting to know those who didn't make it because they were the future fans of baseball as well as amateur scouts who might see a youngster someday, somewhere who really can play. I saw all of those kids who attended my tryout camps as additional sets of eyes in the stands, and I encouraged them to call me anytime they saw someone they believed to be a prospect. And they did.

Red's Random Thought . . .

As I sat in the dugout the day before I was to start my first major-league game, I gave myself a pep talk. *You gotta be all business to be here, Red. It doesn't get any bigger or more serious than this.* The next thing I knew, I looked at manager Charlie Grimm and his shoelaces are on fire!

Chapter 22

Dugout Fun

As a young man I never dreamed I'd pitch in the big leagues, become a minor-league manager, or spend more than twelve thousand days of my life scouring nooks and crannies for baseball players. Sure I thought about baseball as a kid, but I recognized at an early age how difficult pitching is at the top level of competition. On top of that, I had a late start in professional baseball and didn't make it to the major leagues until I was thirty-four-years old, an age that usually finds most pitchers well on the downside of their careers.

So I believed I would have to bear down more, be more businesslike and serious about the game if I intended to be successful. I guess I thought if I had that "take no prisoners" attitude, the manager and the pitching coach would think I was really in the game and really a part of the team. Forty years after the fact, it now dawns on me I may have overreacted.

I pitched in the first major-league game I ever saw, a relief appearance on a raw, bitter April afternoon, Opening Day 1956 at County Stadium in Milwaukee against the Cincinnati Reds. We won the game, I received credit for a save, and I found out the next day that I would get a chance to start the third game of the season, two days later against the St. Louis Cardinals. I couldn't believe it. I was a member of what was considered one of the top big-league pitching staffs of that time: Warren Spahn, Lew Burdette, and me. In Texas we call that "in high cotton."

I had the next day off. Dressed in my uniform, a Braves jacket, and heavy gloves to keep my hands warm against the early April Wisconsin chill, I headed out of the clubhouse for the dugout to watch the game. I was starting the next day. I had made the major leagues after winning an almost unbelievable five spring training games and had really impressed myself. I was on a terrific pitching staff, and I was deadly serious about being a very important person.

I had only recently been accepted as one of the guys. Lew Burdette, Warren Spahn, and Gene Conley welcomed me to the pitching staff with open arms and kindly included me whenever they were going out after a game for dinner and a movie. Yet I was still wet behind the ears in early April 1956. I was really new to the scene of major-league ball, and I didn't know about the big-league's more, uh, "subtle" nuances.

My buddies ribbed me, saying I was far too uptight and grim for my own good. They laughed all the time about the dark cloud I seemingly had languishing over my head, and they encouraged me to loosen up. Although I had no way of knowing it, my Braves teammates were about to introduce me to the other side of the game.

As the second game of the 1956 season began, I sat at the far end of the home dugout in County Stadium, down the right-field line, almost by myself. Then I heard something strange and felt some movement under the seat in the dugout.

"Holy moly, what's going on under there?" I questioned aloud.

"Shush, Red," whispered Chet Nichols, a Braves left-hander, who also *thought* left-handed, I might add. Chet was a certifiable loose cannon. His bolts weren't all tightened down, and he had too many screws loose, but he was probably the most dogged instigator of mirth and trouble on the entire Milwaukee ball club. Here is a supposedly adult player under the seats, crawling on his hands and knees from the end of the dugout carrying a cigarette lighter and apparently headed for the spot where manager Charlie Grimm was seated.

"Okay, Chet," I whispered. "Sorry."

He headed off with a glazed look and a mischievous grin, creeping stealthily toward his prey. Charlie was as involved in the game as a manager can get and really prided himself on being unaware of anything going on around him except the game itself.

I peered under the dugout seat and caught Chet's toothy, pyromaniacal grin as he lit the cigarette lighter and applied the yellow-blue flame to the manager's shoe laces. Cold as it was, the laces didn't light, they smoldered. When Charlie leaped to his feet and headed out to the third-base coach's box with every Braves player laughing at his smoking shoes, Charlie never suspected anything was wrong and the potential blaze was extinguished by the dampness of the grass.

While Chet failed to ignite Charlie's shoes, he lit the imagination of his teammates. In the seventh inning, Burdette sneaked down into the tunnel to smoke a cigarette between innings. He was halfway through when Grimm got ready to head for the third-base coach's box again. For a short moment, when the manager stopped to talk to another player, Burdette stuffed the burning butt in one of the big, extrawide belt loops on the back side of Grimm's uniform pants.

As Grimm ran to the coach's box, the cigarette lit up. When he bent over to put his hands on his knees, a spiral of smoke billowed out of the back of his pants. It looked like Charlie Grimm's pants were smoking! Charlie went through his customary series of signs to the first hitter as clouds of smoke poured from his backside. Fans seated in the third-base stands pointed at the incredibly hilarious sight and howled with laughter. Charlie assumed they were laughing at his signs, so like an old vaudeville trouper, he guffawed loudly and then shot a set of made-up signs to the fans. Finally, as his pants appeared to be sending up smoke signals, he good-naturedly waved at those who continued to laugh uproariously.

Finally the cigarette burned itself out. How it kept from setting Charlie's pants on fire, I will never know. Until the day he died, he never knew why those folks had tears streaming down their faces that day in County Stadium.

In the wake of the hullabaloo I began to rethink my future. I had always wondered if I'd ever be able to adjust to life in the business world outside of baseball. I mean, in your wildest dreams, could you ever imagine me giving someone a hotfoot or trying to incinerate my plant manager's pants in Texas City? Certainly not! I'd have been fired on the spot because I wasn't serious enough about my job. I started to realize that baseball was just the place for me, because there is so much camaraderie and so many funny, wacky characters in the game. Hijinks are just as much a part of baseball as fly balls. You just don't hear nearly as many zany stories about people in other professional sports. I mean, can you imagine any member of the Green Bay Packers ever stuffing a lit cigarette in the late, legendary Vince Lombardi's pants? Or any of the Dallas Cowboys doing the same thing to Tom Landry or Jimmy Johnson? Hah! Suddenly baseball became fun to me again, and I learned to relax that frigid April day, after my first (but not my last) brush with outrageousness.

The first time we played the Cardinals in St. Louis, I was about to head down to the bull pen to warm up for my starting assignment. As I stood in the dugout, the St. Louis club was taking infield practice with Stan Musial playing at first base. From behind the water cooler in our dugout, I heard a high-pitched voice squeal, "Stanley, Staaaaanley, your mother wants you. Stanley! Call your mother, she waaaants you."

It was Warren Spahn on the prowl, looking for trouble and hiding behind the dugout water cooler.

"Stanley . . . Stanley . . . your mother wants you," the irritating high-pitched wail continued.

Spahn and Musial spent their careers hooked in a fierce on-the-field rivalry and off the field they continually engaged in friendly antagonism. This time Spahn was doing his best to irritate the Cardinals first baseman, and he was succeeding handsomely. Musial had no idea where the voice was coming from, but he knew good and well who the culprit was.

Stan walked over to the edge of the Milwaukee dugout and hollered, "Spahn, where are you, you hooked-nosed son of a gun?" There Warren was, hunkered down, out of sight, behind the water cooler, and there was no way he was coming out and facing Musial's wrath. Finally a frustrated Stan walked away with no answer from his nemesis.

But Spahn was far from finished. The incessant, "Stanley, Stanley, your mother waaaants you," continued for three or four innings, driving all of us crazy. As competitive as Musial was, there was no way he was going to be shoved over the edge and allow old Spahn any satisfaction. Every time Musial wasn't looking, Spahn would sneak out from behind the water cooler muttering to everyone within earshot, "He's gonna kill me. He's gonna pay me back for this." Spahn escaped Stan's clutches that day, but he knew the paybacks would be costly and painful.

And were they ever.

The next day Spahn faced Musial in the first game of a doubleheader. In his first two at-bats Stan hit doubles off Spahn, and that drove Warren crazy. Stan's third time up, Spahn threw two strikes, then he went to work. To keep Stan from digging in, Spahn sailed a fastball right at Musial's cap, forcing him to duck out of the way. Spahn blew the next pitch right under his enemy's chin, knocking him down. As Stan crawled out of the dirt, he began screaming at Spahn, and Warren screamed back.

Stan got up, dusted himself off, made sure Warren saw him determinedly dig in, and then he slammed the next pitch for a double off the right-center-field wall. As Musial ran the base paths, Spahn followed alongside, shouting at him all the way to second base. The play was close, but Stan slid in safely. When he got up and dusted himself off, he smiled at Spahn and said, "Call me Stanley now. Tell me to call my mother now, you hook-nosed little jerk!" That's the way their ongoing deal went—the jeering and jibing of two future Hall of Famers, just finding little ways of keeping themselves loose in the throes of pressurized battle. While relentless, there was humor and sportsmanship in their rivalry.

They taught me a good lesson about the seriousness of the game. You can't be all business all the time. The season is far too long and so are some careers to take anything in baseball very seriously.

Minor-league dugouts were just as full of goofy characters and zaniness. During my professional career I played in the Evangeline, Gulf Coast, Big State, Texas, American Association, and National League. I made the all-star team in every professional league I played in except the National League, and I prided myself on being able to field my position extremely well.

I played with the same Nokona glove for a dozen years. I called it my Moneymaker, and it played a major role in an escapade late in my playing career. After I had been sent down to Wichita from the big leagues in 1957, I became sort of an elder statesman. We had quite an international crew in Wichita, all with exceptional arms, such as Juan Pizarro of Puerto Rico and Claude Raymond and Ron Piche of Canada. But a great cast of young American arms were also being developed in Wichita that year featuring Joey Jay, Carlton Willey, Ken MacKenzie, and Don Nottebart. I took all those guys under my wing and each day we'd go outside and play Pepper.

Pepper is a great game for developing hand-eye coordination. Players stand in a line and gently pitch the ball to a batter standing about twenty feet away. Quick line drives and quick grounders teach us to field our position properly. Pepper can actually help a pitcher learn to play the sacrifice bunt correctly and perhaps save himself a ball game. Of course nobody plays

Pepper much anymore, but in those days we thought it was an excellent teaching tool. A competitive Pepper game produced its own happy rewards.

In our Pepper game the person who missed a ground ball or line drive went to the end of the line. With the Moneymaker I never missed. *Never.* The loser of our games had to buy Cokes afterward, and I never had to pick up the tab because these guys couldn't beat me or the Moneymaker.

All the guys who played with me had signed for big money bonuses. I teased them about the money belts strapped around their waists, which must have kept them from bending over to field grounders like the Moneymaker could.

One day they told me they'd had enough. They were tired of losing to the Moneymaker, so they planned to stage a ceremony before the Pepper game. We went outside and these guys, with bats and shovels in hand, began a sort of flag corps parade, or funeral march, beginning at home plate, past first base, to some-where way down the right field line where they staged a funeral ceremony and buried my Moneymaker.

Little did they know that I had another Moneymaker I was breaking in; I let them poke a little fun at my expense to build camaraderie. This was the kind of dopey stuff that loosened them up and helped mold them into a real baseball team.

In 1955 our Dallas Eagles Texas League club had that "real baseball" team spirit, even without a group of coaches, like major- and minor-league clubs have today. We had one manager, the manager, and that was it. So starting pitchers who were not pitching on a particular night filled in as first-base coach, and the manager coached third base.

One night we were playing the Oklahoma City Indians in Dallas at Burnett Field, and I was coaching first base for the Eagles. Oklahoma City had a great first and second inning and had a six-run lead when, all of a sudden, the rains came. Not a deluge, just a hard, steady rain, and the umpires allowed the game to continue.

Between innings I had the bat boy run back to the clubhouse and grab an umbrella. When I went out to the coaching box at the beginning of the next inning, I took along the umbrella and stood under it trying to make a point to the umpires that they needed to stop the game. They ignored me and it seemed like only the fans behind the first-base dugout knew what was going on, and they were laughing their heads off.

The next thing I know, the first-base ump looks over at me and says, "Hey, Murff, you can't do that. You can't have that umbrella out here. Take it down. Take it down *now*. And go put it in the dugout!"

"Gosh," I said, feigning disbelief. "Is that in the rule book? I never saw a rule that said you couldn't have an umbrella in a downpour, ump. Didn't your mother always tell you to put on your raincoat and take your umbrella when you went out to play in the rain when you were a little feller?"

Just then, Oklahoma City manager Tommy Tatum spotted me and my rain gear and he began to squawk. Why he did it, I'll never know. His team was on its way to a victory and the last thing he needed was trouble.

"Kick him out! Kick Murff out! Just kick him out of the game!" Tatum yelled at the ump.

I folded the umbrella, handed it to the bat boy, and went back to the coaching box as Tatum continued his tirade.

"Kick him out for mocking you. He's mocking you. He's mocking your decision to play in the rain. It's your decision not his!" he screamed at the umpire, "Get him out of here."

"Shut up and sit down, Tommy, or I'll run you out of here," the ump yelled back. "We've got it taken care of, so mind your own business."

Well, as fate would have it, Dallas staged the comeback of comebacks. Within an inning we tied the game and then went ahead by one run when manager Dutch Meyer came looking for me.

"Can you warm up quickly and go in and hold this lead?" he asked.

"Sure, no problem," I said.

I did my job by striking out the first two batters and forcing the third batter to hit an easy grounder to the shortstop for the final out. The fact that I got into the game and held the lead sent the Oklahoma City manager into a frothing frenzy.

"He shouldn't have even been in the game! He was mocking you and mocking your decision to play in the rain!" Tatum screamed at the umpire. "You should've run him and his umbrella out, early on, but no, you let him stay and he beats us! I'm filing a protest with the league office!"

"Fine, file it," the ump said. "We told him to take away his umbrella and he did it. Red may have been right. Stopping the game might have been a good idea. But he didn't get thrown out, shouldn't have been thrown out, therefore, it was perfectly legal for him to pitch. So file your protest."

Of course no protest was filed, but I never did take an umbrella out to the coaching box again.

Red's Random Thought . . .

After you find the first Nolan Ryan, you think you'll never find another. But if you're worth your salt as a scout, you never give up, you keep looking. The first time I saw Todd Van Poppell, I thought I'd been struck by lightning twice!

Chapter 23

Lightning Strikes Twice (Maybe)

As far as I can tell, not a lot of good comes from losing games at the major-league level. Losing creates all sorts of problems between the players themselves, between players and management, and between the players and the fans. In their own quiet way major-league scouts can turn around a losing team, but it takes time.

In 1989 my team, the Atlanta Braves, finished the season in the National League West cellar. In fact the Braves had the worst record in baseball that year. That meant that we would have the number-one choice in the 1990 free-agent draft. More importantly it meant the Braves would be getting the young man they believed would be the best free-agent player in the country, someone who could become a true building-block for the club's future. I knew who that player was more than a year before the 1990 draft.

I first saw Todd Van Poppell when he was fifteen years old and had just finished his first year in high school. He was pitching for his Arlington club in a summer league tournament in McKinney, Texas. Todd pitched much better than his senior teammates. In fact the first time I turned a radar gun on one of his fastballs, it clocked ninety-two miles an hour! From a fifteen-year-old!

The next year I saw the sophomore pitch against another professional prospect, and Todd threw the ball two miles an hour faster than his opponent. He never had to strain to throw the ball that way either. Todd was six-four and he had that smooth, loose motion that told me he'd only get faster as he matured. His fluidity also meant he would be an unlikely candidate for arm problems. He was the closest thing I had seen to Nolan Ryan. In fact no one I ever saw besides Nolan was anywhere near as fast.

After watching him pitch three or four times, I backed off. I knew other scouts were watching and there was no sense trying to hide out this kid. We'd had the draft for years, and Todd played in Arlington, Texas, just a stone's throw from the Texas Rangers ballpark. I knew he'd attract tons of attention, even as a sophomore in high school. I decided to move quietly, and I tried never to come around when I knew there would be a pack of scouts watching him. I often tracked the young man through newspaper accounts only.

By Todd's junior year in high school, I had struck up a friendship with his father Hank. In fact he once told me the family had only allowed two scouts into their home the whole time Todd played high school ball, and I was one of them. I liked Hank Van Poppell. He was a first-class business executive in the Dallas-Fort Worth area and he was a really friendly fellow to deal with. He was enjoying the attention his son was getting. I liked Todd too, both as a young man and as a pitcher. Hank let me know early on, though, that he intended for Todd to go to college and not sign a professional contract. When he first told me that, I had no idea how serious he was, but I didn't give up.

In November 1989 I was inducted into the Texas Baseball Hall of Fame in ceremonies at the Arlington Convention Center, and I asked Nolan Ryan to introduce me. Weeks before the ceremonies I extended an invitation to Todd and his family to be there. Of course there was method in my madness. At that point, just before Todd's senior high school season, I knew the Braves would be getting the number-one choice in the 1990 draft, and I was convinced if Todd and his family went to the induction ceremony that I might be able to do something to sell the Van Poppells on the idea of professional baseball, specifically the Atlanta Braves.

About a week before the ceremony I called Braves scouting director Paul Snyder in Atlanta and told him about my plan. We both knew that Todd was a certain first-round choice. I explained that I believed the Braves should make it very clear to the Van Poppell family, in public, that we and not some college coach would be the ones to make Todd a number-one draft choice. I've seen it happen so many times that a college coach will recruit a great young player by promising to turn the young man into a number-one choice. That's not the way it works. I wanted the Van Poppell family to know that the Braves planned to make Todd their first choice, no questions asked, something a college coach could never have the power to accomplish.

Right after Nolan introduced me to the crowd and I acknowledged the applause, I made a couple of opening remarks and threw the dice.

"Would Todd Van Poppell please stand up?" I asked. "I want all you baseball fans in the Dallas-Fort Worth area to meet one of the finest young arms in the game today. In all my years scouting since I found Nolan Ryan, Todd Van Poppell is the only young man I've ever seen who has the capabilities that might one day allow him to challenge some of Nolan Ryan's records. And if the June baseball draft was tomorrow morning, Todd would be the Atlanta Braves number-one draft choice, the number one in the nation!"

Mike Capps was sitting with the Atlanta scouting contingent at a table several rows away from the Van Poppells and he said my remarks caught all the scouts off guard. Once he regained his composure, one of my colleagues uttered, "Red doesn't know it, but he just cost the Braves an additional four hundred thousand dollars by telling the kid that!" I don't think Hank Van Poppell was surprised by my remarks one bit.

I'm glad I made my pronouncement, but once Todd's season began, his father was still saying forget it to every scout who asked. "Todd," his father promised, "will be attending the University of Texas on a baseball scholarship. It's a waste of a major-league team's time and effort to draft him." That caused most big-league teams to back off. But not the Braves.

Shortly before Todd's senior year, I met with Braves scouts Charley Smith, Ralph Garr, and Joe Campise along with Braves general manager Bobby Cox and scouting director Paul Snyder. Just like the meeting Red Gaskill and I had before the beginning of Nolan Ryan's senior year, we made our plans for scouting Todd Van Poppell. Just like the Murff-Gaskill plan, the Braves planned to see Todd pitch every inning of every game that year. After that meeting I told one of the Braves national cross-checkers to buy as much Delta stock as he could afford. I told him, "You are going to be spending a lot of time flying from Atlanta to Dallas-Fort Worth to see Mr. Van Poppell."

Scout him we did. Just as we planned, either I or another Braves scout saw every pitch Todd threw in his senior year. His whole season never discouraged us. His fastball was great. We clocked it at ninety-five miles an hour. He was developing a breaking pitch. Todd displayed composure far beyond his eighteen years. He easily was the Braves number-one pick until 2 P.M. on a June Sunday, one day before the draft.

During the final hours before the draft, Bobby Cox and I kept in constant contact with Hank Van Poppell. We made the family a generous contract and bonus offer. I don't know the exact figures, but I have heard it was in the neighborhood of $1.2 million. The family, however, continued to insist that they were not going to sign, that Todd was going to honor his scholarship to the University of Texas.

I have no proof, but I will always believe a player-agent was helping the Van Poppells decide. The instructions were apparently very, very clear. "Tell the scouts you won't sign. Don't let anyone think you are going to sign and do everything in your power to dissuade the major-league people from believing you will sign."

The Van Poppells' attitude placed the Braves in an awkward position. As the worst team in baseball that year, we desperately needed to pick up some top talent with that number-one choice, talent that would commit to signing a contract with us. The Braves simply could not run the risk of drafting a youngster who would never sign.

At 2 P.M. on Sunday, with the draft less than twenty-four hours away, Bobby Cox and I dejectedly got in my car and left our Arlington hotel, having made our best offer. We were mentally exhausted, and the Van Poppells had stood firm. If drafted, Todd would not sign, his father decisively insisted. On the way to the airport, Bobby stopped and made a phone call to Paul Snyder in Atlanta.

"Put Chipper at the top of the list," Cox instructed. That's how Florida high school infielder Chipper Jones replaced Todd Van Poppell as the Braves number-one choice. For Atlanta the pick turned out to be a great one. Despite losing the 1994 season to injury, Chipper Jones appears to be a potentially great major-league player. Unless he's seriously injured, he should have a fifteen-year career.

The Oakland A's took Todd Van Poppell with the fourteenth pick in the first round. Even after the draft, Hank Van Poppell continued to insist that his son was going to the University of Texas, so you can imagine how surprised a lot of baseball people were when the A's flew the family to California and Todd signed a contract.

To this day the Van Poppell case remains a mystery to me. I don't know what happened to make them change their minds. I am certain we offered more money than the A's. I am convinced the Braves would've been a better organization to develop and nurture Todd's pitching talents. He's struggled but still has great stuff and may one day turn out to be the second coming of Nolan. As the old cliché goes, only time will tell.

The same day Todd signed with Oakland, sportswriters' calls lit up my telephone. Was I upset? Had the Van Poppells pulled a fast one? Was Todd's dad a liar? Had they violated any draft rules or the spirit of the draft rules? Were the Braves set up? Was there a conspiracy against the baseball establishment?

I answered all those questions the same way, with an emphatic no. "An eighteen-year-old," I explained, "has the right to change his mind. He has the right to sign a professional baseball contract rather than go to a senior college and waste two valuable years of development. What Todd Van Poppell and his dad did does not upset me at all."

From the Braves standpoint you have to ask, what if they had drafted Van Poppell and he had not signed? They would almost assuredly have lost Todd *and* Chipper Jones. The Braves did the right thing in moving on to Chipper Jones, and I guess the Van Poppells figure they did the right thing.

Still I can't help wondering about them and the many other families who have agonized over this kind of thing, knowing how very important each move is to a young man's career. Do the Van Poppells now secretly wish they'd have signed with Atlanta and taken advantage of that club's incredible pitching development program? I also can't help thinking that maybe, just maybe, the second Nolan Ryan *did* get away from me. But then in the quiet bottom of my soul I always smile, knowing that Red Murff got the real thing.

Red's Random Thought . . .

I didn't come into this game starry-eyed. I quickly became a student of it, and I know this: Baseball needs strong leadership that is unafraid to make a critical decision, unafraid to ruffle the owners' or players' feathers but capable of building a consensus among ownership, players, and fans. Right now the game is a rudderless, engineless, leaderless ship adrift in a stormy, stormy sea, fast approaching the rocks.

Chapter 24

Back to the Basics

I am a product of what was arguably the grandest generation in baseball. I entered the game when memories of the Great Depression lingered and World War II had barely ended. A time believed by many to be the game's golden age. Major League Baseball was confined mainly to the East Coast. Because there were only sixteen teams at the top level, that meant only the cream of the crop played in the big leagues. Ballplayers played for their livelihoods, of course, but more importantly they loved the game and cherished their relationships with the fans.

Ballplayers who had survived D-Day and Iwo Jima and Okinawa felt privileged to get another chance to play. As a result these players possessed impeccable habits and work ethics. The attitude in the 1950s was simple: Work hard, learn from your elders. If you don't, you'll lose your job and your family will starve. Players from my generation took the time and made the effort to learn how to play the game correctly. For so many the game became their life.

We were lucky to have come along then. Vets knew what they had fought for. Baseball was so ingrained into the American way of life that the very liberty to play the game for a living was a major part of what they risked life and limb for during those terrifyingly bloody years. One of my friends who had fought on Guadalcanal told me that thoughts of making an important play in a big game, the thought of getting hold of one and knocking it out of the park, kept him going through some bitterly tough, cruel battles. Are there those who think baseball didn't really mean something to my generation? It meant more to us than people today will ever know.

Players in my day had their animosities and heated rivalries. Fights broke out between players on opposing clubs and some teams even had those who bickered relentlessly among themselves. During my glory days, 1950–59, I never heard a player talk badly about the game itself. Now, unfortunately, you hear gripy, whiny, selfish rich kids complaining all the time about how bad they have it. Hah!

The fans were different then too. The marketing boys hadn't gotten hold of the game with special giveaway nights like Bat Night, Ball Night, or Pennant Night, all of which today's fans have come to assume as their due. All any fan in that era wanted to see was the game played at the peak of a player's skills, with few if any mental mistakes. Fans didn't expect The Chicken. They demanded that players know how to play and always be mentally in the ball game. During the golden era of baseball, that's what players gave the audience. I believe we need to get back to those basics.

As baseball expanded to Houston and New York in the National League and Washington and Los Angeles in the American League, I watched attitudes slowly begin to shift about the same time that American automobiles started to sprout fins. Sometime in the early 1960s the talent pool thinned as young players badly in need of minor-league seasoning were rushed to the big leagues and forced to learn to play the game under major-league pressure. *Inept, hapless,* and *disgusting* were adjectives used by sportswriters to describe the play of the Mets and the Colt .45s, two of the early 1960s expansion clubs.

Sportswriters began to take on the Win! WIN! WIN! football mentality and became jaded and caustic, using more critical, judgmental, and generally crueler words than did the sportswriters of previous generations. The game's heart beat with an unsteady rhythm. Ballplayers, management, and even scouts expect harsh analysis and criticism from sportswriters, but it's extremely difficult to accept sometimes because the criticism comes from those who never played the game themselves. Although there have been some tremendously talented sportswriters in the past thirty years like Frank Deford, Will McDonough, Roger Angell, and Sally Jenkins, too many other men and women seemed to have no idea how difficult a game baseball is to master, or even to appreciate how many games it takes to get to the World Series. They don't realize that you have to lose a lot to win.

So much of baseball is about overcoming failure. If you win 60 percent of the time, you will win the pennant, but that still means you lose 40 percent of the time. Many major-league clubs have equal talent, but with the early expansion clubs we saw new towns with novice sportswriters who often didn't understand that the difference in winning and losing baseball often came down to whose players were the healthiest or which player had the best year of his career and carried a team further than it should have gone. They also started to focus on celebrity and personality rather than skills.

Writers who don't know baseball have a hard time appreciating that an extremely successful hitter fails seven hundred times out of a thousand. They don't comprehend that the Mets were not the first team in big-league history to lose one hundred games. In the 1960s this kind of reporter couldn't understand the Colt .45s management had little if any talent to compete with on the major-league level. That didn't seem to matter. The ringing criticism never relented.

Compare the early problems of the Mets and the intense scrutiny they were under to a situation that occurred only a few years before in my 1955 twenty-seven-win season with the Dallas Eagles. A foul tip broke the right thumb of our Texas League all-star catcher Ray Murray, and he was lost for the season. Murray's loss was personally difficult because he was a great handler of pitchers and he knew my pitching style better than anyone.

To replace Murray, Dallas management brought in a young man named Nick Testa and put him in the lineup. Immediately Texas League pitchers began giving young Nick fits. He couldn't buy a base hit. In fact, during the entire thirty games he played for Dallas, Nick got only one, *one*, base hit. Everyone on the ball club, all the fans, even the sportswriters were pulling for him to break out of the slump. Nick kept the negative press away by always hustling, always fielding his position, always throwing out base runners, and always, always smiling and associating with the fans. Mr. Popularity. When Nick finally got a base hit, the fans gave him a standing ovation and made him feel welcome. Dallas pitcher Joe Kotrany, who was coaching first base, called time-out and asked the umpire for the ball and even handed it to Nick! Can you imagine how a young man like that, suffering through such an dismal hitting slump, would survive now in the big leagues? The 1990s press corps would ride him out of town and destroy him.

Even though the press often gave them a rough time, the early Mets were the fans' darlings but not for the right reasons. It was very evident the novelty of having the worst team in the world could only have a certain amount of appeal and New York's fans seemed to love that. They loved Casey Stengel's antics, even though his club's play was a sorry joke. Of course many New York fans felt jilted when they lost the Giants to San Francisco and the Dodgers to Los Angeles only three years before expansion. Those National League-hungry fans were ready to cheer for any- one in a uniform with the words *New York* on it.

• • • • • • • • • • •

By about 1963 baseball owners and general managers began to feel critical pressure because a great many mistakes were being made by clubs reacting the wrong way to negative publicity. Baseball executives worried excessively about the public's opinion of their clubs instead of developing talent and giving fans the best-trained product on the field.

I think it was in this era that the mistrust between players and management began to build to the crescendo that has yet to abate. Owners now consider themselves the stars of the show, and the fans react negatively in some cases to their shenanigans. Charley Finley and his pet mule drew more attention to himself than to his ball club when he moved the A's from Kansas City to Oakland. Ted Turner did the same thing when he decided he could be a field manager.

Now Milwaukee owner Bud Seelig thinks he can run baseball as its acting commissioner. White Sox owner Jerry Reinsdorf prevented Gaylord Broadcasting from buying the Texas Rangers and putting them on their Dallas-Fort Worth superstation, then Reinsdorf arrogantly turned around and put his White Sox on the Chicago superstation. He's the same mover and shaker who later helped cause the 234-day baseball strike. While we're criticizing ownership, let's not forget the George Steinbrenner show in New York and his latest soap opera, *I Love Drug-Abusing Ballplayers.* Those owners who seem to prefer to replace their players in the headlines are just plain dumb if they think the game revolves around their pinky rings. It doesn't.

I'd like to see Steinbrenner *try* to hit a Nolan Ryan fastball. I'd bet the house that Seelig can't hit the cutoff man. I know beyond a shadow of a doubt that Reinsdorf can't steal a base or stretch a single into a double. Ownership must learn to be smart enough to stay out of the limelight. They can massage their massive egos in ways other than seeing their names in the headlines. More than a year after the 1994 strike began, the owners and the players still have not resolved any of the issues that brought on the labor stoppage. One of the players deeply involved in negotiations, Brett Butler of the Mets, told *USA Today* he believed baseball would never be the same, that the fans would not forgive. The owners themselves are crying in their milk, claiming they will have lost somewhere between six hundred and eight hundred million dollars as a result of the strike and the backlash of the fans staying away from the ballpark. It's hard to feel sorry for anyone in this situation. They brought it on themselves!

All is not lost in the entire ranks of ownership, however. I certainly admire the tact Astros owner Drayton McLane has taken. He hired a veteran baseball man in Bob Watson to run his club and began holding management accountable for all its actions. There's no buck-passing in the Houston organization, and others should take note.

· · · · · · · · · · ·

I'm not letting the players off the hook for baseball's current troubles. Both parties didn't care about anyone else and carried this latest labor dispute to ridiculous lengths all because of simple greed and selfishness, completely ignoring the fact that the ones who really pay the freight are the fans. Besides the fans, the ones who really suffered during the strike were those front-office people and ballpark concessionaires and all the ones peripherally involved in staging the games. They were laid off during the strike and lost badly needed money. You can't blame those folks for resenting baseball's ownership and players.

I think the players and owners owe the fans one simple thing. An apology. Are ya'll listening? Without the people who love the game there is no future. As of this writing no agreement has been reached on a new labor contract, and fans have no guarantee there won't be another strike. In my opinion baseball is headed down a treacherous path. One more player strike and the sport might lose whatever fan base it has left.

The average American workingman or woman simply cannot relate to players who make an average salary of slightly more than a million dollars a year yet feel the need to charge kids a fee for an autograph. Over the decades one of baseball's charms was the fact that fans viewed ballplayers as well-paid, hard-working, blue-collar characters much like themselves. It's not that way anymore. No one can understand this cry-baby song and dance from men playing a kid's game with the best equipment in the finest parks anywhere. A caller to a Dallas radio sports talk show recently told the host, "Hey, baseball will never get me back in a park. They took my game away from me. All of them, every single one, owners and the players, are a crude, vulgar, greedy bunch of spoiled brats. They ruined my game, and I hate them for it!"

That broke my heart because that caller is only one of millions of American baseball fans who are convinced their game has been cruelly taken away by people who just don't care about anything but money. Baseball must give disaffected fans a reason to change their minds and turn around this perception fast. A thousand bat nights or a million "Chickens" aren't going to scratch the surface of the problem. Diehard older fans, the ones who pass the game's wonder on to youngsters, were raised in the days when players were happy to sign autographs and talk to the fans, when in turn fans were indulged and honored in the right way by players who cared about honing and displaying their craft. Baseball, unlike any other professional sport, allowed its fans to get close to the players, or at least it did once. Those fans are some of the most bitter ones because they know the difference between these players and those from earlier generations and they can't share the same experiences they had with their grandchildren.

Here's a message from a fiery old baseball man and many of his friends: To the players and owners, go back and study how the Branch Rickeys of the world built this game. They developed players the right way. They kept them in the minor leagues for years, really learning their craft. The result? They gave the fans an appealing game of truly special skills, played by normal-sized, gifted athletes and men whom fans could relate to, not some giant seven-foot-tall- or steroid-infested hulk. It's the fans who are suffering, and you guys aren't doing anything significant to win them back.

I don't understand why it's not easy to be appreciative of the fans. Does it take backbreaking effort to be nice to people and to sign a few autographs? Certainly not. I think clubs should require their players and coaches to sign autographs for the fans on the field, before games, for at least an hour a week. I think that's a start. It would be so much better if the players themselves had the decency to take this responsibility upon themselves, but that's not likely to happen. Make the players do it or fine them if they don't. Make the fines substantial, not some hundred-dollar joke.

I don't understand why players can't take the time to visit with the fans in the stands. Why not come over to the stands after batting practice and chat with some fans? What would that hurt?

I am so embarrassed for the game of baseball when I hear callers to radio talk shows who echo a similar complaint to this one. A young man in Dallas, despondent about the game, called in to tell the host that he had relented and decided to give base-ball one more chance. So he bought good tickets and took his eight-year-old son to a Rangers-Yankees game. He dressed the youngster in a Yankees cap and T-shirt, armed him with pen and ball, and stood the boy in the stands right behind the Yankee dugout forty-five minutes before game time to get some auto-graphs from his heroes, the Yankees.

According to the caller, several Yankees glanced at the little guy who was waving his pen and ball frantically, calling each player by name, and begging them to sign. But no Yankee could find it in his heart to do even this small courtesy. Only one Texas Rangers player, who had spotted the teary-eyed youngster, came over from the other dugout and signed the kid's ball. Shame on the Yankees and shame on baseball for allowing players to ignore fans, especially a kid with stars in his eyes! I've heard all the insipid arguments that some players won't sign because some autograph seekers are only trying to make money from their signatures. Too bad. What about the players who charge exorbitant sums to sit and sign at card shows? Baseball is in too much trouble for its players to shirk the fans. What has happened to the people playing my game? I am astounded every time I hear a story like that, and unfortunately I hear more and more stories like that about baseball's heroes.

Today's players could learn something from Ray Murray, the catcher with the Dallas Eagles in the 1950s. Before Ray was hurt and once he finished his pregame work, he belonged to the fans. Whether we were at home at old Burnett Field in Dallas or on the road, the fans always had a chance to visit with Ray and he would always make them feel welcome. The Dallas fans knew him so well, they'd ask about his family and he'd ask about theirs. Some days he would sit on the dugout steps, invite the kids over, show them his catcher's gear, and then give them playing tips for Little League. Once in a while he'd turn his bat upside down and begin strumming it like a guitar, serenading nearby fans with one of his favorite country music songs. Corny? Maybe. But the fans loved the interaction, and Ray figured he owed them something for coming out to the ballpark day in and day out and cheering for him. Ray knew who paid his salary! He made them feel like a big part of the game, and he truly brought baseball closer to the paying customers. Our young millionaires today apparently think we owe them everything and they owe us nothing.

Just because today's players are multimillionaires and have no financial worries, they are not so far above everyone else that they cannot give something back to the game. This is the most blessed baseball generation ever, financially, and they owe their existence to the people sitting in the stands. Their days will be further numbered if they don't start realizing who pays their inflated salaries. Look at the television ratings, especially for the last all-star game, and don't forget this game is operating without a national television contract. A lot of folks are trying to tell the players something. They are so turned off by players who act churlishly, they're turning off their televisions. If more television revenue is lost, I hope the millionaire players have put enough cash away to see them through the corporate cutbacks. Today's players need to get with it or risk losing what they have. Take it from old Red, they need to apologize to their fans and show their appreciation for the fans' loyalty. When that happens, the fans will be back in the ballparks in droves.

Those people who pay their hard-earned money to underwrite this game have simply had to put up with too many sideshows while watching watered-down talent on the field. In return they're asked to pay increasing prices for a product that is badly flawed. Fans stayed away in record numbers at the beginning of the 1995 season. Do the owners think this is a fluke? Do they understand what the fans are saying?

There are a few exceptions. Mo Vaughn with the Red Sox and Frank Thomas with the White Sox constantly devote time, energy, and money to kids' programs in their cities, and they buy thousands of dollars' worth of tickets each season so underprivileged kids can see a big-league game. Unfortunately those great guys are rare exceptions, and I don't see a lot of evidence that either the players or the owners are doing anything about helping the game regain its place as the national pastime.

• • • • • • • • • •

"Okay, Murff," you're saying, "you think you're so smart. Solve the problems."

I'd be glad to, but before I start, please understand that I love this game, and when I criticize what's going on it's only done in a constructive manner. I want the game to make a comeback, but some positive things have to happen first.

First baseball must address its leadership problems. Appointing a commissioner won't do it. The game of baseball must reinvent its management structure and run itself through a three-member baseball commission. The minutia of this plan must be developed and refined by the owners and the players union, but one man simply cannot run a sport that has become so complicated. The man currently trying to run the sport cannot remain in charge. He's an owner, and as such he has an automatic conflict of interest. It's human nature to be prejudiced toward fellow owners.

THE SCOUT

The temptation is to say, "Well, why don't we find one old, tough bird like Judge Kennesaw Mountain Landis? Landis ran baseball with an iron fist during the 1919 Black Sox scandal that tarnished the game when some White Sox players threw the World Series. He stayed on through World War II. As tough as he was and as much authority as he wielded, he only answered to sixteen owners, not thirty rich, egomaniacal businessmen. When the Judge ruled the roost, the reserve clause, binding players to their original clubs, was still baseball's backbone. Landis's job wasn't complicated by intricate, confusing television contracts, player unions, negotiating committees, player strikes, and constant media attention. One-third of the game's survival issues can be solved within a commission. The idea of a single commissioner is terribly outdated and unrealistic.

Some sage once said that baseball is a mirror of society. I think that's right, and I think baseball can make positive changes and become the proper example for our kids and for society. In my opinion this commission must set a new moral agenda for the sport, and this begins with better policing of drug and other criminal violations. Tougher penalties for baseball's criminal element must be at the top of the priority list. There should be no room in the clubhouse for repeat drug offenders. What kind of a message does it send to kids and to drug offenders that all one has to do is go on television and cry some alligator tears and babble an apology? Suddenly he is back in the lineup again, and I don't care how good he is, he shouldn't be there. One strike and you're out! If you get caught with drugs at your home or workplace, how long do you think your boss would keep you on the payroll? Is it too much to expect top-flight players to exercise enough discipline to stay away from drugs, drug dealers, and anyone involved with drugs? Ownership has become too lenient with men who should be in either rehab clinics or jail. The public thinks baseball's drug policy—if there really is such a thing—is about as effective as treating Alzheimer's with aspirin. I'm talking about policing misuse of all drugs and that includes alcohol and tobacco. In stepping up this policing effort, the sport is showing America that it is setting the highest possible ethical standards and setting the proper example for its younger fans. I don't care what any of today's players think. Like it or not, gentlemen, you are role models for kids, whether you accept that responsibility or not. The old saying goes, You can't legislate morals. Well, it says here in the Murff manual that baseball must!

Unfortunately the sport lost a potentially great leader in Bart Giamatti who appeared to be on the way to fulfilling the requirements I'm talking about. He suspended Pete Rose from the game for life for betting on baseball. That was a positive step toward turning around the sport's image, but we need more. We must get tougher on baseball's criminal element and purge it from the game.

This commission must also have the personal courage to stand up to both ownership and the players union and force them to settle all labor differences by signing a solid contract of ten years or more in length. They must make a serious commitment to the fans, ensuring that the game won't be interrupted in the foreseeable future. The fans are sick of this nonsense. Baseball left its loyal spectators at the altar one time too many, and now the game better get the ring on its fingers or forget about it. The fans will find some other sport—football, soccer, basketball, hockey—to cheer for.

As soon as I mention a commission to please the fans, the owners will scream, No way! We have too much money invested! Really? Where do your profits come from? The fans and the advertisers. You don't have one penny in your coffers that isn't somehow related to the fans or their interests.

This commission must be empowered to work out business deals that will allow Major League Baseball to be played worldwide. Given how easy it is to travel, there's no reason why major-league ball shouldn't be played in Tokyo, Moscow, Rome, London, Barcelona, Rio de Janeiro, Sydney, Mexico City, Caracas, or anywhere fan interest is sufficient enough to support such a venture. Once such worldwide play is established, we truly could have a legitimate World Series.

To work out the details of how this commission would be chosen, include the players union and owners in finding a top-notch, independent headhunter who can accept candidates from both parties. Representatives from the groups could gather and secretly vote on the strongest candidates available, and the three with the most votes win. This system worked for the Founding Fathers, so it can work for baseball.

Once the commission is chosen, its membership should sit down with the players and help them decide if they've really got the kind of union in place that will benefit them and the game for the next fifty years. I think a change is in order. Too much animosity, too much angst, and too much grief has filtered from Donald Fehr through the player ranks and into the game. I think it may be time for a change, not only in union leadership, but in the way the union itself operates. But that's up to the commissioners and the players. Both parties need to keep in mind that bad faith negotiations and labor troubles have done nothing to endear anyone in baseball to the fans.

Past that, I think the commission must find a way to end the arbitration process and force players and management to agree to sign ballplayers to one-year contracts only. Now I realize that will upset those who play the game, but the idea makes sound economic sense. If ballplayers are forced to give it their all from year to year, they'll have no choice but to produce. If they don't, forget salary increases. It's called a work ethic.

Those little mechanical adjustments will only signal the beginning of the healing process for baseball. Since scouting is my area of expertise, we've got a load of player procurement problems to solve. Baseball must begin to recruit more former professional players and managers into the scouting ranks and make it attractive enough financially so they'll stay. We have too many scouts who have little or no professional playing experience, too many who aren't craftsmen in the scouting profession. They don't work independently, using their own wits, instincts, and personal knowledge. Instead scouting has become a game of copycat.

When an Arlington, Texas, college-league coach found out we were writing a book about the scouting profession he said, "Well, I hope you mention that too many scouts are looking over each other's shoulders, trying to find out who's a ballplayer and who isn't." He's right. They do. We did.

If part-time coaches are noticing the scouts' lack of conviction and individuality and ability to make player judgments, then it truly is a problem. I fear too many of today's younger scouts listen to a bunch of gossip about prospective ballplayers they've never seen and then write the names of a thousand ballplayers into the club's scouting computer bank. I never turned in the names of more than a dozen ballplayers in my region during a given year, and that's about the number today's scouts should be filing. Those kids should be surefire big-league prospects who the scouts have seen and evaluated personally. No more paying attention to hearsay.

I'll give you a couple of cases in point. Two years after I retired from scouting, I saw a young catcher named Casey Smith from Newman-Smith High School in Carrollton, Texas, in the Dallas-Fort Worth area who was a junior in high school. This kid had it all. He could run, throw, and hit. He was tall, lean, strong, and almost cocky. I mentioned to a scout friend that someone needed to take a look at Casey during his senior year. Well, someone did way too early in the season when he didn't have a good game. The scouting grapevine began to talk, and almost immediately a young man who, in my opinion, should have had a good shot to be drafted, was being undermined by gossip. Scouts unfairly voiced excuse after excuse. Someone said Casey had a bad attitude. Another said he couldn't handle pitchers. All this after having seen this kid only once. It's extremely easy to disqualify a young player who may have talent.

Mike Capps saw Casey during a high school playoff game, loved his talents, and then started asking Newman-Smith fans some questions about the young catcher. Had scouts been look-ing at him? Did they like him? Why not? Did he have a college scholarship? Mike called me to brag about finding Casey, and between us we sort of made it a secondary job to find someone to take a look at him, but we couldn't get anyone interested.

In the late summer of 1995 Mike was talking with an editor at Word, Nancy Norris. She told him about her son, Stephen. He was six-three and 185 pounds and pitched a ninety-five-mile-per-hour fastball. He had been a pitcher at Texas A&M but had transferred to Tyler Junior College. Now Mike has been around me long enough and is a good enough scout to know how skep-tical I am of parents' claims about their sons, so he really didn't believe all of what Nancy said. He had to see this player himself. Mike politely asked Nancy if her son would pitch for him. She okayed it, and Mike took Stephen and a catcher's mitt to a nearby ballpark. Before they were through, Mike was convinced. Stephen had a fastball that was alive, that moved down and out and up and in, and he was fast, really fast! His fastballs tore up Mike's mitt, hit Mike on the knee, and bent Mike's thumb back three different times! Mike called me excitedly, saying, "Red! Red! This kid can really throw!"

I arranged for Mike and Stephen to meet me in Belton, Texas, at Mary Hardin Baylor University—Red Murff Field, of course—so Stephen could throw for me. Mike brought Casey Smith along because he had had all the physical punishment he could handle trying to catch for Stephen earlier.

Stephen Norris proved to me that Mike was right. I had the Mary Hardin Baylor coach bring out his radar gun, and Stephen consistently hit ninety-two miles an hour. After we were done, I sidled up to Mike and said, "Hey, he really can throw!"

Mike replied, "Well, heck, Red, did you think I was lying?"

"No, but I figured if you could catch him, he wasn't throwing very hard."

Mike has yet to forgive me for that remark because he thinks he can still play at age forty-four. But he was right about

Stephen. Here are the scouting reports we filed on Stephen and Casey:

> Stephen Norris: Strong-shouldered, handsome athlete, outstanding arm strength. Norris has the physical potential to be a major-league starting pitcher. His mechanics and ease of delivery enhance his tenure and productivity in the major leagues. This young player wants to sign today!

> Casey Smith: Excellent build for rugged duty. Good hands with quick feet. Needs to work on blocking pitches and mental determination to catch every pitch thrown. Front liner!

We projected Casey as a late second-round draft choice and Stephen as a late first-rounder. But no one else thought so. Mike and I cannot wait to see how well these young men do in junior college and beyond. I just wonder what is going on in a profession that missed these two excellent prospects.

The above stories are just one more reason the scouting grapevine must be replaced with the lone-wolf mentality and scouts must become better baseball ambassadors. Instead of sitting in the stands at ball games with a tightly knit group of their peers, scouts should spread out, away from their buddies, visit with fans, pass out business cards, and talk to people. You never know, you might find out about another ballplayer who might be a better prospect than the one you think you've cornered.

To survive and prosper, baseball also must find ways of attracting the great athletes of all races and backgrounds who are being led toward basketball and football. I realize baseball is a harder game to play and a harder game to practice, but great inner-city and small-town athletes are being drawn into these other sports, not knowing all of the personal and financial rewards baseball offers. Our scouts need to spend more time in backwater places and urban ballparks talking to young players and explaining the merits of a baseball career. Its longevity, camaraderie, monetary rewards, and, most of all, its wonderful, loyal fans. Better public relations for baseball is needed in those areas immediately.

While we're on the scouting subject, let's open up a long overdue can of worms. We need to go back to a system in baseball where real scouts are at work. I mean real scouts in the sense that we return to the days when scouts operated independently.

"Well, Murff," you're thinking, "sounds like you want to do away with the amateur draft?"

Precisely.

I can hear the uproar already but bear with me a moment and listen to my reasoning. If baseball rids itself of the amateur draft, it immediately cuts the cost of player procurement. How? If you eliminate the draft, you find ballplayers and sign them as soon as possible, before the scouting pack or grapevine finds them, before their names appear in *Baseball America*, before the scouting grapevine falsely upgrades their monetary worth. I'm not criticizing *Baseball America*. It's a fine newspaper, containing loads of valuable information, but when its writers get hold of information from scouts and begin to write about these unproven kids, parents get an inflated sense of their son's worth, and everybody stops looking at how to develop a kid's real potential over a period of time.

Along those same lines, economic survival dictates that baseball quit this silly practice of paying a young man one million dollars or more as a bonus before he's ever proven he's a major-league player. If the owners are really concerned about losing money, if they're really losing as much as they claim they are, they can start saving money by listening to the following suggestions. This bonus-up-front practice focuses everyone's attention on the money rather than the fact that this seventeen- or eighteen-year-old is receiving a coveted chance to play. It's all backward. It's like telling a teenage genius you'll pay him a million dollars right now just in case he finds a cure for cancer later in his life. He gets rewarded before taking his first biology exam, and that turns the smart boy into a know-it-all who doesn't think he has to study. When a high school senior receives a big bonus the only thing he's ever proven is that he can buy himself a car.

It's a different story once an experienced ballplayer has shown convincingly that he has great talent and has become a successful drawing card in the major leagues. Then, at that point in his career, he's bringing fans to the park, so he's worth the money.

I've said this a thousand times and I am serious when I say that young players should pay baseball for a chance to play. Why not? Players consider themselves show business people, right? How many aspiring actors or actresses receive a million dollar bonus before ever learning their craft? Those hopefuls sling hash, park cars, wait tables, and spend those earnings on lessons that will help them perfect their craft, and they consider it extremely good fortune to get picked for a teeny part in a movie, a Broadway show, or theater performance by the time they're thirty. That's a far cry from the way baseball's economy is currently set up.

Think about it. Baseball fattens a young man's pocketbook with a million dollars before he ever picks up a bat or throws a pitch. Where is the economic sense in that?

Here is the way to solve this dilemma. Adopt the Hemond-Murff idea for the Baseball College of America. Allow every club to sign twenty prospective ballplayers each year to stock a rookie league team as a part of the college that also educates these boys. Each player is signed for a minimal bonus, maybe an annual salary of ten thousand dollars, with the club picking up all living expenses while he attends the baseball college and plays for the rookie league club. It's an apprentice baseball program that allows young players the benefit of playing professional ball and gaining college credit.

If you really want to do something for baseball that makes economic sense, give the players union financial and developmental responsibility for this college. All other unions are responsible for developing its craftsmen. So let the players develop their own, then sit back and see if the players would stand for these million-dollar-up-front bonuses to unproven players. Wanna bet how they'd react to that?

In our program, and we'd recommend this to the union if it decided to take over player development, if a young man makes the big leagues, then he still makes his half-million- or million-dollar-bonus, but not until after he's proven that he's a big-league player. The payment could be stairstepped. Give him a part of it when he makes AA, another portion when he steps up to AAA, and the largest bonus when he makes the bigs. Doesn't that make more financial sense for baseball? This would be an incentive for a player to develop and practice the skills needed for the Big Show. You'd see kids going at this game full throttle once they know that's where the million-dollar-pot-of-gold lies.

Few kids are going to do what it takes to improve if they get rich in advance. Where is the incentive? Where is the hunger? How does a thirty- or forty-thousand-dollar-a-year minor-league coach instruct a kid like that? How is that man supposed to be able to keep a spoiled rich kid's attention, let alone motivate him?

With the draft we are failing 95 percent of the time to find major-league talent. Only 5 percent of all drafted ballplayers make it to the big leagues. The whole thing is an expensive gamble, and that's why, ultimately, you and your family cannot go to the ballpark for under a hundred bucks. Right now baseball has a wholesale marketing mentality when it comes to scouting and drafting a ballplayer. The thought is, He might be a ballplayer, so let's draft him. We have to do away with that attitude.

If baseball ownership considers this and does its homework, they'll realize they don't have to be at odds with star talent to save money. The draft is a big reason baseball's costs are sky-rocketing.

Young players generally want to play baseball. They followed the rules before the draft and signed with major-league clubs.

They'll play by the new rules. You think young men are going to refuse to sign? They'll sign and play, and those who are really good will know the money is there once they make the big leagues, and they'll play like fiends to get a chance at it.

Some might criticize this plan as a return to a system that allowed the richest teams to sign the best ballplayers and monopolize the game. All baseball has to do to prevent that is place a cap on the amount of bonuses any team can pay its players up-front to sign a contract. Then allow them to earn their money once they make the big leagues.

To do this, baseball must hire and keep scouts who know how to find and develop fledgling ballplayers. Baseball executives need to find experienced baseball men they believe in and trust and then give them the freedom to do their jobs. The current system causes scouts to work more for the benefit of college coaches, player agents, and the trade papers than in discovering talented players.

The first step to an improved scouting system is to change the rules to allow players to be signed at any time after they turn seventeen. This rule could include player-students who have just finished their junior years in high school. This would be a refinement of the Hemond-Murff baseball college idea.

Young men attend military prep schools. Why not a baseball prep school run by Major League Baseball? In our school these talented kids would have a chance to compete, graduate from high school, start work on a college degree, and progress into the professional ranks in the proper order. Abuse drugs, break the law, or act like jerks and they're out before they ever have a chance. They'll have teachers and peers who understand what it's like to be a student-athlete and can keep their players' minds and bodies engaged in the pursuit of top performance. With a major financial commitment from big-league baseball and lots of hard work and the proper planning, this idea could work wonders.

You don't need a draft to start a program like this. You don't need rookie leagues. Thus the costs of player development are reduced. All you need are scouts who can find ballplayers to fill the ranks of such a program and a willingness on the part of major-league ownership to be aggressive enough to make it happen.

Do away with all those rules that prevent a young man from signing a professional baseball contract until he's twenty-one or has finished his junior season in college. Those rules take away a kid's right to practice his chosen profession. It's not like these kids are always getting a real education. How many players are taking remedial classes just to stay eligible? I'm in the professional baseball player recruitment and development business, and I promise that the professional ranks can do that work better than anyone else in college or amateur ball. If the baseball college becomes a reality, we'll prove we can educate young men as well as turn them into first-class ballplayers.

Beyond scouting the next major change needed is to replace the marketing and bean counters in the front office with professional baseball people. We could do this through business-related programs at the baseball college. The current experts have gutted the game by mistakenly thinking ballplayers are just another commodity. How can a commodities sales expert understand that ballplayers have very unusual, specialized skills and talents? The problem has festered over the course of several years and these executives have come to resent the players. One major-league executive, still around I might add, told me one time, "Those players think they know it all, they think they own the game! Well, the —— with them!"

For that executive's information, without players he would have no job. The animosity goes both ways, which is why baseball is in the mess it's in now. These people ought to be collaborators, not adversaries. Sure a lot of players are overpaid cry babies, but only a few great athletes are born every year, and this lack of respect is at the heart of player-owner disagreements. Neither side thinks the other appreciates them. It's also indicative of the breakdown between corporate America and working women and men. Baseball can do better than bow to the bean counters.

As I've said many times before, fans don't flock to major- or minor-league parks to watch business people make deals. They come to see the players play. Such negativity toward the players on management's behalf mirrors a leech attached to the game's jugular, draining the life from it. Such negativity toward the players on management's behalf makes negotiations almost impossible because the bean counters don't understand what they are selling! Profits come from loyalty to the team and to its fans, not from clever marketing campaigns. Putting MBA's in charge of baseball is like appointing John Dillinger to head the U.S. Treasury.

● ● ● ● ● ● ● ● ● ● ●

Sometimes these people simply don't know their own ball clubs, and I've seen that firsthand. For instance, when the Atlanta Braves went from worst to first from 1990 to 1991, everyone in the front office except Bobby Cox and Red Murff was unaware that this potential existed.

Cox was general manager in the middle of the 1990 season, and he and I were sitting in a Dallas hotel room watching a Braves game on television, when the announcer declared, "Boy, there will be wholesale changes on this team next season because the Braves have got to do something about this losing record!" He was obviously echoing something he'd heard from someone in the Braves front office.

I looked at Bobby Cox and I said, "You know, we don't need wholesale changes. At any given time we have a young pitching staff assembled that can jell into a winning combination. We have four or five young pitchers who will give us four or five well-pitched games in every pitching rotation. I'm not guaranteeing they'll win all those games, but they'll make us competitive and we can be more than a .500 team next year if you *don't* make wholesale changes."

"Oh yeah, Red? Whaddaya mean?" Cox asked.

I continued, "This young pitching staff looks a lot like that young staff the Mets had in 1968, the year before they won the whole thing. I don't think we need to do anything on our staff except let them gain some experience. The other scouts and I think we need a third baseman, but other than that we are close, really, really close."

Some of the scouts had already decided the Braves needed Cardinals third baseman Terry Pendleton. Pendleton, we felt, would provide leadership, a potent bat, and excellent fielding abilities sadly lacking in the Atlanta infield. The front office listened to us on this one and acquired Pendleton, and he played a key role in the Braves unbelievable comeback in 1991.

Once again I played the prophet. Bobby Cox moved from the front office to the field manager's job late in the 1990 season. The Braves operated basically without a general manager until John Schuerholz took over as general manager, about sixty days after Cox became the field manager. When he came on-board, Schuerholz had no idea he had such a terrific organization. The Braves had won the National League championship and were set for years, and Schuerholz inherited all the makings of a championship club.

His first major move was a serious mistake. He fired one of the best scouting directors I ever worked for, Paul Snyder, and replaced him with the worst director I ever worked for. That was a dumb move because no one in the Braves organization knew exactly how talented its players were except its veteran scouts, and Schuerholz took away their leader.

• • • • • • • • • • •

Innovation is good, but it seems to me that one big change made more than two decades ago added dubious value. The designated hitter rule in the American League provided some offense, but at the expense of changing the way the game is played and managed.

Baseball needs to forget the designated hitter for several reasons. First the economy of baseball cannot allow for a one-dimensional ballplayer who hits and usually plays no other position, but draws big money. To be a true major-league ballplayer, a young man has to possess several skills, but the designated hitter concept rewards guys with limited talent. That reasoning is the exact opposite of what makes baseball players the most versatile, gifted, and entertaining athletes on earth.

There's another reason the designated hitter rule bothers me. Through the ages half the fun of the game comes from sitting around with your friends, arguing about and comparing players from generation to generation by their statistics. Was Babe Ruth a better ballplayer than Hank Aaron even though Aaron broke Ruth's record for the total number of career home runs? Was Rose or Cobb the better hitter? Would Ted Williams have broken Ruth's record if he hadn't spent more than four years in the military? Statistical debates preserve historical perspective and bless the game with its heritage, keeping the love and language alive and kicking. With the designated hitter, a player might tally an additional fifty to sixty home runs or an additional three to five hundred base hits to his career totals and appear to be a better ballplayer than he actually was. To me the DH unfairly skews hitting statistics.

There's another problem with the designated hitter. Let's say an American League pitcher intentionally knocks down or hits a batter. In the National League, if a pitcher does that, he can be sure the next time he comes up to bat he's going to have to face a fastball aimed at him rather than the strike zone. In the American League a pitcher doesn't have that worry. By rights he should.

If you're a baseball purist like me, you know this rule has altered the game. Luckily the National League hierarchy will never adopt the DH. It doesn't add a thing to the game of baseball, and I wish they'd do away with it altogether. The bottom line on the DH is that it caters to a person who can perform only one task—hit the baseball. To me the DH is like trying to train a donkey. You can take him to the track, work him like a racehorse for 364 days, but when it comes time for the Kentucky Derby, and he goes into the starting gate, he's still a donkey and he'll never win the Derby! Baseball has given its American League fans too many one-dimensional donkeys. Baseball players *must* be all-around athletes.

Admittedly pitchers will need more training in offensive skills. In my generation several pitchers, including Warren Spahn, could handle a bat. I had a young pitcher who pitched for me at Jacksonville named Tony Cloninger, who not only could throw hard—he won more than a hundred big-league games—*and* hit. He hit so well, in fact, that he banged out a couple of grand slams in the big leagues. Pitchers are often the best athletes on high school and college ball clubs and there is nothing to preclude them from improving their hitting skills. We already have several different kinds of relief pitchers. Enough is enough. Let football have the specialists. The DH is out!

• • • • • • • • • •  • • • • • • • • • •

Despite its glaring flaws and shortcomings, I predict this golden goose called baseball will overcome its troubles and survive and go on to become a truly global game. I believe the Internet will one day be jammed with a frenzy of readily available information about a young player who is about to break Nolan Ryan's strikeout records or Pete Rose's record for the number of lifetime hits or Joe DiMaggio's consecutive game hitting record. I believe people secretly need the discipline baseball brings to life, and that discipline is one reason people are attracted to baseball. Through that discipline fans will learn to forgive, forget, and love the game again. I hope those in management and the players once again begin to honor those who pay the bills.

The only way this great game can be turned around, however, is for the two sides to come together, shake hands, and grow up. I recently read an article about how baseball's troubles are analogous to a family. When mom and dad are fighting, the kids are insecure and unhappy. A more harmonious relationship between players and management is the only answer to easing baseball's decline. They are responsible to their fans!

It's true indeed that baseball mirrors life in America. We're a little confused about our priorities in this country, and the latest strike proves that baseball is just as muddled. Even as upset as I get at the stupidity I see in our society and in baseball, I think all of us involved in the game are still on a winning streak, even though we sometimes stumble and lose our way. Baseball has never stopped being a game for the average Joe. That's me. A regular good old boy who used to take a punch in the nose to get someone to play catch with him and who later searched the world for thirty-three years to find others who can do five things really, really well.

Red's Random Thought . . .

At the 1995 state high school baseball tournament in Austin, Texas, I felt it. The nervousness, that lump in my throat I used to get on the days I pitched. The jitters at age seventy-four? When they played "The Star-Spangled Banner," I stood there misty-eyed, and it hit me just how much I love this game. And how much I miss it.

Epilogue

If one of my Baton Rouge Red Sticks teammates way back in the Evangeline League days of 1950 had asked me if I'd love the game of baseball in 1995, and if they asked me if I'd do it all again, the same way, I'd have to say, "You bet your sweet patootie I would!"

I miss the camaraderie with my first professional club, the Red Sticks. I miss taking care of the team trainer's money so he wouldn't go on alcoholic binges. Five years later that same trainer showed up drunk at Burnett Field in Dallas during my twenty-seven-win season with the Eagles. Showed up, he said, to celebrate my success. That poor fellow died a pauper's sad, miserable death from problems related to alcoholism. I miss him and wish I somehow could've helped him stop drinking.

I miss Willie, the clubhouse man and philosopher at Nashville. It was Willie who asked me, "You gonna make this club, Red?"

"I sure hope I do, Willie," I replied.

"With 'hope' in one hand and a cow pie in the other, you make a note of which hand is fuller, Red," he replied.

Willie was right. I didn't make that ball club.

I miss the sweaty palms, the irritability, and the lump in my throat in anticipation of making my first pitch in a ball game. I miss the man-to-man competition, playing mind games with the batter, trying to make him hit my pitch, break his concentration or his bat.

I miss never knowing just how good I could've become as a player. An injury held me back from fulfilling my reach for the brass ring. I was just too old when I started to play professional ball and too old once I made the big leagues. My baseball mistress simply whispered one day, "You deserted me for too long, and now you're gonna have to pay a price." I did as far as playing the game went, but I reaped so many other benefits because I couldn't play anymore.

I miss the competition with other scouts. We were the same fierce competitors scouting talent that we were as players. I remember each one's "take no prisoners" attitude when we were trying to sign ballplayers, and I loved that.

I miss all those telephone discussions I had with my fellow scouts and subscouts. I miss the plans we made and the visits we had. I miss those incredibly hot, steamy tryout camps we all staged. How many did we put on? Thirty-three? The hard work didn't seem difficult at all and, my, how time flew! We gave thousands of young men a chance and we found some great ballplayers and we took a lot of pleasure doing it!

I miss walking into a ballpark, smelling the aroma of grass and pine tar and dirt. I miss hearing parents and girlfriends and little brothers and sisters cheering. I miss hearing the coaches yelling instructions. I miss hearing the infielders' chatter. I miss greeting fans, seeing old friends, and making new ones. I miss the excitement of taking out my radar gun, aiming it at the pitcher's hand and seeing "90" flash in red digits. I miss timing a right-handed hitter's sprint to first base in 3.8 seconds! I miss watching a young right fielder pick up the ball and make a howitzer-style throw to third base, nailing the runner by three feet. I miss hearing the crack of a wooden bat as a seventeen-year-old clobbers a fastball four hundred feet into the black of a Southwest night. I was the happiest man on the face of this earth when I was looking at a big-league prospect!

I miss the conversations I had with fresh-faced, eager young ballplayers. I always told each one, "You can do more than you're doing." Every time each one did. I miss that incredible work ethic that seems absent in the big leagues these days. Thank God this generation of kids still seem to have fire in their bellies. I pray they don't lose it.

I treasure the friendships of each and every one of the prospects I signed and many I didn't sign. They never blamed me for their failures, but they *always* rejoiced in my success. I treasure the friendships of those who would've given their eye-teeth to have signed with me. They are as much a part of baseball as anyone.

I miss talking to parents. There were so many class acts among these ranks. Those people, for the most part, have sacrificed so much for their sons, and almost every one of them would've done anything to make sure baseball had a place for their boy. They so often looked to me for guidance, and I miss giving it to them. I miss the appreciative words they always gave me.

I miss talking to high school baseball coaches in Texas, New Mexico, Louisiana, and Oklahoma. What a marvelous brotherhood! I had so many favorites, some of whom are still with us, some have passed on. Two of the best were Bobby Moegle at Lubbock Monterrey who won more than a thousand games and Ray Knoblach at Bellaire High in Houston. There were so many others. You overcame the football mentality in your states, a mentality that often unfairly relegated you to second-class status in the eyes of some of your coaching counterparts. But you never let that small-minded attitude deter your intent. You improved through the years. You produced some terrific ball clubs. You produced some marvelous young ballplayers who often went on to major-league stardom. You also tipped me off on some fantastic ballplayers whom I signed and sent out. We all helped raise the baseball standards in this part of the world. You were first class all the way! Nice going!

I miss so many of the college coaches I worked with across the country. Some of them are still living, some are gone. I so admired Bobby Winkles and Jerry Kindall out in Arizona, Rod Dedeaux at USC, Jim Smith at LSU, Uncle Billy Disch and Bibb Falk at Texas, Al Ogletree at Pan American, Ray Benge at Sam Houston State, Enos Semore and Chet Bryant at Oklahoma and Oklahoma State respectively, Bob Finley and Alex Hooks at SMU, Frank Windegger at TCU, and Jim Mallon at Southwestern. These men shaped college baseball into the great game it is today. I don't always agree with what happens in the college game, but those coaches fought athletic directors who placed too much emphasis on football. They won their battles against football and developed incredible programs and excellent ballplayers.

I miss working with the great scouting directors—the Bing Devines, the Wid Mathews, the Paul Snyders, and the Jim Fannings. I miss all the bull sessions and selling my ballplayers at predraft meetings. I always knew mine were the best, even if my fellow scouts didn't always agree!

I don't miss working with the bean counters who've wormed their way into the baseball apple, who've never—as my old friend Buzzy Keller so precisely puts it—"Worn a wet jock, so what do they know?" But even in their ignorance, they can't dampen the enthusiasm for this game I treasure.

When I sit down in a tranquil moment in my living room in Brenham and reflect on my career, I often think of General George Patton. I remember that scene from the movie where he's gazing across a quiet, charred battlefield littered with smoldering war vehicles and human carnage and utters, "God, forgive me, I do love it so."

My mind regularly produces its own baseball feature film. In it I see images of Nolan and Koosman on the mound and Grote and Bateman behind the plate and Kenny Boswell on second. I visualize a mirage of dozens and dozens of other ballplayers hitting line drives, running the bases, managers arguing with umpires, fans cheering, and scouts taking it all in, trying not to let a good one get away. These very real, very graphic scenes deliciously dance in my head, and then a tear runs down my cheek. In the peaceful stillness of that moment, when no one else is around, I quietly whisper, "Thank you, God, for baseball and its wonderful people and all the game has done for me and meant to me. God, I do love it so!"

Glossary

PITCHING

CIRCLE CHANGE:

Pitch similar to straight change except the pitcher holds the ball in the palm of his hand, with the thumb and forefinger held together at the side of the ball. The circle change movement usually will be in and down to a left-handed hitter if the pitcher is right-handed and vice versa.

CURVE:

Any loose-gripped pitch thrown with rotation that is an asset to the gravity pull already on a baseball. The curving motion takes place when a pitcher spins the ball downward, with a chopping or breaking motion with his wrist.

FASTBALL:

Also called "heat," "smoke," "gas." Any pitch thrown with a tight grip at a pitcher's maximum velocity with the wrist open and facing toward the catcher. The velocity of a major-league pitcher's fastball is between 83–102 miles an hour.

KNUCKLE BALL: Contrary to popular belief this pitch is held with the fingertips off the seams instead of with the knuckles. The ball is snapped away from the fingers, not propelled with wrist action. This movement takes the spin off the ball, leaving air currents to determine which direction the ball will take. A knuckle ball's peak velocity is 75–80 miles an hour, and its slowest velocity is 64–68 miles an hour. An extremely difficult pitch to throw and almost impossible to control, the knuckle ball has been mastered by few. Los Angeles Dodger and Chicago Cub Burt Hooton threw a controlled knuckle ball he called the knuckle curve, a pitch he threw at about 80–85 miles an hour.

"LIFE" ON A FASTBALL: Any horizontal or vertical movement that occurs when a fastball is thrown, depending on the way the ball is held in a pitcher's hand as he releases the pitch.

LONG RELIEF PITCHER: Able to pitch well for one to four innings. Long relievers are used to bail out a starting pitcher who has been taken out of the game in the early innings. The long reliever's role is to hold the game in check until his team can generate offense. Big-league clubs usually carry three long relievers on their pitching staffs.

SHORT RELIEF PITCHER: Short relievers are skilled in working during pressure situations and must be resilient enough to perform nightly if game situations dictate. The game is almost always on the line when the short reliever enters the game. He only enters the contest when his team has a lead or is tied. His job is to stop the other ball club. These relievers are also called "Firemen," or "Stoppers" for obvious reasons. Has nothing to do the size of the pitcher.

SINKER: Tight-gripped pitch thrown at fastball speed with the wrist cocked, similar to a slider. The sinker, however, will break the opposite way. If a right-handed pitcher's slider breaks or slides away from a right-handed hitter, the sinker will break toward the hitter. Old-time pitchers called this the "In Shoot." Overhanded motion or sidearm motion determines the arc of the sinker's delivery.

SLIDER: A tight-gripped pitch thrown almost exactly the same as a fastball but with a minute adjustment made by the fingers, resulting in the ball being thrown slightly off-center, creating a spiraling torque that breaks away, sailing or "sliding" horizontally away from the batter.

SPLIT FINGER: A pitch thrown with a loose grip, in the change-up category, with the forefinger and middle finger of the pitching hand spread or split while holding the baseball. This pitch is also called the *fork ball*, popularized by the late ElRoy Face of the Pittsburgh Pirates in the 1950s and 1960s. The pitch features a backward spin, with the ball dropping straight down. A skilled split-finger pitcher can make the ball drop down and in as well as down and out.

STARTING PITCHER: One of the top four or five pitchers on a ball club who have regular assignments to start the ball game. Starting pitchers are chosen because of their overall talent and the fact that they adjust well to pitching at peak performance once every four or five days. For instance, the current starting rotation for the Atlanta Braves includes Greg Maddux, John Smoltz, Steve Avery, and Tom Glavine.

STRAIGHT CHANGE: Loose-grip pitch thrown from the fastball delivery. The ball travels to home plate at a speed of 8 to 10 percent slower than the fastball. The slower pitch, thrown with the fastball motion, is deceptive to hitters.

WARMUP: An improper term applied to the tune-up time a pitcher spends acclimating himself to how his muscles are reacting and the weather conditions before his starting or relieving assignment. A pitcher must adjust to wind direction and speed, heat, humidity, and altitude. The density of the air changes with any of these conditions, and pitchers must make allowances.

Catching

HIND-CATCHER:

The only ballplayer on a club who has the entire game in front of him. His job is to call every pitch a pitcher will throw. If pitching is 75–80 percent of the reason the game is won or lost, the catcher bears half that burden. He must also assist the manager in aligning fielders and keeping fielders alert to potential base running situations. He must make the difficult catch of foul popups behind home plate, and he wears hot, sometimes heavy equipment called the Tools of Ignorance, an incorrect name. Men who wear those tools have to be baseball experts and have a manager's eyes on the field.

Hitting

LINE DRIVE:

Also called "frozen rope," "clothesline." Any ball hit on the sweet spot of the bat in the power part of the swing. The ball does not attain great height.

QUICK BAT:

A hitter who uses his hands to make

the bat move extremely fast, bringing the bat's sweet spot in contact with the ball.

STRENGTH OF A HITTER: Scouts can determine a hitter's strength by judging how quickly he can stop his swing with his hands once he's been fooled on a pitch.

STRIKE ZONE: Hypothetical area umpires use to determine if a pitch is a strike or ball. At one time the strike zone was an area from the letters or the armpits on a batter's uniform to his knees. Now the zone has shrunk to an area from the belt buckle to the knees. We use the word *hypothetical* here because each umpire interprets the zone differently. This shrinking strike zone, in my opinion, is one of the primary reasons major-league games now run as long as three hours and more instead of the two hours and ten minutes they once ran.

SWEET SPOT: The portion of the barrel of the bat that provides the best, hardest hitting surface. On a wooden bat the sweet spot is an area about three inches long, measured from the top of the bat toward the label. On an aluminum bat the entire barrel is a hitting surface or sweet spot.

TEXAS LEAGUER: Describes a base hit that is not hit extremely hard, nor hard enough to be called a line drive. The hitter who gets a Texas Leaguer base hit has not used quick hands.

WHEEL HOUSE: The powerful arc of a hitter's swing.

Good hitters are able to adjust their *wheel house* to hit pitches in different parts of the strike zone. Pitchers love hitters who cannot adjust.

Fielding

GROUND SKINNER: Scouts sometimes say a young infielder or outfielder can really "catch a ground skinner." That means a fielder does an excellent job fielding a ball hit sharply on the ground either through the infield or to an infielder.

TWIN KILLING: Another nickname for a double play, an amazing show of skills after the ball is thrown, hit, picked up, thrown, caught, thrown again, and caught, all within the time frame of four seconds or less.

General

BUSHES: The minor leagues.

DINGER: Home run.

THE OLD HORSEHIDE: The baseball, once made from horsehide, now made from cowhide.

THE OLD SOUPBONE: A player's arm. A term most commonly used in the old days when pitchers described getting the "old soupbone" ready to throw.

PINE TAR: Black, sticky substance applied by rag to the bat handle to help the hitter hold on to the bat.

RHUBARB: Phrase incorporated into baseball by the late great announcer Red

	Barber. This word describes an argument between the umpire and players or managers.
ROSIN:	Sometimes mixed with pine tar for additional tackiness. The pitcher's rosin bag is placed on the mound and may be used to help him hold on to the baseball.
THE SHOW:	Players often refer to big-league baseball as the Show.

Scouting

ADVANCE SCOUT:	Major-league clubs employ scouts to watch games involving the next opponent on the schedule. The advance scout fills out reports on each position player and pitcher he sees, noting strengths and weaknesses. The reports include information on how to pitch to a particular batter in a game situation and how certain pitchers handle hitters in given game situations.
THE BIG FELLOW:	Scouts sometimes leave a ballpark early to see "The Big Fellow." This means they have seen enough of the young man they are looking at and are heading to another park to see another player.
DRAFT AND FOLLOW:	A player procurement tactic begun during the early 1990s. A major-league club will draft a young man in the late rounds and offer little, if any, signing bonus money. The

intent is to follow the young man's progress for the next year (baseball rules allow a drafting team to keep draft rights for one year) then either sign the young man or allow him to reenter the draft.

FIELD SCOUT: A major-league scout who finds and grades prospective big-league ballplayers in a designated area, such as a state, several states, or a portion of a state.

FREE AGENT: Young man eligible to be drafted and signed by a major-league ball club or signed as a nondrafted free agent.

NATIONAL CROSS-CHECKER: A major-league scout who appraises and assigns a national grade to all top prospects in each area of the country. The national grade of each top prospect is compared to grades of every other top prospect at each position. The national cross-checker's grade report is the final determining factor in ranking prospects before the draft. The ranking determines which prospects will be drafted in which rounds.

PROSPECT: Any young man judged by a major-league scout to have the potential to play major-league baseball.

SCOUTING DIRECTOR: Supervises and schedules the itinerary of each national cross-checker. The director receives reports from field scouts concerning each prospective big-league ballplayer. The scouting director oversees the player draft with the aid of field scouts, national cross-checkers, and the general manager.

Most Important People in Baseball

FANS:
The driving force behind the game. Once the most revered species, now the least appreciated. The smartest baseball people know, however, that the game could never take place without them.

The Authors

John "Red" Murff spent forty-three years in professional baseball; ten as an accomplished minor-league pitcher, winning twenty-seven games and *The Sporting News'* minor-league player of the year award while a member of the Dallas Eagles in 1955 (the only time a player from Class AA received the prestigious honor). Murff also spent parts of two seasons as a pitcher with the Milwaukee Braves and one season as a minor-league manager before he began a thirty-three-year career as a scout, scouring the Southwest and Central and South America for baseball talent.

He scouted for the Houston Colt .45s, New York Mets, Montreal Expos, Atlanta Braves, and Chicago Cubs. Murff's most noteworthy discovery was future Hall of Famer Nolan Ryan, but he has signed no less than *two hundred* young men to professional contracts during his career.

Murff now lives in Brenham, Texas, with his wife, Sara, an elementary-school teacher . . . and he still drives around Texas, stopping at small-town ballparks whenever the mood strikes.

Former CNN Correspondent Mike Capps met Red Murff in high school and later worked part time with him, scouting talent for five years. Highlighting his twenty-five years in broadcast news, Capps received an Emmy nomination and a 1994 Cable Ace Award for his live coverage of the siege at the Branch Davidian compound in Waco, Texas. He also reported live for CNN from events in the Gulf War, the Midwest floods, and the overthrow of Haitian President John Bertrand Aristede.

Before CNN Capps had worked ten years with WFAA-TV in Dallas. There he co-produced investigative coverage of the fall of the football program at Southern Methodist University. That coverage won the coveted Alfred I. DuPont-Columbia and George Foster Peabody Awards for excellence in broadcast news coverage.

Capps and his wife, Dee, have four daughters and live in Dallas. Like Murff, Capps is also known to be drawn like a moth to the lights of a small-town ballpark . . . anywhere in the world.